WITHDRAWN

STUDIES IN ROMANCE LANGUAGES: 23

GALDÓS
The Mature Thought

Brian J. Dendle

THE UNIVERSITY PRESS OF KENTUCKY

To Tanya and Nancy

Library of Congress Cataloging in Publication Data

Dendle, Brian J   1936-
   Galdós, the mature thought.

   Includes bibliographical references and index.
    1. Pérez Galdós, Benito, 1843-1920. Episodios
nacionales. 2. Historical fiction, Spanish.
I. Title.
PQ6555.E463D4   1980   863'.5   80-51013
ISBN 0-8131-1407-1

Scholarly publisher for the Commonwealth,
serving Berea College, Centre College of Kentucky,
Eastern Kentucky University, The Filson Club,
Georgetown College, Kentucky Historical Society,
Kentucky State University, Morehead State University,
Murray State University, Northern Kentucky University,
Transylvania University, University of Kentucky,
University of Louisville, and Western Kentucky University.

Editorial and Sales Offices: Lexington, Kentucky 40506

Contents

Acknowledgments

I wish to express my gratitude to the following, but for whom this book would not have been written: to the late Alberto Jiménez, of Oxford University, whose teaching of *Mendizábal* first stirred my interest in the *episodios nacionales:* to Professor Vicente Llorens and to Professor Joseph Schraibman, whose illuminating seminars at Princeton University rekindled my enthusiasm for Galdós's historical fiction; to Professor Salvador García and to Gwen Kirkpatrick, of Ohio State University, and to Dr. Lois Barr, of Northwestern University, for their assistance in locating otherwise unattainable works of reference; and to Professor John E. Keller, of the University of Kentucky, for his constant encouragement. I am also most grateful for the financial assistance provided by the National Endowment for the Humanities in the summer of 1973, which enabled me to carry out preliminary research in Spain into the historical background of the *episodios nacionales.*

Introduction

Despite the marked increase in interest in Galdós's novels over the last fifteen years, the study of his works nevertheless remains in its infancy. Basic research materials are scattered or unavailable. The preparation of a scholarly edition of the complete literary works of Galdós is still to be undertaken; important textual variants are revealed by chance discoveries; the listing of editions of Galdós's works has tempted no bibliographer; significant biographical information (for example, details of Galdós's relations with women) is only now being brought to light, and this piecemeal. Many of Galdós's journalistic articles, such as his political commentaries in the *Revista de España*, await editing; other articles, one assumes, remain undiscovered.[1] Furthermore, despite Galdós's role as leader of the Republican party in the early years of this century, only a few isolated examples of his political oratory and political correspondence have been located and republished. Although figures of lesser political consequence have attracted the interest of historians, the account of Galdós's political activities has yet to be written.

The sheer volume of Galdós's literary production—he was the author of seventy-seven novels and eighteen plays published during his lifetime—has rendered overall assessment of his work all but impossible. Studies of individual novels have lacked the evidence of a wider context (whether literary or historical) to confirm the critic's findings. Treatments of Galdós's total work, however, have perforce been impressionistic. Because the discussion of individual novels in such studies is necessarily brief, the reader is compelled to accept the author's conclusions on faith. As Geoffrey Ribbans observed some time ago, detailed investigation of aspects of Galdós's work is needed before general conclusions may safely be ventured: "Until much more spade work has been done on individual novels (and *Anales Galdosianos* is already contributing powerfully in this direction) general studies of Galdós will almost inevitably be at best cautious and groping and at worst woolly and misleading. At this stage anyone embarking on an overall study of Galdós would be well advised to start off with a close analysis of carefully selected specific examples before venturing any firm conclusions."[2]

Of all Galdós's literary works, the *episodios nacionales* and the dramas have most suffered from scholarly indifference, even though the *episodios,* both in number and bulk, comprise over half of Galdós's novelistic production. Studies of individual *episodios* are rare or, in the case of many novels, nonexistent. Those critics of an earlier generation who ventured to examine the *episodios* were for the most part concerned with Galdós's handling of sources and treatment of the historical past. The student interested in individual *episodios* written in 1898 and subsequent years will find little guidance beyond the bland reviews penned by Gómez de Baquero for *La España Moderna* and the cursory summaries of Emilio G. Gamero y De la Iglesia (*Galdós y su obra* [Madrid, 1933], vol. 1). In recent years, interest in the *episodios nacionales* has been stimulated by the ambitious studies of Hans Hinterhauser, Alfred Rodríguez, Antonio Regalado García, and José Montesinos. All four scholars offer notable insights into the *episodios;* their works, nevertheless, are introductory rather than definitive. All take as their unit of discussion a series of ten novels, not the individual *episodio.* The value of such treatment for those seeking information on a specific *episodio* or on Galdós's ideological posture at a determined moment is correspondingly limited.

My present study is of the twenty-six *episodios nacionales* written between 1898 and 1912. These later *episodios* offer, I believe, greater interest for an initial treatment than those of the first two series: they have received very little scholarly attention; they are to my mind artistically superior to the twenty *episodios* published between 1873 and 1879;[3] they afford—because Galdós was reacting so directly to the events of his own day—a singular opportunity to establish the ideological profile of the mature Galdós.

Galdós resumed composition of the *episodios* at a time of national crisis: war with the United States was imminent (war broke out during the composition of *Zumalacárregui*); the defeats of 1898 shattered national self-confidence and placed in question the Restoration political settlement; many Spaniards now regarded the recent past of Spain with revulsion and anxiously sought the means to construct a new nation.

In the *episodios* written between 1898 and 1912, Galdós's ordering of the past reflects a vision born of the present. In the *episodios* of the third series (1898-1900), he shares contemporary reactions to defeat and hopes for "regeneration." In these novels, he projects onto nineteenth-century Spanish history the concerns of 1898: fears of national suicide, an abhorrence of politics and of solutions based on verbal formulas, dismay at the disarray of Spain's leadership, opposition to Catalan claims for special privileges, the avid search for drastic remedies for a "sick" nation (a temporary dictatorship, material development, change in individual behavior, avoidance of adventures and "fantasy"). The *episodios* written in the spring of 1900, when the failure of Silvela's "Ministry of Regeneration" to effect change had become apparent and when Costa's ambitious movement for "Regeneration" had been reduced to one more selfish pressure group, reveal a disillusionment with national prescriptions and a flight into personal life.

In the *episodios* of the fourth and fifth series (1902-1907, 1907-1912), Galdós continues his analysis of defects in the national character (inability to perceive reality, a "Romantic" sickness). He also reflects in these novels Liberal—and Republican—political concerns of the early twentieth century. Thus, the bitter anticlericalism of certain *episodios* accompanies contemporary Liberal campaigns to submit the Church to a *Ley de Asociaciones;* Galdós warns against Spanish involvement in Morocco; he acknowledges, although gingerly, social and agrarian problems. In early 1907 Galdós committed himself to political activism; he joined the Reformist Republican party, sat in the Cortes as Republican deputy for Madrid, played a leading role in the *Bloque de Izquierdas,* and presided over the *Conjunción Republicano-Socialista;* the analysis of Republican errors correspondingly looms large in the *episodios* of the fifth series.

In order to elucidate Galdós's ideological posture and to trace shifts in his attitude, I have chosen to examine each *episodio* separately. My concern is above all with defining for each *episodio* that part of Galdós's message, whether implicitly or overtly stated, which addressed or reflected the contemporary situation of Spain. In my handling of intrigue and characterization, considerations of ideological reference have been uppermost; Galdós, in any case, subordinated in these novels character and plot to thesis. In every case, the basis of my study has been the novel itself. Only after determining the teaching or implication of the novel in question have I attempted to place this message in a wider context, whether of other *episodios* or of the historical and political climate in which Galdós addressed his remarks.

The present study is organized to facilitate its use as a work of reference by those who seek information on and an introduction to individual *episodios;* because Galdós's teachings evolved but slowly from novel to novel, a certain repetitiousness, for which the reader's indulgence is craved, is inevitable in such an arrangement. Individual chapters are devoted to the discussion of the *episodios* of the third, fourth, and fifth series respectively. Each of these chapters is introduced by a summary of the major features of Galdós's ideology in the series under discussion; the reader interested in conclusions, rather than in treatments of individual novels, is invited to consult these sections.

To assist the reader in understanding the political climate in which Galdós wrote the later *episodios,* I have treated, albeit briefly, the historical and political background to the periods of composition of these novels. In Chapter One, I discuss 1) the Spain of 1868 to 1898 (the failure after the Revolution of 1868 to achieve a stable constitutional system of government, the Restoration compromise, the Cuban problem, etc.), that is, the formative period that preceded Galdós's return to the *episodios* and against which Galdós and his contemporaries were to react so strongly; and 2) the historical moment (1898-1900) in which the *episodios* of the third series were composed (reactions to the defeats of 1898, Silvela's ministry, the "Regenerationist" movement). Chapters Three and Four are introduced by a discussion of the contexts in which the fourth and fifth series, respectively, of *episodios* were written.

In my treatment of the historical background, I make, of course, no claim to supplant the labors of the professional historian. I wish merely to isolate those features that had most impact on the contemporary Spanish consciousness. I have endeavored to indicate not only those aspects of the national scene that merited Galdós's attention (and also those attitudes that Galdós, perhaps unconsciously, shared with his contemporaries) but also those problems (such as the social question) that Galdós manifestly shirks.

I have refrained from establishing comparisons between these later *episodios* and the earlier novels of Galdós. Such comparisons should, I believe, only be undertaken after a detailed study of the novels in question and of the contexts in which they were written. It is my intention, however, to publish in the near future a study of the first two series of *episodios nacionales* of Galdós, in which I shall discuss differences of approach and of ideological attitude between the Galdós of the earlier *episodios* and the Galdós of the last three series.

Chapter One

The Historical Background, 1868-1900

In early 1898 Benito Pérez Galdós (1843-1920) resumed composition
of the *episodios nacionales,* a task that he had abandoned, supposedly
forever, some twenty years previously. Galdós was, of course, still
concerned with popularizing in the *episodios* selected aspects of Spanish history; he also, however, in the *episodios* written in 1898 and
subsequent years, used the past as example to comment on the problems of his own day and to afford his contemporaries instruction in
which national modes of conduct are best avoided. Galdós returned to
the *episodios nacionales* at a time of national crisis: the long-expected
war with the United States broke out as he was writing the first novel
of the new series, *Zumalacárregui.* The *episodios* of the third series
reflect the obsessed national soul-searching of the Spain of 1898 and
1899, the proposals of the Regenerationists for the radical restructuring
of Spain, and, gradually, Galdós's disillusionment with imposed solutions to Spain's problems.

Galdós's ideological message, like that of the Regenerationists, can
only be understood in the context of the Restoration system, under
which he had spent most of his adult years. His political formation had
begun in the mid-1860s when, as a student in Madrid, he had witnessed
the harsh repression by Queen Isabel's government of the student riot
of April 1865 and of the rebellion of the artillery sergeants in 1866.
After the Revolution of 1868, the young Galdós was close to the center
of the Spanish political scene, first as parliamentary correspondent for
Las Cortes and then as editor of *El Debate* and the *Revista de España.*
In this period, Galdós observed, and in all probability shared, the
optimism of the liberal revolutionaries who hoped to make of Spain a
second England, the increasing pessimism as Spain degenerated into the
anarchy of 1873, and the relief of most middle-class Spaniards when a
stable system of government (the Restoration) was imposed by the
military. Galdós counted among his friends many of the leading political figures of the Restoration and sat as a Liberal deputy in Sagasta's

"Long Parliament." In his novel *La desheredada* (1881), he defends the values of the Restoration: a commonsense need for survival, a distrust of solutions based on fantasy.

In the third series of *episodios,* Galdós explores the defects of the Spanish character, expresses his disgust with the nineteenth-century past of Spain, attacks the "fictitious" nature of Spanish institutions and the Spanish tendency toward Romanticism, and seeks a new direction for national energies. His vision reflects Spanish middle-class experience between 1868 and 1898: the initial optimism and subsequent disillusionment of the revolutionary period (1868-1874), the ensuing fear of disorder and distrust of the ability of Spaniards to govern themselves, the relief with which the many years of Restoration "peace" were accepted, and, finally, in 1898, the overwhelming recognition that the Restoration system was based on lies, had ignored the fundamental needs of Spain, and had served as a lengthy preparation for national humiliation.

In this chapter, as a necessary prelude to the discussion of the ideology of the later *episodios nacionales* of Galdós, I shall briefly discuss the major features of the Restoration settlement and the impact of the disaster of 1898 on Spanish life, Silvela's "Ministry of Regeneration" (1899-1900), and the programs of selected Regenerationists. Because, despite the lip service paid in the *episodios* to *fulano* and *mengano* (the "man in the street"), Galdós was, like most of his middle-class contemporaries, above all conscious of the political (rather than the social and economic) organization of Spanish life, political history will be the main concern of this summary.

THE RESTORATION SETTLEMENT AND 1898

In September 1868 Queen Isabel II, in the eyes of many Spaniards the fickle tool of corrupt and reactionary clerical interests, was expelled from Spain by a military coup organized by Generals Prim and Serrano and Admiral Topete. The revolution, supported by an uneasy alliance of centrist parties (*Unionistas, progresistas,* and *demócratas*), brought with it, at least in theory, such constitutional rights as universal suffrage, religious freedom, freedom of the press and of association, and the inviolability of the home. Such high hopes of reform were conceived that many believed Spain would enjoy a peace and prosperity rivaling that of Victorian England. Thus, immediately following the

September Revolution, the liberal Albareda (the future employer of Galdós and editor of the influential *Revista de España*) wrote: "Las naciones de Europa que nos miraban con desdén vuelven a nosotros la vista con admiración, y sólo nos falta enseñar a los que aún duden de las altas y nobles condiciones del pueblo español, que si hemos sido fuertes para llevar a cabo tan glorioso alzamiento, tenemos el juicio, madurez política y las costumbres necesarias para consolidar un orden social en el que se realice el desenvolvimiento de todos los intereses legítimos, y que sea la manifestación más completa del espíritu civilizador del siglo en que vivimos."[1]

The optimistic hopes for liberal reforms and national stability held by the revolutionaries of 1868 were never fulfilled. The ensuing turmoil and manifest inability of Spaniards to agree to a common form of government were to leave a legacy of disillusionment that marked a whole generation.[2] Republicans and Carlists staged isolated attempts at rebellion. The throne of Spain was ignominiously hawked around the courts of Europe before its final acceptance by Amadeo of Savoy (who reigned from January 1871 to February 1873). Days before Amadeo's arrival in Madrid, the strongman of the Revolution, Prim, fell victim to unidentified assassins.

Amadeo's well-intentioned attempt to rule as a constitutional monarch proved abortive. The war against Cuban separatists (who had risen in revolt in 1868) drained the treasury and made abolition of the unpopular draft impossible. Government continued, as before the September Revolution, to be by the established methods of fixed elections, violence, and widespread bribery. Constitutional guarantees were suspended. Personal vendettas, such as that between Prim's two former henchmen Sagasta and Ruiz Zorrilla, made individual resentment and ambition the deciding factor in political questions.

Amadeo abdicated in February 1873. The Spanish Republic was immediately proclaimed by the Cortes. The Republic enjoyed no greater support than had Amadeo: Ruiz Zorrilla, the Radical leader, sought immediate exile; many conservatives fled following an abortive coup of April 1873; the Republicans themselves were bitterly divided between partisans of federal and unitary republics, and of authoritarian and democratic presidential regimes. In the ten months of existence of the Republic, four presidents (Figueras, Pi y Margall, Salmerón, and Castelar) held office. The Cuban struggle continued; much of the north and east of Spain was in the hands of the Carlists (the Third Carlist War broke out in 1872); military indiscipline was widespread. Furthermore, the Republic was sabotaged by the enthusiasm of its own supporters. Federal Republicans staged revolts in many cities of the south and east of Spain. In Cartagena, where Spain's Mediterranean fleet was based, the Federal Republicans proclaimed an independent canton which attempted to levy taxes on neighboring cities and which held out against the central government from July 1873 to January 1874. Such was Spain's degradation that, after Castelar, the conservative fourth president of the Republic, had declared the rebellious fleet to be pirates, three Spanish warships were seized by the German navy.

In January 1874, immediately following Castelar's defeat in the Cortes, the captain-general of Madrid, General Pavía, dissolved the Cortes by force and brought the Republic to an inglorious and un-mourned end. Throughout 1874, General Serrano, as head of the executive power, restored order throughout Spain.

In December 1874 Prince Alfonso, Isabel's son, who had just attained the age of sixteen, issued the Sandhurst Manifesto. In this document, penned by the politician-historian Cánovas with the aim of appealing to as broad a spectrum of Spanish opinion as possible, Alfonso avowed his patriotism, Catholicism, and liberalism (the last two terms being considered antithetical by many Spaniards). Before the end of the month, Colonel Martínez Campos proclaimed without opposition (but also, apparently, without the connivance of Cánovas) the Restoration of the Bourbon monarchy, the last successful *pronunciamiento* by the Spanish military until Primo de Rivera's coup in 1923.

Alfonso XII ("constitutional King of Spain by the grace of God") reigned from 1875 until his premature death from tuberculosis in November 1885. His ready intelligence, gift for easy relationships, willingness to heed such political mentors as Cánovas, and talent for gestures (such as his visit to the victims of cholera in 1885) evoking popular enthusiasm increased the acceptance of the restored throne. Above all, the weariness of most Spaniards with the constant constitutional changes of the revolutionary period made them loath to seek alternative systems. The monarchy received further reinforcement in a time of vulnerability when Alfonso's widow, the Austrian princess María Cristina, earned widespread respect for the dignified manner in which she bore the burdens of Regency (the heir to the throne, Alfonso XIII, was born in 1886 and came of age in 1902). Her deference to

Sagasta and Cánovas enabled the Restoration political system to survive with little change until the end of the century.

The Restoration was above all the creation of Cánovas del Castillo (1828-1897), a historian whose political career had begun with his drafting of the Manifesto of Manzanares for General O'Donnell in 1854. Cánovas was determined that Spain should be ruled by civilians and that, as in England, the constitution itself should be removed from the political arena. Above all, he was committed to preventing the dismemberment of the nation by sectarian forces.

To this end, his policies were of expediency and conciliation. Many of the civil liberties won by the Revolution of 1868 were conserved (if not enforced in practice) in the Constitution of 1876; to the scandal of certain Catholics, even a measure of religious toleration was allowed. As broad a spectrum of political opinion as possible was included in (or "swept into," as contemporary usage expressed it) his system. The head of the Liberal party, Sagasta, consented to play the role of leader of the loyal opposition; Cabrera, the "hero" of the First Carlist War, recognized, to the horrified dismay of his former coreligionaries, the Restoration; Pidal and his *Unión Católica* (an offshoot of the Carlist movement) joined Cánovas's Conservatives in 1884; Castelar, the strongly conservative Republican, regarded the Restoration "with benevolence" and finally allied himself with Sagasta's Liberals in the 1890s.

As the years passed, threats to the regime, however flimsy it may have appeared in 1875, lessened. The Carlists split in futile ideological quarrels; Ruiz Zorrilla and his revolutionary Republicans (whom Cánovas unsuccessfully wooed) placed their increasingly frustrated hopes in a military *pronunciamiento* (although by now attempts at army coups were finding little support); workers' movements were few in number and ill organized; sporadic violence (such as that of the "Black Hand" in the region of Jérez) was easily controlled by the *Guardia Civil* and served merely to titillate bourgeois fears of the collapse of respectable society.

Although later generations of Spaniards were to attack the Restoration for its supposed indifference to social problems and, above all, for the elaborate artificiality on which its parliamentary system was based, it offered Spain a stability in government that it had lacked in the preceding years of the nineteenth century.[3] Cánovas was committed to a two-party system that would guarantee the preservation of the constitutional monarchy. Each party—the Conservatives led by Cánovas and the Liberals or Fusionists headed by Sagasta—would work within the constitution and could reasonably expect to have its turn in power.

Whereas the earlier practice of the "liberal" Spain of Queen Isabel had made military coup the necessary prerequisite to accession to power—and the power thus gained was preserved by the restructuring of the constitution to eliminate all opposition—Cánovas relied instead on *el turno pacífico,* the peaceful and regular exchange of power between the two major parties. The president of the Council of Ministers was appointed by the Crown; "elections" would then be arranged to give the new president a sizable majority in the Cortes. To prevent discouragement and consequent recourse to extraconstitutional means of obtaining power, prominent members of the opposition party were also assured of "election."[4] Save for a handful of Republican deputies from large cities and Carlists from the north of Spain, deputies to the Cortes were chosen by the minister of the interior and "elected"—as was Galdós for Puerto Rico during Sagasta's "Long Parliament"—by telegram. At the local level, corruption, the voting of the dead, and pressure by *caciques* assured that there were no upsets. Indeed, if we are to believe Fabié, the constitutional amendment of 1890 introducing universal male suffrage led to even greater abuses than had previously prevailed.[5]

Differences between Conservatives and Liberals were minor and were based as much on personality as on ideology; both parties benefited from the system.[6] The great majority of Spaniards (women, the poor, the illiterate), however, had neither the opportunity nor the knowledge to express themselves on political issues. Nevertheless, despite these obvious shortcomings, the governments of the Restoration were not entirely unresponsive to certain powerful sectors of the public. Vested interests—the wheat growers of Castile, wine producers, the industrialists of the Basque Country and Catalonia, the army, those profiting from the Spanish presence in Cuba—were able to bring considerable pressure to bear on the government. Thus, tariff questions were bitterly debated in the Spain of the Restoration; the army prevented reforms that implied a lessening of its share of the budget; popular patriotic opinion made resolution of the Cuban question impossible.

The *turno* functioned with only minor stress—the feared crisis following the death of Alfonso XII was solved with ease when Cánovas insisted that Sagasta be granted power—until the 1890s. Here in schematic form are the governments of the Restoration and some of the major events of each period of rule (apart from minor "bridge ministries," Cánovas was president of the Council of Ministers when the Conservatives ruled; Sagasta, when the Liberals were in power:

1875-1881	Conservatives	End of the Third Carlist War Constitution of 1876 Peace of Zanjón (1878) ending Cuban War Emancipation of the slaves in Cuba
1881-1884	Liberals	The "Black Hand" in Jérez Attempted Republican *pronunciamientos* Royal visit to Central Europe
1884-1885	Conservatives	Cholera epidemic Difficulties with Germany over the Caroline Islands Death of Alfonso XII
1885-1890	Liberals	The *Parlamento Largo* Scandals in the Madrid municipality Introduction of universal male suffrage
1890-1892	Conservatives	Campaigns in the Philippines and Cuba Strikes and terrorism in Barcelona Silvela breaks with Cánovas over the scandals of the Madrid municipality *Bases de Manresa*
1892-1895	Liberals	General Margallo killed near Melilla Guerrilla warfare in Cuba Terrorist attacks in Barcelona
1895-1897	Conservatives	War against Cuban separatists Martínez Campos's conciliatory policy in Cuba Weyler's harshly aggressive policy in Cuba War in Philippines Triumphant reception of General Polavieja on his return from Philippines MacKinley elected as president of U.S. Assassination of Cánovas

Sagasta and Cánovas maintained control over their respective parties, and thus of the Restoration system, until the early 1890s, when the age of the two leaders and the increasing independence of certain of their followers led to the rise of dissident groups. Thus, in 1892 Francisco Silvela, an austere Conservative lawyer who had campaigned incessantly against governmental tolerance of the corrupt Madrid municipality, broke with Cánovas, a dissidence compounded by Silvela's personal distaste for Cánovas and, to an even greater degree, for his roguish electoral manipulator, Romero Robledo. Similarly, in the 1890s Gamazo, Montero Ríos, Moret, Canalejas, and Maura (the last four of whom were later to become president of the Council of Ministers) pursued policies increasingly independent of those of their nominal leader, Sagasta. Nevertheless, it was the unresolved question of the Cuban War which shattered the smooth functioning of the political settlement of the Restoration.

Although the long struggle (1868-1878) between Spain and Cuban Separatists officially ended with the amnesty granted in the Treaty of Zanjón (1878), the peace had proved to be little more than a truce. The relatively humane and conciliatory policies of Martínez Campos, the captain-general of Cuba, were not continued, nor was General Polavieja's plea heeded that Spain prepare the island for peaceful accession to independence.[7] Almost immediately, a fresh insurrection (the *guerra chiquita* of 1879-1880) broke out. Over the next decade, Cuban exiles continued to agitate and to send arms to the island; the banditry with which Cuba was rife was often indistinguishable from the guerrilla warfare of the insurgents; the corruption of the Cuban administration was notorious; the Ten Years' War and the example of the independent countries of Spanish America contributed to the Cubans' feeling of nationality (Cuba was officially not a colony of Spain but an overseas province of the mother country, with representation in the Cortes); partisans of a limited Cuban self-rule increasingly tended to accept the views of the separatists.

Lack of understanding of the Cuban problem, the strength of vested interests, and a facile and ignorant patriotism contributed to the reluctance of Spanish politicians to propose other than feeble and belated measures for the reform of the administration of Cuba. Even Cánovas experienced difficulty in obtaining passage of the law to abolish slavery in Cuba. Perhaps the last chance to deal with the Cuban problem came in 1893 when the Liberal Maura, then minister for the overseas provinces, suggested a modest and limited autonomy in local affairs for Cuba and Puerto Rico. Maura's plan was attacked as "anti-patriotic" not only by the Conservatives but also by many Liberals. Sagasta, never celebrated for political courage or farsightedness, failed to support Maura, who was obliged to resign his ministerial post.

Guerrilla warfare had continued in Cuba throughout the 1880s and early 1890s. In January 1895 the exiled José Martí gave the order for the insurrection that plunged the island into civil war. Sagasta, whose policies—refusal to back Maura's reforms, weakening of the Caribbean garrison with his "peace budget"—had contributed to the rising, found an opportunity to resign as president of the Council of Ministers; his successor, Cánovas, dispatched Martínez Campos to the island with reinforcements. Martínez Campos, who had no stomach for brutal policies and who realized the strength of separatist sentiment in Cuba, was unsuccessful in halting the revolt. In early 1896 he was replaced by General Weyler (who was notorious for his energetic, even cruel, methods) and, on his return to Madrid, was received by a hostile, howling, "patriotic" mob. (By way of contrast, General Polavieja, supposedly successful in quelling the Philippine revolt, received a delirious welcome on his return to Spain in 1897.)

To the Cuban rebels' policy of burning plantations and waging guerrilla warfare, Weyler replied with an equally harsh policy of "concentration" of the civilian population in protected areas. By the summer of 1897, much of Cuba had been "pacified" and Weyler's forces numbered 200,000 men. Nevertheless, Spanish casualties in the war were enormous, losses being caused above all by disease; it was calculated at the time that four men had to be sent to Cuba to produce one soldier in the field. Furthermore, there were fears that the conflict would become international: the United States was rumored to have plans for the annexation of Cuba (and also of Canada); Cuban exiles in the United States supplied the rebels with arms and recruits; an American jingoistic press attacked the "savagery" of Weyler's policies. Nevertheless, United States policy, even under MacKinley (who succeeded Cleveland as president in March 1897), was at first cautious, being limited to offers of mediation and protests against the mistreatment and damage to property of American subjects.

With the exception of Pi y Margall's minuscule grouping of Federal Republicans, all Spanish political parties supported policies of intransigence toward the Cuban rebels. Indeed, with the climate of war fever reigning in Madrid, it would have been politically impossible, even had the inclination existed, for Cánovas to accept American offers of mediation. Sagasta and Cánovas followed identical Cuban policies: too few reforms offered too late; the dispatch of troops; a massive and costly rebuilding of the Spanish fleet to protect the Cuban coast from the raids of filibusters. Sagasta avoided creating problems for Cánovas while the war was in progress. Criticism, whether by Liberals or by Silvela's dissident Conservatives, was leveled at Weyler's methods, not at the war itself. Cánovas and Sagasta expressed, indeed, their patriotic resolution to continue the war at whatever cost in almost identical terms: Cánovas, in the Cortes in July 1891: "Es preciso que tengáis la seguridad de que ningún partido español abandonará jamás la isla de Cuba; que en la isla de Cuba emplearemos, si fuese necesario, el último hombre y el último peso."[8] Sagasta, in the Cortes in April 1895: "España está dispuesta a sacrificar hasta la última peseta de su Tesoro y hasta la última gota de sangre del último español antes que consentir que nadie le arrebate un pedazo de su territorio."[9]

The burden of the Cuban war fell unequally on Spanish society. The sons of the rich and of politicians were not sent to Cuba; they were legally allowed to purchase exemption from the military draft, which therefore affected only the poor and those without connections. As the journalist Francos Rodríguez observed, the sacrifices demanded were always of others: "Quedaba sobreentendido que era hasta la última gota de sangre ajena y la última peseta del prójimo."[10]

On August 8, 1897, Cánovas was assassinated by an Italian anarchist. The accession to power in October of the Liberals under Sagasta (following the brief "bridge ministry" of Azcárraga) brought an immediate modification of Spain's Cuban policy. Weyler was relieved of his command. (He was given a tumultuous reception on his return to Spain and was courted, to no avail, by politicians representing every shade of opinion, ranging from the Carlists to the Republicans.) Weyler's successor, General Blanco, had orders not to take offensive military action. In the Cortes, legislation granting self-government to Cuba and Puerto Rico was obtained by Moret.

Moret's reforms were, however, harshly attacked in the Spanish press as offering no advantages to Spain and were rejected out of hand by the Cuban separatists. At the same time (October 1897 to January 1898), the Liberal ex-minister Canalejas visited the United States and Cuba in a private capacity; his communiqués to Sagasta evaluating the strength of the United States fleet and the desperate straits of the Spanish army in Cuba passed unacknowledged; his letters to the press were, following governmental pressure on the editor of *El Heraldo,* never published.[11] Indeed, only in the Philippines, where Aguinaldo and his followers submitted at the end of 1897, did Spanish policy show signs of success.

Meanwhile, the Conservatives, left leaderless by Cánovas's death, regrouped—save for the dissident band headed by Romero Robledo—in January 1898 under Francisco Silvela (1845-1905) in the *Unión Conservadora.* Silvela, a self-declared "creyente impenitente en la fuerza de las ideas morales," called in his program for a fundamental change in Spanish life: "justicia para el humilde; justicia y severidad para los poderosos . . . la profunda modificación en nuestra manera de ser social."[12]

On February 15, 1898, the American battleship *Maine* exploded and sank in Havana harbor. The cause of the explosion was never adequately determined, but the American press attributed to Spain responsibility for the disaster. From this moment, despite the concessions and frenzied diplomatic activity of Sagasta and his representatives, American intervention became inevitable. A secret and, given the climate of opinion reigning in Spain, politically unacceptable American offer to purchase Cuba was rejected. A joint resolution of the United States Congress called on Spain to abandon Cuba; the American ultimatum expired on April 23. Overshadowed by the fear of war with the United States were the massive uprisings that took place in the Philippine Islands in March 1898.

The events of the Spanish-American War are too well known to merit more than mention here. On May 1 the Spanish Pacific fleet was destroyed at Cavite. Cervera's fleet, dispatched to the Caribbean despite the protests of its officers to the Spanish government that it was incapable of offering a challenge to the American navy, was first bottled up in Santiago de Cuba and then destroyed by the markedly superior American fleet on July 3. At the end of July, American troops landed in Puerto Rico, the islanders offering no opposition. In August, while Spain was suing for a suspension of hostilities, Manila fell. In October, American and Spanish diplomats met in Paris; on December 10, by the Treaty of Paris, Spain agreed to surrender to the United States all Spanish overseas possessions, save for the African colonies which were, in any case, of only minor importance. On January 1, 1899, American troops took possession of Havana.

Leonard Williams, the correspondent of the London *Times* in Madrid during the war, has commented on the bleak national situation as it appeared to many after the disastrous defeat: "For Spain the annals of the nineteenth century were principally sad ones. Beginning with a war, ending with a war, with various wars between the two, the glory she has won from those deplorable campaigns is utterly disproportioned to the miseries they have caused her. Civil and other strife, her children without schools, tens of thousands of her sons gratuitously slaughtered, her industries and commerce paralysed, her fields and factories uncultivated and unmanned—such is the record, crimsoned with her blood, of almost all she has accomplished or omitted to accomplish in a hundred years of history."[13]

The impact of the defeat was all the greater because so few Spaniards expected such a denouement. The war was welcomed with frenzied enthusiasm: crowds offered delirious ovations to departing troops; the Spanish colors were everywhere displayed; patriotic subscriptions belatedly raised funds to purchase warships; newspaper chroniclers and café gossips pondered the equality, if not the superiority, of Spanish naval might to that of the United States; indeed, the press had for years—and articles by Maeztu and Pi y Margall form honorable exceptions—encouraged the war fever that swept Spain. The following lines from Federico Balart's imbecilic poem " ¡Guerra! ", published in *El Imparcial* in early 1898, give some indication of prevailing sentiment:

> ¡Mejor!   ¡Así al villano
> verás por fin desnuda la mejilla
> y en ella estamparás, para mancilla,
> los cinco dedos de tu fuerte mano!
> No temas que tu honor reciba ultraje
> de esa imbécil canalla
> que por táctica tiene el agiotaje
> y los dollares por única metralla.[14]

But after the defeat, an attitude, not of indifference as some have claimed, but rather of weariness and disillusionment prevailed. Spanish reaction to the defeat, with its questioning of the Spanish past, distrust of the state and its institutions, and introspective search for change, has been summarized by Cepeda Adán:

Si hubiéramos de expresar gráficamente la reacción madrileña ante la guerra, diríamos que hay una primera parte, los seis primeros meses del año, en que el entusiasmo, la confianza, el orgullo son la tónica dominante. Madrid, engañado por unos políticos y por una prensa que presentaba una realidad de color de rosa, se lanza a las manifestaciones más ruidosas para testimoniar su firme creencia en la derrota del enemigo, al que se considera un pueblo primitivo, de mercachifles, cuyos barcos sufren averías constantes, sus políticos son unos zafios y sus soldados correrán ante las bayonetas españolas. Luego, a partir de Cavite y Santiago de Cuba, ante la espantosa catástrofe, no tanto por lo que se perdía—siendo mucho—como por lo fulminante y desastroso del final, se cae en un estado, primero, de sorpresa; luego, de rabia contenida, y, por último, de desilusión, de escepticismo. "Nos han engañado," es la frase que se piensa o se pronuncia en todos los corros. Desde este momento se produce un divorcio entre la nación, y el Estado, y la política. Ya no se confía ni en personas ni en Instituciones, y cada uno se encierra dentro de sí en busca de sus propias soluciones, y algunos van a intentar un proceso de revisión de todo el pasado inmediato y remoto de España.[15]

The effect of the defeat on Spanish political life was at first muted, if only because no politician wished to take Sagasta's place until after the peace treaty was signed. Popular discontent was scattered, unorganized, and without coherence in its choice of target. (Thus, news of the defeat at Cavite had led to mob demonstrations against the houses of Sagasta and Moret and to acclamations of Weyler.) There was, in any case, little opportunity for the expression of dissent: constitutional guarantees were suspended in July 1898 and the press was censored.

Sagasta, continuing Restoration policies of expediency and consensus, took care, before suing for peace, to obtain the advice of leaders of all political parties and of prominent figures in the Spanish military; only Romero Robledo, who had Cuban financial interests, defended continuance of the war. The aging Sagasta's hold over his own party was, nevertheless, slender. Before the end of 1898, Gamazo, with a large number of dissident Liberals, rejected Sagasta's leadership. In March 1899 Sagasta abandoned power.

By the late summer of 1898, there was, as Cepeda Adán remarks, a growing feeling of divorce between what were seen as "two Spains": the fictitious Spain of the government, institutions, and organs of the press, and the "real" Spain which had seen its blood and savings squandered in defense of "national honor." Many now perceived this same "national honor" to be a rhetorical device of politicians, a mask for administrative corruption and incompetence, both in Spain and in its former overseas provinces.

Demands for investigation of responsibilities were widespread. When the Cortes met in September 1898, the Conde de las Almenas embarrassed his Conservative fellow senators (he was ultimately disowned by Silvela) with his violent attacks—which he was to continue throughout the coming year—on Spain's military leaders. At the same time, the Liberal Canalejas accused the government of having systematically lied to the nation about the true military and diplomatic situation; it was Canalejas who coined the phrase "Se perdieron las colonias, pero el honor no se ha salvado."[16]

Symptomatic of the widespread desire to put an end to the Restoration political system is the article "Sin pulso" which Silvela published in *El Tiempo* in August 1898. Silvela acknowledged the apparent lack of reaction to the defeat; he demanded that policies of "lies" be abandoned and replaced by "reality." National life should be restructured on a basis more in accordance with the modest circumstances of Spain:

Todos esperaban o temían algún estremecimiento de la conciencia popular; sólo se advierte una nube general de silenciosa tristeza que presta como un fondo gris al cuadro, pero sin alterar vida, ni costumbres, ni diversiones, ni sumisión al que, sin saber por qué ni para qué, le toque ocupar el Gobierno. Es que el materialismo nos ha invadido, se dice; es que el egoísmo nos mata; que han pasado las ideas del deber, de la gloria, del honor nacional; que se han amortiguado las pasiones guerreras, que nadie piensa más que en su personal beneficio. . . . Hay que dejar la mentira y desposarse con la verdad; hay que abandonar las vanidades y sujetarse a la realidad, reconstituyendo todos los organismos de la vida nacional sobre los cimientos, modestos pero firmes, que nuestros medios nos consienten.[17]

Silvela's call for "reality" touched a nerve in public consciousness. On September 1 General Polavieja (1834-1914), the hero of successful campaigns in Cuba and the Philippines, launched a manifesto to the nation. Polavieja, like Costa, directed his appeal outside the party system to all those Spaniards who felt an "anhelo de mejora y de enmienda de España." Denying any aspiration to military dictatorship (a constant fear of Spanish politicians after the breakdown in 1898 of the Restoration settlement), Polavieja nevertheless demanded radical changes in the political structure of Spain: the extirpation of *caciquismo*, the incorporation into national political life of *la masa neutra* ("the silent majority"), administrative decentralization—a policy that attracted the support of Catalan regionalists[18]—and compulsory military service. (The injustice of allowing the rich to purchase exemption figured prominently in working-class complaints.) Above all, Polavieja called for a sense of reality, for policies of material reforms to replace the rhetorical abstractions so favored by Spain's rulers: "a la política de las abstracciones sustituya en el Gobierno la política agraria, la política industrial, la política mercantil."[19]

Polavieja's manifesto was echoed almost immediately by Joaquín Costa and Basilio Paraíso, whose programs equally demanded national regeneration, administrative decentralization, a realistic acceptance of Spanish limitations, material reforms, and the abandonment of hollow political abstractions. Costa's program will be described later in this work; at this point, I wish merely to indicate the publicity that it received at the end of 1898. In early November the *Cámara Agrícola del Alto Aragón* met in Barbastro and distributed its program, composed by Costa, throughout Spain. In the same month, the *Asamblea de las Cámaras de Comercio* met in Zaragoza, under the leadership of Paraíso and Santiago Alba; their proposals resemble closely those of Costa. In February 1899 Costa founded in Zaragoza the *Liga Nacional de Productores,* a pressure group of those whose interests he felt were not sufficiently represented in national life.

The arrival of, and publicity accorded to, new elements on the political scene indicate the disarray and unpopularity of the Restoration settlement. Furthermore, neither Costa nor Polavieja could easily be described as belonging to the right or the left. Costa's program bore many points in common with that of the Carlists. Polavieja, despite the adherence to his cause of the Catholic right, was for a time considered by many as an ally of Canalejas.[20] (Canalejas's support was, however, lost by Polavieja's manifest predilection for Catalan regional aspirations.)

In January 1899, in a radical restructuring of Spain's political leadership, Silvela, acknowledging the similarity between the program of Polavieja's manifesto and that of the *Unión Conservadora,* formed an alliance with Polavieja. Both Silvela and Polavieja, because of their reputed sympathies with Catalan aspirations, came under attack from leaders of such diverse opinions as Romero Robledo (independent conservative), Weyler (Liberal), Martínez Campos (Liberal), and Castelar (Republican).

Catalan demands met with neither sympathy nor understanding in the ruling circles (Madrid, the press) of late nineteenth-century Spain. Catalan claims for special treatment were dismissed as selfishly motivated (the pressure of commercial and industrial interests for economic protection) or unpatriotic (the pleas for measures granting linguistic and legal autonomy to Catalonia).

Catalan industrialists strongly opposed the free-trade principles to which many Spanish Liberal politicians (who were responsive to the agrarian interests of south and central Spain) were committed. The Catalan textile industry depended on a protected market, which was granted high tariffs from 1891 onwards.[21] Moreover, Catalan manufacturers were keenly interested in preserving the Spanish connection with Cuba;[22] after the defeat of 1898, they demanded that the government compensate them for their lost markets.

While Catalan businessmen obtained the protection of the state for their markets, they were firmly opposed to governmental intervention to protect workers from exploitation. The success of the cotton industry depended on the payment of low wages; many women and children were employed in atrocious conditions, even after Dato's reforms of 1900. Workers' movements were for the most part ill organized and by policy abstained from participation in Restoration politics. Symptomatic of strong underlying social discontent were the acts of anarchistic terrorism in the Barcelona of the 1890s. Thus, in 1893 bombs were thrown at the captain-general of Barcelona, Martínez Campos, and, in the same year, some thirty people were killed when bombs were hurled in a crowded Barcelona theater. Vigorous police repression of terrorism and allegations of torture employed in the Citadel of Montjuich earned Spanish authorities a reputation for cruelty in European left-wing circles.

Catalonia was also separated from the rest of Spain by its self-imposed exclusion from the Restoration political settlement. The Restoration system, with its rotation in power of the two dynastic parties, excluded Carlists and Federal Republicans, who possessed considerable strength in Catalonia. As hopes of overturning the Restoration system diminished, former Carlists and Republicans stressed from their former creeds a regionalism that increasingly took account of the peculiar economic and social needs of Catalonia. Whereas Cánovas had strived to include parties of the left in the Restoration framework, the conservative Mañé i Flaquer, the director of the influential *El Diario de Barcelona*, attracted Carlists to the cause of Catalan traditionalism by his emphasis on the *fueros* (regional privileges).

The Catalan movement was a fluctuating grouping of disparate, even inimical, elements: former Carlists, traditionalists, and Federal Republicans who united to defend the regional distinction of Catalonia from the centralizing tendencies of Castile, businessmen who sought high protective tariffs, and latter-day Romantics whose defense of Catalan cultural separateness took on increasingly nationalistic tones. Despite their grievances, Catalan workers showed little inclination to join a separatist movement dominated by the middle class and by business interests.

Attempts at giving political focus to regional sentiment were at first timid. Vicente Almirall (a former Federal Republican) protested to Alfonso XII in 1885 the smothering of regional life by the centralizing policies of the government, a gesture that aroused the ire of the Madrid press. Shortly afterwards, Guimerà requested of the queen regent that Catalonia be granted its own Cortes and that Catalan be declared the official language of the region.

Catalan autonomist aspirations—the dream at that time only of a handful of middle-class intellectuals—received their most notorious expression in the *Bases de Manresa* (1892). The demands included that Catalonia have a separate Cortes, that Catalan be the sole official language of Catalonia, that only Catalans hold public office in the region, that Catalonia have its own legal and taxation systems, that Catalonia contribute volunteers to the Spanish army (in place of the hated draft), that corporations be granted representation in the Catalan Cortes,[23] and that Catalonia be responsible for its own educational system (which would stress technical education[24]). These last two demands—for corporative representation and vocational education—were to appear again in Costa's program.

Throughout the 1890s, distrust and hostility between Madrid and Barcelona increased. Prat de la Riba's *Compendi de la Doctrina Catalanista* (1894), in which he taught that Catalans have but one *patria* (Catalonia), was widely circulated. In 1897 the *Unió Catalanista* intervened in foreign affairs, to the outrage of the Madrid press and the Spanish government, when it sent a message of encouragement to the king of the Hellenes in support of Cretan aspirations to unite with Greece. The resultant governmental overreaction won fresh adherents to the Catalan cause.[25]

After the Spanish-American War, which cost Catalonia her Cuban market and the incompetent conduct of which could safely be blamed on Madrid,[26] middle-class sentiment in Catalonia increasingly favored decentralization, if not separatism. Thus, Polavieja's manifesto and Costa's program, both emphasizing decentralization, won much Catalan support. Symptomatic of the divorce between Madrid and Barcelona was the Catalan gesture on the occasion of the visit of the French fleet to Barcelona in July 1899: the Spanish national anthem was hissed, while the Catalan *Els Segadors* was received enthusiastically.

SILVELA AND THE "MINISTRY OF REGENERATION," MARCH 1899-OCTOBER 1900

Silvela's "Ministry of Regeneration" (March 1899) was perceived by many as an opportunity to break with the tired politics of the Restoration. The Liberals, held responsible for the defeat of 1899 and divided by Gamazo's refusal of Sagasta's leadership, were in disarray. The Conservatives, on the other hand, offered hope of national renovation. Their new leader, Francisco Silvela, had in the past demonstrated his independence of spirit by rejecting the "immoral" leadership of Cànovas. His cabinet represented a rupture with the traditional *turno*, including, as it did, ministers drawn from outside the conventional political structure. Thus, Catalan aspirations were acknowledged with the appointments of Durán y Bas to the Ministry of Justice and the politically independent General Polavieja to the Ministry of War.[27] Furthermore, breaking with the normal procedures of party patronage and heralding a promised decentralization, Silvela appointed the prominent Catalanist Bartolomé Robert as mayor of Barcelona.

Silvela's program echoed that of the "Regenerationists." He called for "morality" in government and personal sacrifice in the cause of national redemption.[28] His ambitious proposals for the material reform of Spain resembled those of Costa: compulsory military service, a stable civil service, decentralization, and the development of agriculture, irrigation, and railroads. The radical reforms that he demanded in the political, administrative, and social structure of the nation were to constitute (and Silvela employs the same phrase as Costa) a "revolution from above": "tiene que ser una obra de reformas radicales, de verdadera *revolución hecha desde arriba,* de empeños que representan profundas modificaciones en nuestra manera de ser política, administrativa y social" (my italics).[29]

In practice, Silvela's program proved impossible to accomplish. Lasting achievements of the government were limited to Dato's social legislation (regulating the employment of women and children in factories) and the "hydraulic policy" of the Regenerationist Rafael Gasset. (Gasset, as head of the newly founded Ministry of Agriculture, published in the *Gaceta* of August 1900 ambitious plans for afforestation and for the construction of railroads, experimental farms, and highways.) The most difficult task of the government, however, and the one that sapped its energies, was to obtain passage of the budget. The budget, introduced by Villaverde in June 1899, was finally, and only after bitter parliamentary and extraparliamentary struggles, voted in March 1900. To restore the credit of Spain and to pay for the debts incurred in the war, the budget included numerous new taxes. Furthermore, to the dismay of many, the budgetary allocation for the army and navy was increased. (Silvela himself demanded the rebuilding of the Spanish fleet; it was in any case politically dangerous to interfere with the military establishment, even more bloated after the repatriation of troops from the overseas provinces.[30]

Silvela's task was rendered all the more difficult by a political instability that placed in doubt the very continuance of "constitutional" rule in Spain. Apart from the agitation of Costa's followers and the exacerbated Catalan question, there were throughout the period rumors of republican conspiracies and minor attempts at risings by Carlists. Constitutional guarantees had twice to be suspended during Silvela's government. In Barcelona, workers' movements demanded a revision of the Montjuich cases. In the Cortes, the dissident Liberal Maura referred to the urgency of reforms in a manner that left no doubt as to the threats which loomed over the government from extraparliamentary sources: "Si la revolución no la hacemos aquí, se hará en la calle." Above all, there were fears of a military *pronunciamiento.* Generals Martínez Campos and López Domínguez bruited vague plans for the formation of a party of national concentration. General Weyler, under the extreme provocation of the Conde de las Almenas's intemperate demands for the attribution of responsibilities for Spanish military defeats, scandalized the Cortes with his threatening remark (July

1899): "No olvidéis que, en tiempos no muy lejanos, la patria se ha regenerado por medio de sublevaciones."[31]

The most constant opposition to Silvela's reforms came, however, from the two groups he had most hoped to associate with his projects for national regeneration: the various associations of Chambers of Commerce (organized by Costa and his collaborators) and the Catalan regionalists. The announced policies of the Chambers of Commerce and the *Liga Nacional de Productores* were almost identical to those of Silvela and Polavieja: morality in government, decentralization, state intervention to foment material development. Nevertheless, the Chambers of Commerce protested vigorously the new taxes and military expenditure in the Villaverde budget and the government's alleged rejection of the program of the Assembly of Zaragoza. Throughout the summer of 1899, Chambers of Commerce carried out a propaganda campaign against the budget, inciting their members to close their commercial establishments and to refuse to pay taxes. In January 1900 Paraíso, Alba, and Costa founded the Unión Nacional. In meetings all over Spain and in well-distributed publications, they called for a taxpayers' strike and announced that, having broken all relations with the Spanish political establishment, they would no longer communicate with Silvela. By July 1900, however, the taxpayers' strike had completely collapsed. The Unión Nacional (and with it, the influence of such self-proclaimed "regenerators" as Costa) was reduced to a mere curiosity.[32]

The most serious threat to national stability came from Catalonia. Silvela's appointments of Polavieja, Durán y Bas, and Bartolomé Robert did little to calm Catalan agitation. Many Catalans considered Villaverde's budget a betrayal; they held that Polavieja and Silvela had promised a *concierto económico,* that is, that Catalonia itself be responsible for raising the taxes to pay its share of the national budget. Throughout the summer of 1899, Catalan businessmen, encouraged by the propaganda of Paraíso and Costa, refused to pay taxes. Robert, the mayor of Barcelona, accusing Madrid of "catalanophobia," refused to assist the government. In October 1899 Robert resigned as mayor, as also did Durán y Bas as minister of justice. The government was forced to seize the goods of businessmen; a state of war (which lasted from October to December 1899) was declared in Barcelona; strict press censorship was imposed; and a warship was anchored in Barcelona harbor. By the end of 1899 the commercial classes of Barcelona had manifestly lost confidence in the government and in the political system directed by Madrid. In January 1900 the *Unió Regionalista* was founded by ex-followers of Polavieja. What had started out as a protest by the bourgeoisie against new taxes—and the proletariat of Barcelona had remained indifferent to the taxpayers' strike—had evolved into a strong movement for regional autonomy. When the elections of 1901 were held, the political system of the Restoration (the two-party *turno*) no longer functioned in Barcelona. The struggle was now between Republicans and supporters of regional self-government.

Support for Silvela steadily eroded throughout the eighteen months of his "Ministry of Regeneration." Polavieja resigned from the cabinet in September 1899, refusing to accept the cuts in the military budget proposed by Villaverde. Durán y Bas resigned in the following month, in sympathy with Catalan protests. Villaverde, exhausted by the budgetary struggles, resigned in July 1900. Finally, the resignations of the reformers Dato and Gasset in October 1900, protesting the appointment of General Weyler as captain-general of Madrid, occasioned the fall of Silvela's ministry. It was, however, according to Silvela, the insolubility of the Catalan problem that had rendered his government an impossible task.

THE REGENERATIONISTS

The humiliating defeats of 1898, defeats for which the nation was emotionally ill prepared, created a receptive public for the theories of those thinkers who anxiously probed the causes of national decadence and proposed ambitious plans for the regeneration of Spain. The wide currency given to the ideas of Ganivet, Costa, Maeztu, and Macías Picavea (and there were many other "Regenerationists") is to be explained neither by the penetration of their analysis of Spain's problems nor by the pertinence of the measures that they proposed to solve them. Rather, their importance lies in their giving expression to the discontent and ill-channeled search for positive action prevalent in the Spain of their time.

The following brief summary of the thought of Ganivet, Costa, Maeztu, and Macías Picavea is in no sense intended to be exhaustive. My present concern is with noting, even at the risk of omitting other more striking features in the reformers' programs, those proposals and attitudes that the "Regenerationists" share with the Galdós of the later *episodios nacionales:* the hatred of rhetoric and rash adventures, the dismissal as fraudulent of the constitutional progress of nineteenth-century Spanish liberalism, the call for material development of the nation, the appeal to authoritarian solutions and contempt for politics, the claim that Spaniards are afflicted with defects of temperament and behavior that ill fit them for participation in modern European civilization, and the diagnosis of Spain as a "sick," even "moribund," nation.

Ganivet's analysis of the Spanish soul, the *Idearium español*, was first published in 1897. His characterization of the defects of Spaniards, however, is that of the Regenerationists and of the Galdós of the later *episodios*.

Spaniards, Ganivet claims (as also did Galdós), lack common sense and measure. They fritter away their energies in empty talk: "se discute todo y se discute siempre. La fuerza que antes se desperdiciaba en aventuras políticas en el extranjero, se pierde hoy en hablar; hemos pasado de la acción exterior a la palabra."[33]

Referring, before 1898, to possible "regenerators," Ganivet (and Galdós makes the same pessimistic claim in *Mendizábal*) affirms that the nation will never allow these reformers to complete their task: "en España no puede haber moralizadores, es decir, hombres que tomen por oficio la persecución de la inmoralidad, la corrección de abusos, la "regeneracion de la patria." . . . si los paladines de la moralidad no se paran a tiempo y pretenden continuar la obra hasta darle remate y digno coronamiento, se hallan frente a frente del mismo espíritu que al principio les alentó" (*Idearium*, p. 57).

The sickness of Spain, Ganivet claims, is a failure of the will (abulia), that is, a chronic irresolution, a vacillation between apathy and violent impulse. The origin of this malady is to be sought in the fixed nature of Spanish thought, in Spanish inability to see things as they are. The remedy (and Galdós teaches the same lesson) lies in moderation and in subordinating action to prudent judgment. Before Costa, Ganivet demands that a "padlock" be placed on the Spanish spirit of adventure.

The most trenchant and best publicized expression of Spanish aspirations for change and revulsion at the policies that had led to defeat are found in the writings and speeches of Joaquín Costa (1846-1910).[34]

Costa's ideas received wide distribution after the defeats of the summer of 1898. In speeches, pamphlets, and books, he vehemently attacked the political establishment and called for a radical restructuring of Spanish institutions. By the end of 1898, Costa was working to organize the "productive classes" into a pressure group that would cleanse the body politic of corruption. Thus, in the second week of November 1898, Costa drafted the manifesto that the *Cámara Agrícola del Alto Aragón* forwarded to corporative bodies (Chambers of Commerce, artisan guilds, etc.) throughout Spain. In February 1899 the *Liga de Productores*, under the presidency of Costa, was formed in Zaragoza; its program, calling for a "revolución honda y rápida desde el poder," was presented to the Cortes at the end of July.

In January 1900 Costa's *Liga* and the Assembly of the Chambers of Commerce amalgamated to form the Unión Nacional, headed by Paraíso, Costa, and Alba. However, after its encouragement in the summer of 1900 of the taxpayers' strike (which Costa had opposed) against the Villaverde budget, the Unión Nacional—and with it Costa's political fortunes—declined rapidly. Nevertheless, for the next three years Costa continued to publicize his program. His speech to the Floral Games of Salamanca in September 1900 (published as *Crisis política de España*) and the report that he presented to the *Ateneo* of Madrid in March 1901 (*Oligarquía y caciquismo como la forma actual de gobierno en España*), for example, found a wide audience.

Costa's program was vague, rhetorical, and authoritarian.[35] It was, however, the very simplicity of Costa's political thought that contributed to its wide diffusion in the Spain of the years following the disaster. The slogan form to which Costa reduced the outlines of his program gave his proposals a directness and popular impact achieved by few other Spanish political thinkers. Thus, such words and phrases as *regeneración, revolución desde arriba, cirujano de hierro* (the Cromwellian protector who would impose summary reforms), *escuela y despensa* (the massive material and educational changes needed to "deafricanize" Spain, *política hidráulica* (the development of Spanish agriculture), *política de alpargata y calzón corto* (attention to the laboring classes), and *doble llave al sepulcro del Cid* (the end to foreign adventures) rapidly became part of contemporary vocabulary.

The major features of Costa's program were contained in two works: the *Consulta* of the *Cámara Agrícola del Alto Aragón* (distributed all over Spain in late 1898), and *Oligarquía y caciquismo* (published in 1901; the proofs were read by Galdós[36]).

The *Consulta* consists of two sections: the analysis of the present (and past) degradation of Spain, and Costa's proposals for reform.

For Costa, the Disaster of 1898 had revealed the official organs of the state (press, universities, Parliament, etc.) to be without substance, to be mere "scenery in a theater": "Donde estábamos acostumbrados a mirar prensa, escuela, pensadores, Parlamento, crédito, partidos, hombres de Estado, clases directoras, etcétera, no había más que lienzos pintados, verdadera tramoya a estilo de la de Poniatowski, que el estampido de unos cuantos cañones ha bastado para hacer venir al suelo sin estrépito."[37] The sterile political ambitions of Spain's recent rulers had distracted the nation from consideration of its true needs. Military and civil unrest had brought Spain to ridicule; the pompous rhetoric of past victories could not compensate for current hunger and serfdom. Spain's rulers were too cowardly to carry out the retrenchment that the impoverished nation required. The material development of Spain had been sacrificed in the "insane and criminal" involvement in the Cuban War.

Costa demanded the immediate material reform of Spain: the development of agriculture (the "hydraulic policy" of investment in irrigation works and settlement of barren lands), improvements in communications, a vigorous pruning of the national budget, social reform (insurance, factory inspections), municipal self-government, simplification and independence of the judicial system, the reduction of the number of universities (to reduce the "proletariado de levita" in number), and the creation of technical schools.

Costa's hostility to the Restoration political system is marked. Costa was willing to accept the status quo in constitutional matters, but only to avoid distracting the nation from more important tasks. The Spanish Cortes, he considered, was a danger and an obstruction to progress; the strengthening of local government and of ministerial power would attenuate their "virulence."

Costa's calls for a *política sumarísima* and for the strengthening of the ministerial system reflected the authoritarianism of his proposals. Disgusted by the impotence of the parties of the *turno* to effect reform, Costa demanded instead leaders of a different calibre, leaders who would combine the qualities of Bismarck and Saint Francis: "Necesitamos en el Gobierno 'impersonales': Bismarcks, injertos de San Francisco de Asís, con más de San Francisco que de Bismarck" (Pi, p. 1505). Furthermore, Costa called for an iron social discipline which would purge Spain of corruption and feudalism: "No con expedientes, sino "con el hierro y el fuego," hasta que Ceuta haya recibido en custodia mayor número de levitas que de chaquetas, y la península quede purgada de feudalismo, señor el pueblo de sí mismo, y España en los pórticos de Europa en punto a justicia y a libertad" (Pi, p. 1521).

In his report to the *Ateneo, Oligarquía y caciquismo,* Costa stridently assailed the trappings of nineteenth-century Spanish liberal regimes. In appearance, Spain was a nation ruled by a parliamentary system; in reality, it was the fief of an inept and corrupt oligarchy of some thousand Spaniards (deputies, senators, newspaper proprietors). The Revolution of 1868 had changed nothing; its political reforms were mere theater, "firework displays." Despite liberal rhetoric and revolutionary zeal, the same degraded Asiatic system of *caciquismo* ruled the nation in 1900 as it had in 1868:

pero el verdadero obstáculo tradicional, el trono del cacique, quedó incólume, y todo aquel aparato teatral, manifiesto de Cádiz, juntas revolucionarias, destronamiento de la reina, Constitución democrática, soberanía nacional, no pasó de la categoría de pirotecnia: la graduamos de revolución, y no fue más sino un simulacro de revolución. Todo aquel estado de corrupción y de servidumbre, trasunto de las naciones decadentes de Asia, que acabo borrosamente de bosquejar, subsiste íntegro treinta y dos años después, salvo haberse agravado con la hipocresía de la soberanía nacional y del sufragio universal, escarnio e inri de la España crucificada. Lo mismo que entonces, la nación sigue viviendo sin leyes, sin garantías, sin tribunales, sujeta al mismo degradante yugo de aquel feudalismo inorgánico que mantiene a España separada de Europa por toda la distancia de una edad histórica.[38]

Once Spain's sickness was recognized, the imperative task must be to extirpate oligarchic rule and to combat the "africanization" of Spain: *caciques* and oligarchs must be suppressed "with an iron hand"; the reforms of the *Consulta* must be imposed immediately and by decree, thereby avoiding the "systematic obstruction" of the Spanish Cortes.

The journalist Ramiro de Maeztu foresaw in November 1897 the impending disaster. With harsh bitterness, he denounced the exploitation, poverty, ignorance, and inane illusions of a nation that blindly and without forethought sacrificed its sons in a futile war:

Arrastra España su existencia deleznable, cerrando los ojos al caminar del tiempo, evocando en obsesión perenne glorias añejas, figurándose siempre ser aquella patria que describe la Historia. Este país de obispos gordos, de generales tontos, de políticos usureros, enredadores y "analfabetos," no quiere verse en esas yermas llanuras sin árboles, de suelo arenoso, en el que apenas si se destacan cabañas de barro, donde viven vida animal doce millones de gusanos, que doblan el cuerpo, al surcar la tierra con aquel arado, que importaron los árabes al conquistar Iberia; no se ve en esas provincias anchurosas, tan despobladas como estepas rusas: no se ve en esas fábricas catalanas, edificadas en el aire, sin materia prima, sin máquinas inventadas por nosotros . . . no se ve en esas ciudades agonizantes, donde la necedad ambiente aplasta a los contados espíritus que pretenden sustraerse a su influjo; no se ve en esas Universidades de profesores interinos; en este Madrid hambriento; en esa prensa de palabras hueras: mírase siempre en la leyenda, donde se encuentra grande y aprieta los párpados para no verse tan pequeña.[39]

Maeztu continued his attack on Spanish pretensions in *Hacia otra España* (1899). Like Costa and Galdós, both of whom he fervently admired, Maeztu dismissed the political rhetoric of nineteenth-century Spanish liberalism as hollow sham. "Liberty and order," he claimed, were words devoid of meaning in Spain, a slogan for politicians who wished solely to gain power and create jobs for their hangers-on. The constitutional struggles of the nineteenth century, the ardent debates on forms of government, were scathingly resumed by Maeztu (and Galdós uses identical terms) as "nuestra política romántica."

Maeztu's cure for Spain's ills was that of Costa: the padlocking of the Cid in his tomb, the massive material development of a nation that needed not constitutions but canals, factories, and systems of communications. Totally disillusioned with the accepted "patriotic" values of Spain (and Maeztu was later to regret his words), he bitterly concluded *Hacia otra España* with the declaration that the power of material wealth was greater than that of the spirit: "Cuando sobre la espada del militar, sobre la cruz del religioso y sobre la balanza del juez, ha triunfado el dinero es porque entraña una fuerza superior, una grandeza más intensa que ninguno de esos otros artefactos" (pp. 253-54).

In *El problema nacional* (1899),[40] Macías Picavea blamed defects in the national character for the poverty and decadence of a naturally rich

nation. National ruin was caused by the untamed individualism of
Spaniards: "ese indómito humor individualista, rebelde a toda suave
comunión y armonía, constituye el exclusivo origen de todas las espan-
tosas ruinas y daños morales que a la nación han afligido y afligen" (p.
88). Like Ganivet and the Galdós of the later *episodios*, Macías Picavea
found that Spaniards suffered from a defect of the will. Alternating
between passionate outbursts and apathy, incapable of working steadfastly toward realistic goals, they preferred to live in dreams: "la vida
de casi todos los españoles convertida en un delirio de ensueños difusos,
más que en una vigilia de realidades tangibles" (p. 217).

Macías Picavea's Spain was a sick nation, in imminent danger of
death. Its educational system was bookish and sterile, its commerce in
ruins, its industry backward, its communications ineffective, its religion
hypocritical, its constitutions fictitious. The nation lay in the power of
caciques and was, in the phrase of Revilla, no more than a "tribu con
pretensiones."

Like Costa and Galdós, Macías Picavea considered all official institutions to be hollow and deceptive. Spanish liberalism earned his
contempt, for Spanish liberals were as autocratic, rhetorical, and removed from reality as their opponents ("¡Frailes por dentro, jacobinos
por fuera! "). The Revolution of September was vain and sterile and
had failed to touch fundamental national problems: "Huera por dentro,
estéril en su acción, inconsciente en sus direcciones, sin eficacia honda
ni nacional ni europea, representa sólo una perturbación más, vana y
epidérmica, que deja sin tocar e inerte el fondo de las cosas" (p. 365).

Spain would be cured of its "sickness" only by "surgical" remedies.
Apart from his support for Costa's positive proposals (hydraulic policy,
educational reforms, regional autonomy, public works), Macías
Picavea's analysis included three elements that were repeated by
Galdós: his stress on the will (*la voluntad*) as a means to national
health; his adamant hostility to the Cortes, which he demanded be
closed for at least ten years: "por constituir su morbosa existencia el
más considerable foco de infección social y degeneración nacional,
aparte su impotencia absoluta para toda obra buena" (pp. 388-89); and
his call for a leader to take control of the national destiny: "es el
momento para España de la aparición de *un hombre,* del hombre
histórico, del hombre genial, encarnación de un pueblo y cumplidor de
sus destinos" (p. 502).

Chapter Two

The Third Series of
Episodios Nacionales, 1898-1900

In December 1879, in the concluding paragraph of *Un faccioso más y unos frailes menos*, Galdós announced his abandonment of the "género histórico." While the tedium of composing some three historical novels a year must surely have played no small part in his decision, Galdós cited as reason for his renunciation the lack of historical perspective, the closeness of the years following 1834 to his own day: "Los años que siguen al 34 están demasiado cerca, nos tocan, nos codean, se familiarizan con nosotros. Los hombres de ellos casi se confunden con nuestros hombres. Son años a quienes no se puede disecar, porque algo vive en ellos que duele y salta al ser tocado con escalpelo."[1] By 1898, however, Carlism had been reduced to a mere curiosity, and liberal, constitutional rule had long been institutionalized. In theory, if not in practice, the reign of Queen Isabel II could now be examined with a detachment impossible in the early years of the Restoration.

In early March 1898, Galdós announced plans for a new series of *episodios nacionales;*[2] the first novel of the third series, *Zumalacárregui*, was written in April and May of that year. Galdós, in his introduction to *Zumalacárregui*, cursorily attributed his resumption of the *episodios* to public demand. Later, in his *Memorias*, he referred to the financial difficulties that he trusted the publication of the new series would resolve.[3] Assuredly, however, the sense of national crisis and impending change, as evident in the Spain of the early months of 1898 as in 1873, was reason enough for Galdós to attempt again, through the recreation of Spain's past, the analysis of Spain's ills and the suggestion of possible remedies.[4]

Zumalacárregui was, moreover, conceived at the moment when the bankruptcy of Restoration policies became, for those not blinded by partisan or national prejudice, fully apparent. Spain lacked effective leadership. (The Conservatives were divided and without party head; the Liberals were led by an aging Sagasta of sadly diminished prestige.) The failure of Spain's Cuban policy was manifest, and war with the United States, following the explosion of the *Maine* in February, was imminent. Last-minute appeals to Cuban separatists for a suspension of hostilities fell on deaf ears. Throughout March, jingoistic press and politicians proclaimed Spanish military superiority over the United States. On April 25, 1898, the United States declared war on Spain.

Galdós composed the third series of *episodios nacionales* between April 1898 and October 1900, that is, in the period running from just before the outbreak of war, through the months of defeat, national self-analysis, and attempted regeneration, to the downfall of Silvela's reformist ministry (October 1900). In his popularization of aspects of the First Carlist War and of the liberal regimes of Isabel's minority, Galdós guides his contemporaries to an awareness of Spain's past, an awareness that is a necessary step toward attaining that mature judgment which will prevent the repetition of past errors. Galdós's recreation of history, however, also serves as a forceful commentary on the problems of his own day. Historical events and figures are exemplary; they frequently illustrate defects in national modes of behavior that, continuing into the present, have brought Spain to disaster. Thus, a fictional character such as Fernando Calpena not only witnesses and participates in Spain's past, his attitudes and experiences (rashness, infatuation with abstractions, inability to see reality, downfall) also parallel those of the Spain of 1898. His gradual growth to mature values indicates the path that, for Galdós, Spain must follow if national and personal well-being is to be achieved.

Galdós's analysis of Spain's ills is in many respects akin to (and often antedates) that of the Regenerationists. Like Costa, Galdós treats Spain's past with revulsion. He denounces as shams the apparent liberal advances of the nineteenth century (the constitutions of the 1830s, the Revolution of 1868), savagely attacks a national infatuation with rhetoric that makes a clear vision of Spanish reality impossible, and demands fundamental reforms to save a "sick" nation from suicide. For both Costa and Galdós, Spain is ruled by a corrupt and feudal *cacique* system; official institutions are illusive, deceiving only the gullible. Both Galdós and Costa recognize the poverty of Spain and the sufferings of the humbler classes, and both lament a national tendency to self-destruction. Galdós and Costa also coincide in the remedies that they propose for Spain's "sickness": they call for modest policies, adapted to Spanish reality and directed toward material prosperity;[5] they despise solutions based on politics or ideology; they favor vigorous, even authoritarian, leadership; they reject the facile importation of foreign political systems and demand that reforms be rooted in the history and customs of Spain.[6]

It would be unwise to suggest a direct influence of Costa on Galdós (or of Galdós on Costa). Rather, they both coincided in giving expression to ideas that were in general currency in the Spain of 1898 and following years. Much of Galdós's "message" can be found, for example, in his earlier novel *La desheredada*. However, the force with which he now speaks, his reiteration throughout the third series of key attitudes that he shares with the Regenerationists, his obsession with the "problem of Spain" mark these *episodios* as being as much a part of Regenerationist literature as the writings of Costa. Most of Galdós's comments are couched in general terms; at times, however, he alludes to specific concerns of his day—the Catalan question in *Los Ayacuchos*, Costa's program itself in *La estafeta romántica* and *Bodas reales*.

Throughout the third series of *episodios,* Galdós projects onto the past the pessimistic vision with which many of his contemporaries regarded the Spain of 1898. The spectacle of ragged, crippled soldiers returned from Cuba was a common sight on the streets of Spanish cities in 1898 and 1899. Galdós, echoing the popular complaints of his time, claims that the Spanish people has been sacrificed to satisfy the ambitions of the few: "[El pueblo] lo hace todo; él pelea, él paga los gastos de la campaña, él se pudre en la miseria, para que estos fantasmones vivan y satisfagan sus apetitos de mando y riquezas."[7]

The ready recourse to violence, the anarchical individualism of Spaniards, illustrated in such novels as *Zumalacárregui* and *La Campaña del Maestrazgo,* are destructive not only of national prosperity but of the future of the race itself. Galdós, noting the *escualidez cadavérica* of the Spanish countryside, claims that neglect of agriculture, the flight of natural leaders to the city, will lead to national consumption. Symptoms of racial decline are evident, typified in the sickly offspring of the healthy Maltrana family. The Spanish race, now decadent, is driven to suicide: "Será una manifestación aislada, como otras mil que vemos, del cansancio y pesimismo de la raza española, que indómita en su decadencia, dice: 'Antes que me conquiste el extranjero, quiero morirme. Me acabaré, en parte por consunción, en parte suicidándome con la espada siniestra de las guerras civiles.' Si tuviéramos buenas estadísticas, se vería que ahora muere más juventud que antes."[8]

Like so many of his contemporaries, Galdós is contemptuous of political abstractions. Ideologies serve only to delude the fatuous and mask ignoble desires for self-advancement. The liberal parliamentary system is an exotic foreign plant, ill adapted to Spain's needs. The obsession with politics distracts from more practical concerns; the energies of the nation have been frittered away in futile quarrels over forms; the Cortes are "aquel teatro todo mentira y rencores." Abuse of words is one of the gravest defects in the national character, *palabrería* being in Spain the substitute for will-power and rectitude; the mouthing of high-sounding ideals cloaks the pettiness and vulgarity of personal ambition. The abuse of politics to serve private ends, the cynically hypocritical divorce between the altruistic language of political discourse and the sordid reality concealed by such language, Galdós declares in *Bodas reales,* created in Spain a legacy of corruption for generations to come, a vicious enslaving of national life in which principles have been robbed of all meaning. The relevance of Galdós's criticism to the pompous patriotic rhetoric that preceded the Spanish-American War is obvious.

Galdós's harshest criticism is leveled against attitudes of Romanticism and Quixotry, maladies that divorce Spaniards from reality and that lead them to concern themselves for the affairs of others or for empty abstractions, to the neglect of their own self-interest.[9] Examples of the Romantic-Quixotic sickness abound in the third series of *episodios:* Calpena's Romantic frenzy and sickly life-denying passion for Aura Negretti; Don Alonso de Castro-Amézaga's sacrifice of life and fortune in defense of the dynastic rights of Queen Isabel; Don Beltrán's abandonment of family to search for phantom buried treasure; the Manchegan Bruno Carrasco's attempt to reform Madrid (at the cost of family, honor, and fortune); and the *madrileño* José del Milagro's projected conversion of the land of Don Quixote into a second Garden of Eden, while his daughters are blindly abandoned to prostitution. Similarly, it is *desconocimiento de la realidad* that causes the historical Montes de Oca to pay with his life for his Romantic dreams.

Galdós's assault on Quixotry, his questioning of all but the most severely practical of goals, is nowhere more apparent than in his changing treatment of Costa's program. In *La estafeta romántica* (written in the summer of 1899), iron surgery, the padlocking of Romanticism—Galdós uses Costa's terms—and the dictatorial intervention of practical men of affairs restore Pilar to health. In *Montes de Oca* and *Bodas reales,* however—novels written in the spring and fall of 1900 when the rhetorical nature of the Regenerationist program had become manifest—the catchword *regeneración* and the major features of Costa's proposals for summary reforms are placed in the mouths of cynical politicians. José del Milagro's hydraulic plans (his proposal to make La Mancha bloom through administrative decree and artesian wells) are imbecilic, as also are projects to change Spain's climate through the planting of trees. In a reference to Zaragoza, the headquarters of Costa's movement, Galdós now cuttingly dismisses self-appointed regenerators: "marcharon a Zaragoza, sin acordarse de que esta ciudad es y será siempre la primera de España en no admitir ciertas bromas, y en su aversión a dejarse regenerar por el primero que llega."[10]

In common with Costa and Macías Picavea, and reflecting his despair at parliamentary solutions to Spain's problems, Galdós is obsessed with the need for a leader who will impose fundamental reforms on Spanish life. Of the various leaders praised in the third series of *episodios,* only one—Mendizábal—is a civilian. The others are all generals: Zumalacárregui, Espartero, Córdoba, Maroto, and, above all, Cabrera. Contemptuous of political abstractions, Galdós declares that the leader's ideology is without importance (significantly, three of the generals praised were Carlists). The essential quality of leadership is not correct doctrine but *energía* (the ability to impose one's will). Until the longed-for leader imposes his protectorate on Spain, one character suggests, no progress can be made: "mientras no venga uno que remate, no hemos adelantado nada."[11] For the sickly novelistic characters obsessed by ideologies and abstractions, an imposed solution is the only cure: Calpena blesses the dictatorship of his mother; a forced marriage and maternity give Aura Negretti mental equilibrium; kidnapping frees Santiago Ibero of religious melancholia and restores him to happiness.

The call for a leader who will impose radical (if undefined) reforms reflects not only Galdós's distaste for the selfishness and lack of direction prevailing in Spanish ruling circles but also his obsessive fear of disorder, a fear born of the turmoil that followed the Revolution of 1868. The fundamental demand of the *episodios,* however, is not so much for the restructuring of society from above, but rather for a change in individual behavior. Galdós's proposals for national and personal self-improvement are as vaguely phrased as his pleas for leadership: a healthy morale will work miracles; a combination of the *will* and *judgment* will guide Spain to a happier future. Passages advocating the rather obvious virtues of self-reliance and of work (especially the cultivation of the soil) are frequent: "Haced un país donde sea verdad la justicia, donde sea efectiva la propiedad, eficaz el mérito, fecundo el trabajo, y dejaos de quitar y poner tronos."[12] Pleas for less ambitious goals and for the abandonment of Quixotic idealism are constant. Don Beltrán's advice in this respect is exemplary of Galdós's views, even if the noble Aragonese proves incapable of following his own common-sense mandates: "Mire, hijo, cuando el destino nos pone al pie de un árbol de buena sombra, cargado de fruto, y nos dice 'Siéntate y come,' es locura desobedecerle y lanzarse en busca de esos otros árboles fantásticos, estériles."[13]

In the embittered times that followed the defeat of 1898, Galdós's message is one of reconciliation, of avoidance of strife. Spain, he believes, lacks agreed modes of conduct that would facilitate the handling of private and public life. The tendency to see political questions in terms of angels and demons—an attitude based on the subordination of life to ideology—is the root of much of Spain's disorder. As an antidote to the Spaniard's childish and ill-mannered self-centeredness, Galdós urges respect for others and the practice of courtesy.

In his attack on ideology, on abstractions, Galdós coincides with the Regenerationists. The teaching of the third series is initially—before the failure of Silvela's and Costa's programs became manifest[14]—one of optimism, for Galdós believes reform to be possible; indeed, the very blackness of Galdós's vision of Spain's past is intended as a spur to his contemporaries to change. The emotional lives of four fictitious characters—Fernando Calpena, Aura Negretti, Pilar de Loaysa, and Santiago Ibero—offer obvious parallels to the vision of the Spain of 1898 held by many of Galdós's contemporaries. All four have devoted themselves to an idealistic cause; their illusions are destroyed in a cataclysm, which leaves them morally and emotionally prostrate. But Galdós then indicates the path to health that they (and, by inference, the Spain of 1898) must follow. No program, no ideological commitment, is necessary; indeed, the reformed Calpena affirms the primacy of behavior over thought: "Según vivimos, así pensamos." In periods of turmoil, Galdós advises, the prudent course is to wait, to avoid rash action. Time is the great healer; experience teaches the limitations that reality imposes on all of us; life provides its own solutions. The benign dictatorship offers a period of repose, a halt to break Spain's self-destructive habits. Out of suffering and experience comes self-knowledge and awareness, and it is awareness that distinguishes the Calpena of *Vergara* and *Los Ayacuchos* from the ranting self-indulgent revolutionary of *Mendizábal*. Calpena does once again act Quixotically—to rescue Santiago Ibero—but he is now fully conscious of the motivation for his deeds, no longer the blind slave of literary models. And it is with awareness and detachment, Galdós suggests, that Spaniards can avoid identification with abstract causes, that Romantic *desconocimiento de la realidad* which perverted nineteenth-century liberal politics and which provided fertile ground for the facile optimism of the *patrioteros* of 1898.

I turn now to the teaching of individual *episodios*. My concern is above all with Galdós's message, whether overtly stated or implicit, to his contemporaries of the period 1898 to 1900. His treatment of the historical past, although significant if only for its revaluation of many of the myths of Spanish liberalism, will receive less attention, for an adequate discussion of his approach to history can be found elsewhere. (See, for example, José F. Montesinos, *Galdós,* vol. 3.) In the context of the individual novels, the reader experiences no difficulty in determining which remarks are ironically intended and which represent the views of Galdós. I therefore see no need to burden my commentary with indications that a character is serving as the mouthpiece of Galdós when a normal reading of the text allows no other possibility.

Zumalacárregui (April-May 1898) treats the First Carlist War between November 1834 and June 1835, when Zumalacárregui was killed during the siege of Bilbao. Geographical and temporal limitations in the novel reinforce the almost claustrophobic narrowness of outlook which Galdós attributed to the Carlist movement. The action of the novel is limited to the north of Spain; the outside world—whether conceived spatially or ideologically—finds no place within the novel.[15] No historical background is given; the novel begins, in medias res, with Zumalacárregui's invasion of the Ribera de Navarra. Beyond the briefest of excursions into the *cristino* camp and cursory sketches of the fatuous, self-seeking courtiers of the Carlist court, the novel treats, in its historical sections, only episodes from Zumalacárregui's campaigns. The

Carlist apologists in the novel argue no historical or social justification for their defense of the Pretender's rights. They appeal, outside the historical context, to ideology, to God's supposed support for their divine cause.

The battles described, often little more than skirmishes, have, with the exception of the siege of Bilbao, left little resonance in Spanish history. Against this backdrop of localized, and in the long run fruitless, campaigning, Galdós portrays the courage and powers of resistance of the Spanish soldier, whether Carlist or *cristino*. Examples of charity can be found, but the dominant note of the historical action in the novel is one of brutality and personal vengeance, consciously fomented by Zumalacárregui to build political and military morale. The *cristino* general Valdés is favorably, albeit briefly, characterized, both for the simplicity of his customs and for the affection and respect that he inspired in his troops. The outstanding historical figure of the novel is, however, Zumalacárregui. Despite Galdós's oft-expressed contempt for Carlist ideology, Zumalacárregui is presented in epic terms. His courage, military skill, self-sacrifice, and, above all, breadth of vision combined with attention to detail contrast strongly with the petty scheming of Don Carlos's advisers.

Gómez de Baquero has claimed that in *Zumalacárregui* "la parte histórica ahoga la parte novelesca," that the abundance of topographical and military details weakens the narrative.[16] Galdós's concern, however, is less with the minutiae of history and geography[17] than with the creation, through an imaginative combination of fictional and selected historical elements, of an impressionistic vision of the nature and movement of the period he is portraying. In *Zumalacárregui*, historical action and fictional narrative mutually support each other. The saintly death of the fictional *cristino* Adrián Ulibarri in the first chapter foreshadows Zumalacárregui's exemplary end. It also, in ironic contrast to Zumalacárregui's calculated use of religion for political purposes, undercuts Carlist claims to the exclusive possession of religious truth. In the same scene, the reversal of roles—it is the priest Fago who demands absolution from Ulibarri—establishes from the outset the topsy-turvy condition of Spanish life. The wandering, inconclusive nature of the military campaign finds its counterpart in Fago's personal instability. The attention that Galdós lavishes on such an episode as the recovery of the cannon illustrates the military leader's concern for detail. It also provides for Fago the possibility of channeling, if only

momentarily, his undoubted talents in a useful and personally reward-
ing fashion.

Juan Avalle-Arce, in his perceptive discussion of *Zumalacárregui*, has
suggested that José Fago is, in his insane obsession with the past, for
the biased Galdós the symbol of the Carlist movement.[18] But Fago is
totally lacking in the fanatical devotion to the cause that Galdós
attributes in *Zumalacárregui* to Carlist supporters. Rather, he represents—in his instability, his quest for an ever-elusive meaning for his
existence, his inability to see clearly into his own nature—Galdós's
projection onto the past of the Spain of 1898, of a Spain rent in two,
unable to set firm goals in the future and vainly seeking a past made
impossible by the very violence of the methods used to pursue it. Like
the Spaniard described by Ganivet, Fago is abulic in nature, with fitful
exaltations of the will followed almost immediately by depression and
abandonment of purpose. His internal contradictions and compulsive
behavior, like those of a Spain unable to come to terms with itself, lead
necessarily to his extinction. Unable to resolve the tension between
military ambition and piety, vacillating between self-affirmation and
passivity, he is confused by the occasional intrusion of reality (in the
shape of Saloma's double, the camp follower *Saloma la baturra*). Fago,
like the Spain of 1898 dreaming of past greatness, strives to escape the
limitations of self in his maniacal search for a phantom from his
personal past. The elusive Saloma Ulibarri is, however, rendered forever
inaccessible by Fago's violence and by the gulf of parricide and ideology that must eternally separate them.

Significantly, Saloma Ulibarri plays no part in the novel before its
conclusion. For Fago, seeking his Dulcinea, she is an ideal, representing
hope of personal and national reconciliation. For the Carlists, she is
despised as *cristino* spy and priest's woman. Imagination—and this is
Galdós's constant message in the later *episodios*—deforms, however.
The "real" Saloma, when she finally appears in the novel, is neither
angel nor demon; she is engaged in the humble yet useful task of
washing clothes; she rejoices in the death of Fago's alter ego, Zumalacárregui, the killer of her father and disturbing element in national, as
well as personal, life.

Fago's own identity is as much a mystery, both for himself and
others, as that of Saloma. Priest and warrior, lover and ascetic, egotisti-
cal and yet capable of submerging his personality in that of Zumalacárregui, he is variously mistaken for Mina's nephew and Carlist

prince. Always maintaining an ironic distance, Galdós permits no final judgment on this tormented symbol of national schizophrenia. The priest who hears of Fago's death is unable to determine whether he was good or evil. Earlier, the hermit-seer Bora confesses bafflement when he attempts to decipher Fago's character: "De ti no sé nada . . . No te entiendo . . . En ti veo mucho malo y mucho bueno. En tus ojos hay dos ángeles distintos: el uno con rayos de luz, el otro con cuernos. Yo no sé lo que será de ti. Tú harás maldades, tú harás bondades . . . No sé."[19]

It would not, I believe, be rash to see in *Zumalacárregui* a warning note that Galdós is sounding in the early months of 1898 to his fellow countrymen. Significantly, in view of the disaster that was so rapidly to befall Spain, Galdós chose to portray a losing side. In pointed contrast to the patriotic rhetoric of the day, the lesson is drawn that the long-suffering courage of the Spanish soldier, the inspired military skill of a Zumalacárregui, and the fanatical morale of the Carlists are insufficient to bring victory. Bullets and cannon, not prayers or the supposed justice of one's cause, decide battles; God is impartial, taking no part in the wars of mortals.

Throughout the novel, the pointlessness and horrors of war are stressed. It is the blood shed in the fratricidal struggle[20] —and the relevance to the Cuban situation would have been immediately apparent to Galdós's contemporaries—which makes reconciliation impossible. The conclusion, both of Fago and others, is disillusionment with collective values and a selfish search for individual survival.

Going beyond the immediate Cuban situation, Galdós probes weaknesses in Spanish behavior in search of guidance to future action. As in *La desheredada,* a reform in moral attitudes (self-knowledge, the setting-up of realizable goals, the adjustment of means to ends) is necessary for continued national and personal existence. Such Spanish defects as excessive recourse to violence, overweening ambition, and anarchical Quixotic individualism must give way to a collaborative effort. This common effort requires the direction of a leader who, like Zumalacárregui, can see the broad perspective of historical change and yet also concern himself with the smallest detail of his projects. The leader however, unlike Zumalacárregui, should offer his skills and loyalty to more fruitful tasks than those of war and service to the ambitions of self-seeking courtiers and politicians.

Curiously, *Zumalacárregui* presents many similarities to the very first *episodio nacional, Trafalgar* (1873). In both cases, the setting is provincial. (It is only in the second novels of the first and third series that the reader is introduced to the seat of political power, Madrid.) In both *Trafalgar* and *Zumalacárregui*, a defeat is portrayed, and the heroism and self-sacrifice evoked are expended in a cause that does not answer the true interests of Spain. Above all, both novels illustrate exemplary leadership and a noble acceptance of death. The Battle of Trafalgar, however, was the prelude to the glorious War of Independence; Gabriel Araceli's adventures and moral growth were therefore continued in the later *episodios* of the first series. Carlism, on the other hand, represented for Galdós a false path in Spanish history. Fago, resuming the frustrations and undertain focus of a nation at war with itself, is the victim of internal contradictions and is allowed no transcendence. For the later *episodios* of the third series, a new fictional protagonist, one who can learn from his errors and thereby exemplify the goals to which Spanish society should direct itself, will be introduced in the shape of Fernando Calpena. The only connection between *Zumalacárregui*— representing, like the Cuban War, a dead end in Spanish history—and *Mendizábal*—with its perspective toward the future—will lie in Galdós's exaltation of the qualities of leadership.

Between the time of composition of *Zumalacárregui* (April-May 1898) and that of *Mendizábal* (August-September 1898), the disastrous nature of the policies of Sagasta and his predecessors became fully apparent. Naval defeats at Cavite (May) and Santiago de Cuba (July) spelled the end, save for insignificant territories in Africa, of Spain's colonial empire. In early August, a suspension of hostilities was accepted on American terms. In Spain, Sagasta ruled with a muzzled press. (Constitutional guarantees were suspended in July.) The Cortes, which met briefly in September, were not allowed to inquire into the causes and responsibility for the disaster. A sentiment that the nation had been deceived by its leaders was widespread. Silvela, in August, and General Polavieja, in September, called for a radical restructuring of the organization of the nation, for the replacement of the "lies" and rhetorical abstractions of politicians by policies based on a realistic acceptance of the Spanish situation.

Mendizábal covers the period between September 1835 and the early months of 1836, between Mendizábal's accession to power and the intimations of his rapidly approaching downfall. The overwhelming impression given by the novel is one of life and movement, of a great change taking place in Spanish society. The material scene (details of elegant fashion, of society life, of novel household comforts) is briefly sketched. Numerous references (if only by name) to writers and politicians, brilliant pastiches of Romantic attitudes of love, rebellion, and despair, the assimilation into the text of phrases that the most casual student of literature would associate with the 1830s ("los porteros del Pirineo," "vuelva usted mañana," "Bueno es el mundo, bueno, bueno, bueno," etc.), all serve to recreate a time of mental effervescence, of overheated imaginations furiously seeking an outlet. Energies and ambitions are poured into politics, with its feverish atmosphere of intrigue and counterintrigue, and into art and letters, with the eruption into Spanish life of a generation of young Romantics.

Perhaps in no other novel has Galdós so successfully incarnated in novelistic characters and intrigue his impressionistic vision of the nature and evolution of historical attitudes. The rapid pace of societal change in the Spain of the mid-1830s, such abrupt transformations of personal fortune as Mendizábal's meteoric rise to (and fall from) power and Muñoz's elevation to consort of the queen[21] find their novelistic counterpart in the adventures of Fernando Calpena, who passes dizzily from poverty to financial and social success before, at the end of the novel, his downfall and imprisonment. Calpena (born, significantly, in the very year of Trafalgar) represents the first generation to come of age entirely within the nineteenth century. Like the Spain of the nascent liberal regime, Calpena lacks roots in the past—he is unaware of his parents' identities—and is of partly French formation. Imitating his compatriots in politics, Calpena neglects the counsels of prudence he had received in his upbringing, readily embracing the Arabian Nights atmosphere into which his mysterious protector plunges him. Just as Spanish liberals were blinded for a time by the beauty of María Cristina, so also does Calpena, with in the long run equally unfortunate consequences, become enamored of Aura Negretti.

Aura (Aurora) Negretti is a complex figure. She symbolizes within herself a Spain that is both illusory and real. Her name refers above all to the "crystalizing" (to use the term in the Stendhalian sense) effect that she has on others: the hope of a new dawn which is nonetheless followed by darkness; a bewitching quality (of fundamental void?) which allows others to project on her their own illusions of happiness. (The more experienced *La desconocida* dismisses her as a "false diamond.") She represents also, like the Rosario of *Doña Perfecta*, an ingenuous Spain in need of guidance. Her ancestry is as mixed as the ideologies of the Spain of the 1830s. She is willful yet well intentioned. Her most pressing desire—which is that of a Spain still in the formative stage (and that of 1898 also)—is for instruction: "Vamos, que no tengo educación. . . . No he tenido quien me eduque ni quien me enseñe nada. . . . Y ahora trato de educarme yo misma; pero, la verdad, no sé por dónde empezar."[22]

In his treatment of Calpena's revolt against reason, Galdós sounds a note of warning against the belief of Spanish reformers and revolutionaries that the strength of personal desire, and the clothing of this desire in high-sounding verbal formulas, are of themselves sufficient to transform society. Calpena in his youth had learned from the saintly Vidaurre the classical virtues of charity, moderation, and order. These lessons receive further reinforcement in the novel in the equally balanced and commonsense approach of the sympathetically portrayed "cura, torero y retórico," Pepe Hillo. The days of Vidaurre are nevertheless past ("No nacerá otro D. Narciso Vidaurre, el santo, el justo, el sabio, el discreto," p. 81). New experiences (the favors mysteriously showered upon Calpena) apparently justify Calpena's acceptance of the role of chance in his life. Calpena's abandonment of his guardian's teaching, however, goes beyond the mere reception of unearned benefits. Innocently believing, with Aura, that the world begins afresh with them, he denies the past to declare his independence of society.

But, as Spanish liberals were discovering, historical and social contexts cannot be denied. Just as Mendizábal's freedom of action was circumscribed by the hidden intrigues of courtiers, masons, and foreign ambassadors, so also are the lives of Fernando and Aura controlled by forces from the past, by characters representing the despotism of the *Antiguo Régimen*. *La desconocida*'s attempts to rule Fernando are benevolent. Jacoba Zahón, the facial double of Marie Antoinette, on the other hand, is openly tyrannical and exploits Aura; she symbolizes more narrowly selfish and sordid facets of traditional authority.

In large measure, Calpena, like the liberal revolutionaries of the nineteenth century, is justified in rejecting the despotic manipulation of which he is the object. The manner in which he carries out his revolt, however, is misguided. His declaration of freedom from society and his shaking-off of the tyranny of the past are accompanied by the abandonment of reason, by an enslavement to his own passions, and by an obsessed violence and exaltation (in love, in politics, in personal habits). His behavior is, like the feverish politics of the period, harshly categorized in the novel as a sickness, a madness that has possessed him and many of his generation. Not only are the means he employs self-destructive, but he also lacks sufficient knowledge of the world to choose a worthy goal for his aspirations. Aura's own insanity (in apparent emulation of the French Revolution, she sets out to execute Jacoba) only intensifies that of Calpena. Calpena, like the callow formulators of ideal constitutions, believes that all will come to him without effort on his part; he believes that he can control his destiny without heed of others. He uses his emancipation, however, only to live a bad Romantic drama. His ill-considered rebellion provokes a worse repression than that against which he had protested. At the end of the novel, his inability to use his freedom wisely lands him, as also his better-deserving friend Hillo, in jail.

Like *Zumalacárregui*, *Mendizábal* takes as title the name of a historical figure who, for Galdós, revealed qualities of leadership. Mendizábal appears on the Spanish political scene with the aura of a worker of miracles. He promises a rapid end to the Carlist War and to the anarchy of the juntas, a solution to Spain's financial problems, and the establishment in Spain of the ordered liberty of England. The abilities he brings to his task are many: he is intelligent and genuinely concerned for the welfare of his country; he is a tireless worker; his vision of the needs of Spain is far-reaching—he foresees and weighs the consequences, both good and evil, of the seizure and sale of clerical property—yet at the same time he has a care for detail that enables him to attend to the day-to-day concerns of government. But limitations, both of a personal and historical nature, doom his efforts to a sure failure. He is vain and superstitious, seeking facile, immediate solutions, while possessing no clear vision of the means to arrive at his lofty goals. Despite the almost dictatorial powers granted him, circumstances—palace intrigues, the pressures brought to bear by France and England—restrict his freedom of action. Beset on all sides by the envies of rival politicians and the importunities of job-seekers, fearing replacement by a victorious general, and obliged to devote time to the long-winded and empty rhetoric of the Cortes, he is forced to decide too hastily on too many matters; opportunity for adequate deliberation is denied to him.

Galdós's portrayal in *Mendizábal* of "la fealdad mal oliente de la España de 1836" reflects above all his concern for the similar problems besetting the Spain of 1898, as Ramiro de Maeztu immediately recognized: "Solo un escritor, Pérez Galdós, ha desentrañado del burbujeo de los gérmenes la España capitalista que se nos echa encima. En su libro *Mendizábal* abundan los brochazos en que los ojos del novelista más se han fijado en la patria de hoy, que en la de nuestros abuelos" (*Hacia otra España*, p. 218). Calpena's attitudes and adventures repeat the Spanish experience of 1898: an exalted belief in the justice of his cause, an excess of emotional fervor, a trust in miraculous solutions, a sudden downfall and loss of innocence, all played against a backdrop of national corruption. Calpena's rash abandonment of the principles of his upbringing raises the question (to be explored in later novels) of how change is to be effected in Spain. Galdós's approach in *Mendizábal* is exploratory. His positive proposals for reform (mere insinuations at this point) are tentative and at first sight contradictory.

Change of behavior, not ideological purity, is Galdós's implicit demand. He diagnoses the pervasive national sin as selfishness. Politicians are motivated by self-interest and envy; Mendizábal's flaw is vanity; swarms of self-proclaimed patriots and redeemers strive to live in idleness at public expense; Calpena wastes his energies in a sterile, destructive passion.

A further lesson of *Mendizábal* (and one consonant with the straitened circumstances of the defeated nation of 1898) is the need for less ambitious goals.[23] The three characters who receive most sympathetic treatment in the novel—Vidaurre (with his devotion to duty and balanced cult of classical virtues), Hillo (with his common sense and generosity), and Milagro (who accepts his humble lot and struggles good-humoredly for the survival of his family)—all live modestly and sacrifice self in the service of others. Magical remedies (Calpena's Romantic bliss, Mendizábal's promised miracles) are rejected by Galdós. National and personal self-reliance, so blatantly absent in the characters of *Mendizábal*, will prove a surer guide, as Vidaurre counseled: "Lábrate la dicha con tu trabajo, acostúmbrate a que tu bienestar sea obra de ti mismo, y no esperes nunca favores llovidos del cielo" (p. 89).

However, while humility, sacrifice, and obedience are demanded of the individual, Galdós seeks for national problems an imposed solution. (Compare the entry into national politics of General Polavieja on September 1, 1898.) A total regeneration is needed. Little is accomplished by those who use half-measures, who do not know how to *rematar la suerte*, in Hillo's picturesque phrase. Parliamentary methods are useless (Galdós's contempt for the time-consuming squabbles and hollow inanities of the Cortes is marked throughout the novel); nor, Hillo remarks, will *comerciantes* succeed any better than humanists in ruling Spain.[24] National salvation will come through the efforts of a leader: "mientras no venga uno que remate, no hemos adelantado nada," p. 44). The leader's program is not defined by Galdós. The leader's power will come from success, from the energetic fulfilment of promises: "La fuerza la da el buen gobernar, el cumplimiento de lo que se ha ofrecido, la energía, la rectitud; de todo esto sale al fin el aura popular" (p. 261).

That the nation can be redeemed by a suitable leader is not questioned. Mendizábal, *La desconocida* affirms, fails only through personal vanity (that is, he relies on the opinion of others rather than imposes his own will): "podría indudablemente regenerar el país si se cuidara menos de aspirar el incienso que le echan sus aduladores y paniaguados" (p. 261). The leader may well come from the military, for, Mendizábal wryly observes (and the irony of the remark does not necessarily imply Galdós's dissent), only a successful soldier is capable of imposing salvation on Spain: "no ignoraba que, en nuestra tierra de garbanzos y pronunciamientos, el guerrero victorioso es el único salvador en todos los órdenes" (p. 130).

Although a direct influence must be excluded (Costa's program was not distributed until mid-November 1898), the teaching of *De Oñate a la Granja* (October-November 1898) strikingly resembles the analysis and proposals of the *Consulta* of the *Cámara Agrícola del Alto Aragón*. Galdós, like Costa, attacks the "Romantic" nature of Spanish politics, an arbitrary judicial system that caters to the whims of the powerful, and universities that produce only *leguleyos*. Like Costa, Galdós advocates prudence, proper attention to one's own interests (Costa's "Hacienda, que tu amo te vea"), and the "surgery" of a dictator. It was a common plaint of 1898 that the laboring classes bore a disproportionate burden of the Cuban campaigns. Similarly, Galdós recognizes that the *pueblo* paid the cost of Bourbon dynastic ambitions: "El lo hace todo: él pelea, él paga los gastos de la campaña, él muere, él se pudre en la miseria, para que estos fantasmones vivan y satisfagan sus apetitos de mando y riquezas."[25]

Few historical events, and these often at second hand, are related in *De Oñate a la Granja:* Mendizábal's farcical "Romantic" duel with

Istúriz, Mendizábal's fall from power, the Carlist retreat from the phantom court of Oñate, the sergeants' rebellion in La Granja. The partisan nature of Galdós's approach to history is apparent throughout the novel: *cristino* officers are sympathetically portrayed; Don Carlos and his followers are treated with hostility and scorn. The Carlist court mirrors that of Madrid: it is rent by self-seeking ambitions and petty envies; Carlist courtiers, like the café strategists of the nation's capital, seek to impose their fatuous views on experienced military leaders. Religious hypocrisy abounds in the Carlist camp.[26]

Many aspects of Spanish life in 1836 (and the criticism was equally relevant to the Spain of 1898) provoke Galdós's contempt: the malicious gossip that, with the guerrillas, typifies the national character, the intrigues of court and Cortes ("aquel teatro todo mentira y rencores"), self-seeking professional revolutionaries ("aquella desdichada hez de la plebe revolucionaria") and clerics who mouth the slogans of the left, and a spoils system that leads to the abrupt dismissal of honest functionaries.

The pessimistic mood of late 1898 is reflected in the disillusionment that pervades the novel. The countryside is laid waste by warring bands. Valuable Spanish lives are uselessly sacrificed in defense of a degraded absolutist ideal. Mendizábal, whose fundamental decency is extolled, wisely prefers the peace of domestic happiness to the ingratitude of a nation. Don Alonso, the quixotic champion of liberalism, his stability destroyed by the death of his wife (which occurred, symbolically, on the day that Fernando VII died), insanely sacrifices prosperity and health for the cause of Queen Isabel; he has learned the lesson of experience when, toward the conclusion of the novel, he can but repeat, like the sailor of *Trafalgar*, "A casa."

As in *Mendizábal,* Galdós diagnoses the sickness afflicting Spanish customs and politics as "Romantic" in its inspiration. The extremists of the French Revolution, Robespierre and Saint Just, were "los románticos de la política." *El trovador* contains the germs of social egalitarianism; even Hillo, possessed by the contagious disease of Romanticism, for a while takes leave of his senses. Carlist War and Mendizábal's duel are both manifestations of Romantic insanity: "Para que el romanticismo, ya bien manifiesto en la Guerra Civil, se extendiese a todos los órdenes, como un contagio epidémico, hasta los Ministros Presidentes iban al terreno, pistola en mano, con ánimo caballeresco, para castigar los desmanes de la oposición. En los campos del Norte, la cuestión dinástica se sometía al juicio de Dios. Los políticos, ciegos, medio locos ya, no pudiendo entenderse con la palabra que de todas las bocas afluía sin tasa, apelaban a la pólvora" (p. 91).

In common with the Regenerators of 1898 (Silvela, Polavieja, Costa, etc.), Galdós in *De Oñate a la Granja* demands a total restructuring of Spanish government: "pues el defecto capital está en la quilla, y mientras no se emprenda la reforma por lo hondo, construyendo de nuevo todo el casco, no hay esperanzas de próspera navegación" (p. 120). Continuing the authoritarianism of *Mendizábal*, Galdós suggests, through *La desconocida*, that the salvation of the nation is to be sought in a dictator, in the exemplary General Córdova ("la representación más alta de la inteligencia y la voluntad en tres órdenes distintos, el militar, el político y el diplomático"): "Córdova tiene todas las cualidades de César . . . Es guerrero y político . . . Si él no hace de esta tribu de alborotadores una nación, perdamos la esperanza de redimirnos. Mendizábal ha fracasado, porque no ha sabido rematar la suerte . . . Córdova la rematará . . . Es el hombre único . . . Esperar nuestra salvación del Estatuto o de la Constitución del 12, es vivir en el reino de las pamplinas . . . Córdova es el Bonaparte sin ambición, bello ideal de los dictadores . . . *Una espada que piense: esto es lo que nos hace falta*" (pp. 44-45; my italics).

The Spanish obsession with politics, however, distracts the individual from his true interests. Significantly, immediately after the panegyric of Córdova's qualities, Hillo matter-of-factly proposes that he and Calpena eat. Politics disturb all classes of society. Thus, Nicomedes Iglesias is a Sancho Panza who loses both prosperity and bride in his unsuccessful quest for an *ínsula* amid the sordid politics of Madrid. Similarly, the quixotic Don Alonso's futile defense of the rights of the young queen costs him property, daughters, and life itself.

In tracing the first hesitant stages of Calpena's growth to spiritual health, Galdós indicates the course that the Spain of 1898 should follow on its road to regeneration. In *Mendizábal,* Calpena had revealed too great a selfishness, an infatuation with words, a lack of experience and of prudence.[27] Like a nation in need of a respite from the excitement of politics (and Galdós's proposed remedy is precisely that of Costa), Calpena's frenzied Romantic career is momentarily curtailed by a dictatorial act, by the incarceration that he likens to "surgery." The perils of this "surgery" are acknowledged: deprivation of freedom, Calpena realizes, prevents any realistic assessment of his future conduct;

his imprisonment would, should the "benign tyrant" disappear, become permanent. Nevertheless, the breathing space afforded to Calpena protects him from further imprudence. It also, by forcing on him a change of behavior, represents the first stage of his cure. (Calpena is now amused, rather than exalted, by the popular demagogues who are his prison companions; he is compelled, through dependence on *La desconocida*'s letters for all contact with the outside world, to make some effort to come to terms with authority, however capriciously exercised. *La desconocida* also recognizes the need to adapt to changed circumstances. She determines to relax her arbitrary rule and permit her protégé some measure of freedom.)

Calpena, when released from prison, now has some awareness of the world, a world that bears little resemblance to the creations of his Romantic imagination. Ildefonso Negretti, Aura's guardian, proves to be no ogre; a courtship (provided that the demands of decency be respected) will be permitted; it is the abashed Calpena who is unable to reply to Negretti's reasonable inquiry as to his profession; the Romantic drama becomes, in the light of day, a *comedia casera*. A further sign of the decline in Calpena's Romantic obsession is evident during the disorder of the Carlist retreat from Oñate, when Calpena is forced to choose between a social demand—the appeal to help in saving Don Alonso—and his selfish urge to pursue Aura. Calpena now protects with chivalry and decision those who most immediately need his assistance. He is rewarded by entry into a world that, with its exemplary heroine—the Demetria who is a model of activity, practical sense, good nature, and charity—and fecundity of Nature, is as idyllic as any dreamed of by Pereda. Calpena's self-analysis, provoked by the spectacle of Demetria's cheerful acceptance of responsibility, marks a decisive moment—and the lesson is clearly intended by Galdós for the guidance of his contemporaries of 1898—in his abandonment of the socially destructive bent of his earlier Romantic selfishness in favor of the more fruitful ideal of service to community. His reflections merit quotation in full:

¡Espantosa desigualdad! —se dijo.—Veo a esta mujer tan útil, tan activa, repartiendo alegrías en torno suyo y aumentando el bienestar humano. Luego miro para dentro de mí y observo mi inutilidad, mi insuficiencia. Necesito de estos ejemplos para cerciorarme de que no sirvo para nada, de que no soy nada, de que mi existencia es absolutamente estéril . . . al menos hasta ahora . . . He aquí un hombre sin carrera, sin profesión, que no sabe cómo vive hoy ni cómo vivirá mañana . . . un hombre

que todo lo espera del acaso, que apoya sus cálculos en lo desconocido ... un hombre que desconoce el trabajo, y que no da señales de
vida en la sociedad más que para perturbarla (pp. 326-27).

Reacting against the depressed spirit of the Spain of 1898, Galdós
offers in *Luchana* (January-February 1899) an inspiring vision of Spanish courage and a lesson in the power of the will to overcome all obstacles.
The novel is built on a series of contrasts that reveal both the defects of
Spaniards and the qualities that will enable the nation to overcome
these flaws. Thus, Galdós treats in *Luchana* military indiscipline (the
"comic opera" revolt of the sergeants of La Granja) and Spanish
heroism (the courage of the inhabitants of Bilbao and of Espartero's
troops), bookish Romanticism (that of the dreamer Calpena) and classi-
cism (or "Romanticism of action," that of Zoilo Arratia), an excess of
feeling (the Spanish people, Calpena, Aura Negretti) and prudent direction of conduct (Don Beltrán, the Arratia family), individualism (Calpena) and the strength of union (the Arratia family), passive acceptance
of fate (the Calpena of earlier novels) and the bending of destiny to
man's will (the heroic inhabitants of Bilbao, Zoilo Arratia).

In common with the Regenerationists, Galdós in *Luchana* takes issue
with the obsession of nineteenth-century Spanish liberals with forms,
their willingness to take appearance for reality. Thus, the sergeants of
La Granja substitute for legitimate authority a constitution that they
have never examined. Spanish liberals are content with the mere trappings of change: "Estos pobres liberales son unas criaturas que se pasan
la vida mudando motes y letreros, sin reparar en que varían los nombres
y las cosas son siempre las mismas. Ahora les da por jugar alas
Constitucioncitas ... ; ¡qué inocentes! "[28] Passion and enthusiasm,
rather than thought and fruitful action, are the moving forces in
Spanish political life: "un país que todavía anda buscando la mejor de
las Constituciones posibles, y que no parece dispuesto a dejarse gobernar con sosiego hasta que no la encuentre; de un país que todavía
emplea como principal resorte político el entusiasmo, cosa muy buena
para hacer revoluciones, cuando éstas vienen a cuento, mas no para
gobernar a los pueblos" (p. 11). "Ese sentimiento indefinido viene
siendo la energía que mueve toda la máquina social y política; pero,
¡ay! , andaremos mal si no se traduce pronto en ideas, en hechos

pacíficos, pues no vive un país con el solo alimento de entusiasmos y cantatas" (p. 64).

The defense of Bilbao, on the other hand, demonstrates the tenacity, heroism, and self-sacrifice of which Spaniards are capable, when fighting in an obviously just cause and with proper leadership. In the face of danger, all Bilbao closes its ranks; distinctions of class and ideology cease to count; personal ties are subordinated to service to community.[29] Morale is the deciding factor, while optimism (even if feigned) and collective effort enable the inhabitants of Bilbao to accomplish apparently impossible goals:

Gran virtud es en estos casos la ficción de entereza. Los pueblos viven del sentimiento colectivo, y los bilbaínos supieron en tan suprema ocasión cultivarlo, creándose previamente la atmósfera en que debían consumar sus inauditas hazañas; atmósfera falsa, si se quiere, pero que los hechos, la constancia y tesón de aquel divino mentir convertirían luego en real y positiva. . . . Los histriones dejarían de serlo a fuerza de fingir bien y de mostrarse alegres cuando la realidad les imponía la tristeza. Era un pueblo de imaginativos, y los imaginativos que proceden con intensidad en su labor psicológica, acaban por crear (pp. 211-12).

Qualities of leadership are as valued in *Luchana* as in earlier *episodios*. The leadership of Espartero is exemplary: devoted to his troops and to the cause for which they were fighting, sacrificing health and fortune to obtain victory, he possessed the gift of inspiring enthusiasm in his followers and of boldly seizing whatever advantage chance might offer him. "Desgraciada era entonces España; pero tenía hombres," Galdós admiringly exclaims (p. 387). The passage of time only confirms the greatness of such leaders and renders their failure in peace all the more poignant:

El tiempo, en vez de amenguar la talla de aquellas figuras, las agiganta cada día, y hoy las vemos subir, no tanto quizás por lo que ellas crecen, como por lo que nos achicamos nosotros; y aun lloramos un poquito, ya con todo el siglo dentro del cuerpo, viendo que gérmenes tan hermosos no hayan fructificado más que en el campo de la guerra civil. Creíamos que aquello era el aprendizaje para empresas de superior magnitud . . . Pero no era sino precocidad infantil, de las que luego salen fallidas, dándonos tras el muchachón de extremado vigor cerebral, hombres raquíticos y sin seso (p. 386).

Calpena (the symbol of a sick, "Romantic" Spain) is as demented as ever, blindly seeking his "ideal," Aura. He receives, however, sound advice from Don Beltrán de Urdaneta. Don Beltrán, echoing the teaching of Ganivet and Costa, pleads for the replacement of a restless, sterile idealism by practical, attainable goals (a doctrine of common sense which at this point in the *episodios* neither he nor Calpena is emotionally prepared to follow): "Mire, hijo, cuando el destino nos pone al pie de un árbol de buena sombra, cargado de fruto, y nos dice "Siéntate y come," es locura desobedecerle y lanzarse en busca de esos otros árboles fantásticos, estériles, que en vez de raíces tienen patas . . . y corren . . . Yo desobedecí a mi destino, y por aquella desobediencia no he tenido paz en mi larga vida. Créalo: donde no hay raíces no hay paz" (p. 115). In his portrayal of the magnificent Arratia family, Galdós indicates the path toward a brighter future for Spain. The Arratias are traders and industrialists; one family member (Ildefonso Negretti) is artisan and inventor. They are creators of wealth and thus contribute to the common good.[30] The qualities possessed by this family of entrepreneurial capitalists (an idealized vision, perhaps, of the *clases productoras* that Costa sought to organize) are model: devotion to duty, honesty, candor, spirit of solidarity with family and nation, love of hard work, infectious good humor, willingness to take risks, strength of body and mind. As individuals, their virtues differ, but each in his own way offers an example for Spain to emulate. Thus, even poor, amphibious Churi, deaf and unable to speak coherently (the symbol, possibly, of an older Spain that is unable to adjust to the modern world), unselfishly flees, when disappointed in his aspiration to Aura's hand, rather than bring discord to his family. Martín Arratia, the balanced, far-sighted businessman and courageous *miliciano,* symbolizes the calm acceptance of duty. If Spain was in *De Oñate a la Granja* a captainless, foundering vessel, Martín's values will ensure salvation from shipwreck: "Si terribles son las olas embravecidas, no es menos pavoroso en ciertos casos el cumplimiento del deber, así en la guerra como en el comercio. Todo es navegar; todo es una continuada lucha, un gran derroche de esfuerzos, arte y valor para no ahogarse" (p. 161). In the face of the disaster of 1898, Galdós stresses the avoidance of recrimination and discord. Thus, Martín Arratia accepts with resignation the loss of Aura, preferring to look ahead to the common welfare: "lo pasado, pasado: todos hermanos, todos unidos, y a trabajar por el bien común" (p. 355).

In Zoilo Arratia, Galdós optimistically represents one of the qualities that will enable Spain to recover from the Disaster of 1898: the power of the will to overcome all obstacles. Calpena's Romanticism is derived from books and idle dreams and is, like the phantom constitutions his contemporaries so avidly pursued, *pura mentira*. Zoilo, on the other hand, is "un romántico . . . de acción," or rather, as Aura recognizes, a classic, in the tradition of the ancient gods who imposed their wills on mankind.[31] Affirming a healthy freedom from dependence on others, Zoilo takes pride in the performance of noble deeds.[32] His moral force, his fearless energy, his will of iron are irresistible. The habits of the past (the authority of father and uncle) and present difficulties (Aura's resistance) readily give way to the magnetic force of his personality. In words with which Galdós boldly challenges all those who would despair of the future of Spain, Zoilo affirms the power of man to forge his own destiny: "Todo lo que el hombre quiere con firme voluntad, lo tiene, y más" (p. 320).

The qualities of the Arratias and their contribution to the national good are models presented by Galdós for the future guidance of Spain. His confidence that Spain can indeed be regenerated by such means is exemplified in his treatment of Aura Negretti. Aura's symbolical role in *Luchana* is twofold. She symbolizes, with her waywardness and beauty (a beauty that is a trap for the unwary and that in itself serves no beneficial purpose in society), the restless aspirations of Romantic Spain. Avidly wooed by suitors of all classes, ages, and ideologies, she is, like the Constitution of Cadiz, *la niña bonita,* a lure to distract men from more useful tasks. But in herself, as opposed to the "Romantic" vision which others have of her, she is hysterical, overimaginative, and totally lacking in will-power, a clear symbol of the defective, ill-constituted Spain of 1836 and of 1899.

This second Aura (or Spain) is in *Luchana* nursed to equilibrium by a combination of isolation from disturbing influences, attention to physical health, and contact with life-enhancing ideas (the infectious joviality and exemplary labor of the Arratias). Freedom from disorder, material prosperity, and healthy goals are, however, only part of the remedy that Galdós proposes to his contemporaries. Aura (Spain) is certainly well on the road to recovery (she is able, during the siege of Bilbao, to assist the defenders). She is, nevertheless, still not totally freed from her sickly Romantic obsessions and suffers, notably, from a paralysis of the will. To avoid the relapse of Aura (Spain) into the disastrous attitudes of the past, Galdós offers a drastic, imposed solution, one already intimated in his laudatory treatments of Zumalacárregui, Mendizábal, and Córdova. An exemplary dictatorship will preserve Spain from further suicidal impulses; Zoilo Arratia imposes marriage on Aura.

From the opening chapters worthy of the brush of a Goya, in which crippled and demented fugitives relive their torments, to the denouement of murder and suicide, Galdós presents in *La Campaña del Maestrazgo* (April-May 1899) a nightmare vision of the self-destruction of a nation. Unending atrocities—the *cristinos'* execution of Cabrera's aged mother, Cabrera's savage reprisals, the priest Lorente's pathological cruelty, the massacre of Burjasot—precede and accompany the Carlist *caudillo*'s campaigns of early 1837. The veneer of modern civilization has been stripped away to reveal a fantastic, medieval world, in which superstition, demonic possession, and savagery reign un- checked: "La mezquina civilización *a la moderna* se desvanecía, se borraba como un afeite mal aplicado, dejando sólo las querellas feudales, el ardor místico, la superstición, las crueldades horrendas y e- minentes virtudes, el heroísmo, la poesía, la intervención de ángeles y demonios, que andaban sueltos y desmandados por el mundo."[33]

Galdós sympathizes with neither warring band. God is indifferent to man's cruelty; *cristino* and Carlist alike behave with brutality. The characters of the novel, whether historical or fictitious, have no interest in the religious and dynastic issues supposedly at stake; their struggle is for purely personal gains: "Creo que se lucha por la dominación, y nada más, por el mando, por mangoneo, por ver quién reparte el pedazo de pan, el puñado de garbanzos y el medio vaso de vino que corresponden a cada español" (p. 70).

The savage Carlist War is only incidental to *La Campaña del Maestrazgo*. Galdós illustrates above all the suicidal consequences facing Spain if common sense be lost and ignoble passions allowed free rein. Calpena's adventures—save for the passing mention that Calpena has lost his wager and thus the hand of Aura—are now forgotten; instead, the leading figure is Don Beltrán de Urdaneta. Heedless of the excellent advice that he himself had proffered in *Luchana*, Don Beltrán loses sight of his true interests, fleeing the "despotism" of a daughter-in-law to search for the buried gold of a former tenant; that is, he forgets present reality in favor of dreams of past glory. Like those unfortunate *escarmentados* who had taken part in the Carlist War, Beltrán learns the hard lessons of experience. The gold is, if not fantastic, certainly inaccessible. Because he in his pride rejected the discipline and petty indignities of family life, he must now suffer insults to his honor and the constant threat of death as a hostage in the hands of Cabrera. But Beltrán learns, if with some backsliding, from his suffering. In exemplary contrast to the Carlist priests, with their sanguinary acceptance of the savagery of a "holy war," he humbly submits in the name of Christ to insult. His former pride and greed—characteristics, perhaps, of those who in the 1890s would dream of reviving the past glories of Spain— now give way to the Christian virtue of resignation.

Representative of the sickness and degradation to which the Spanish temperament is prone are two inhabitants of the atavistic world into which Don Beltrán has so rashly plunged: Marcela (a wandering hermit of ambiguous sexuality and sanity, who possesses the same fierce independence as Cervantes's character of the same name) and her suitor the Carlist officer Nelet (a rural Don Juan of violent and perverse passions). Two courses are open to the pair and, implicitly, to Spain. The first, suggested by Beltrán, is one of fruitful union, of redemption of both Marcela and Nelet from their sterile and antisocial individualism, possible only if Nelet succeeds in controlling his instincts by renouncing violence. The second is one of cataclysmic destruction, expressed in Nelet's nightmare vision in which he, in the form of a skeleton, tramples millions of children as he rides a skeleton horse across a barren plain. Nelet's (and Spain's) demons are too strong. Nelet kills Marcela's brother, murders Marcela, and commits suicide. At the end of the novel, only gravediggers, and not Cervantes's shepherds, remain.

Besides indicating the catastrophic consequences, both for nation and individual, of giving way to selfish passion, Galdós preaches through the mouth of Don Beltrán the measures necessary for the regeneration of Spain. National salvation is not to be found in political remedies but will be created by work: "Allanad y afirmad el suelo ante todo, y esto lo haréis con las artes de la paz, no con guerras y trapisondas. . . . haced un país donde sea verdad la justicia, donde sea efectiva la propiedad, eficaz el mérito, fecundo el trabajo, y dejaos de quitar y poner tronos" (p. 242). The nation is destroyed by those who would live idly at the expense of the state: "¿Empleados de qué? Sois muchos a comer rancho; sois muchos a vivir de distinciones, de cintajos y signos categóricos. Y yo os pregunto: ¿quién trabaja? ¿De dónde sale el rancho, el sueldo, la ropita con galones? Esto es absurdo: estáis matando el país y haciendo de él un magnífico cementerio poblado por maniquis, que ostentarán su presunción paseándose entre las sepulturas" (p. 243).

Like Ganivet and Costa, Galdós advocates the avoidance of excess, the adjustment of means to ends: "No seáis pródigos; adoptad con discreta medida las prácticas de los miserables, llevando cuenta y razón de lo que tenéis y consumís, para que nunca os salga la necesidad más larga que su remedio, ni la sábana más corta que la pierna" (p. 243).

The cultivation of useful trades, the avoidance of pretension, and the practice of courtesy in personal relations are Don Beltrán's final lessons:

Y ya no me queda que deciros sino que seáis trabajadores, que os procuréis un modo de vivir independiente del Estado, ya en la labranza de tanta tierra inculta, ya en cualquiera ocupación de artes liberales, oficios o comercio, pues si así no lo hacéis y os dedicáis todos a figurar, no formaréis una nación, sino una plaga, y acabaréis por tener que devoraros los unos a los otros en guerras y revoluciones sin fin. . . . Sed cultos, bien educados, y emplead las buenas formas así en el lenguaje como en las acciones, que la grosería es causante de terribles males privados y públicos (p. 245).

As in previous *episodios*, Galdós is concerned with the leadership that Spain so lacks. Spain, if she is to enjoy peace, needs a forceful government. This force or energy may reside in a person or in the laws:

Ten presente que no se hace nada de provecho sin fuerza, entendiendo por esto, no el poder de las armas, sino una virtud eficaz y activa, que a veces reside en una persona, a veces en las leyes. Ni las leyes tienen aquí fuerza, o llámese energía gobernante, ni hay Rey o Príncipe que tal posea. Puede que nazca algún día; mas yo te aseguro que a la fecha no ha nacido. De modo que paz, lo que se llama paz, no la veréis en mucho tiempo los que sois jóvenes, ni quizás lo vean nuestros hijos y nietos (p. 299).

For Galdós, the savage Cabrera possesses the qualities of a true leader. Of noble temperament, Cabrera scorns the temporizing policies of Don Carlos and his puppet court. His talents are for mightier enterprises than those afforded by the Carlist State: "hombre que por su inteligencia comprensiva, su voluntad potente y sus dotes de organización, había nacido para más altas empresas" (p. 169). His dream is Napoleonic in scope: to create a new society, replacing the old aristocracy with a new leadership drawn from the ranks of victorious warriors. His use of terror is, like that of Zumalacárregui, deliberate, the necessary instrument to power of one whose strength is not derived from institutions and who is compelled to create his own social organism. Allowed to triumph, Don Beltrán declares, Cabrera would be a paternal, even liberal, dictator: "Si este hombre triunfara y pudiera manifestar tranquilo y seguro lo que lleva en su corazón y en su cabeza, sería un dictador severo y paternal, rigorista y clemente, próvido para todo, y hasta liberal dentro de su poder soberano indiscutible" (pp. 169-70).

In *La estafeta romántica* (July-August 1899), Galdós returns to the themes of *Luchana:* Romanticism and Regeneration. The novel was written in the summer of 1899, when hopes for regeneration were still strong. (Silvela had taken office in March; Costa was leading a campaign against the Villaverde budget.) The measures for reform that Galdós advocates in *La estafeta romántica* are those of Silvela and Costa: benign dictatorship (Costa's "iron surgery," Silvela's *revolución desde arriba*), emphasis on material prosperity, and the need to come to terms with reality. Galdós's message is optimistic: our fears and illusions, not outside constraints, cripple us; recovery (exemplified in Calpena's convalescence) is possible. Should, however, Galdós's proposed remedies not be carried out, the Spanish race, exhausted and without hope, risks suicide.

The intrigue of *La estafeta romántica* (Galdós's only epistolary novel) is slender. While Calpena slowly recovers his emotional balance, his mother (*La desconocida* of previous *episodios,* now finally identified as Pilar de Loaysa) plots his marriage with Demetria de Castro-Amézaga. The union of Fernando Calpena (representing intelligence) and Demetria (representing hard work, healthy agricultural and domestic pursuits) will produce "una generación que reúna la voluntad y la inteligencia."[34] Pilar's story dominates a large section of the novel and illustrates the often groundless nature of fear. Pilar (the Spain of the nineteenth century), long unhappily married, living a life of lies, finally decides to embrace reality. She confesses her past errors and, separating from her husband, breaks with the past.

The treatment of history in *La estafeta romántica* is cursory and is limited to little more than mention of such events of 1837 as Espartero's victory at Zornoza, the abortive approach of Don Carlos and his phantom court to Madrid, the petty intrigues of princes, and the military overthrow of the regime established by the sergeants of La Granja in the previous year. References to the Romantic movement are frequent, but are rarely developed: Romantic works read by the characters in the novel are listed; Larra's burial is related in a pastiche of the style of Santos Alvarez.

"Romanticism"—the systematic refusal to see reality (the besetting sin of a Spain that in the years prior to 1898 had lost all awareness of Spain's true role in the modern world)—is the main target of Galdós's criticism in *La estafeta romántica*. Romanticism not only distracts from reality, it is also a dangerously destructive sickness, for moral annihilation follows the shattering of illusions. Calpena had fallen prey to a Romantic malady in *Mendizábal;* now, like the depressed Spain of the months following the disaster of 1898, reduced to an "esqueleto, hecho pedazos en el espantoso choque de la caída," he is unstable, fitfully vengeful, and given to melancholy and graveyard thoughts. Similarly, his mother Pilar, when faced with the pressures of change, becomes *romántica, revolucionaria.* She now suffers nightmares, is feverishly exalted, and is consumed by "ideas tétricas, de complicaciones diabólicas."

The attack on "fiction" (an attack that parallels those of Costa and Silvela) continues throughout the novel. Beltrán declares that "reason" is to be found in practical men (those concerned with power and money), not in the theories of philosophers: "Cuando veas que se pierde en el mundo la razón, no la busques en la guarida polvorienta del filósofo: búscala en la tienda del guerrero, dominador de pueblos, o en el palacio del allegador de caudales" (p. 254). Pilar, sick in body and soul (and the obvious symbol of the Spain of the years preceding the disaster of 1898), has woven her own web of terror and deceit in her pretensions to be other than she is: "¿Imaginas tú algo más enojoso y abrumador que una vida en que tenemos que figurarnos y representarnos de otra manera que como somos? " (p. 195) "¿Qué ganamos con vivir en el engaño social, desempeñando mentidos papeles, decorándonos con una opinión ficticia, y haciendo creer que somos lo que no somos? Cada uno lo que es: bueno o malo, tuerto o derecho, cada ser represente su propio carácter. Apartémonos de la comparsa social, renunciemos a la fastidiosa obligación de marchar a compás, haciendo

figuras más o menos airosas" (p. 216). Life, Hillo proclaims, must not
be confused with literature: "Esas cosas se leen, se admiran, pero no se
imitan, porque acabaríamos por volvernos locos. . . . Una cosa es de-
clamar, querido Fernando, y otra es vivir" (pp. 80-81). Calpena also, in
his sorrow, recognizes that literature is an unsatisfactory guide: "Esos
libros me compadecen; pero no pueden, y bien claro me lo dicen, no
pueden remediar mi mal. Ellos imitan la vida, pero no son la vida; son
obra de un artista, no de Dios" (p. 202).

The stages of Calpena's recovery of health parallel those advocated
by Silvela and Costa for Spain: the rejection of falsehood (Romantic
values for Calpena, political rhetoric for the Spain of 1898), a period of
convalescence imposed by authority, and the development of material
well-being. Calpena, recognizing that his former vision of self and world
was defective, now willingly accepts the despotic authority of Valvanera de Maltrana and of his mother Pilar: " 'Bendito sea el
despotismo—dije entonces.—Soy como un pueblo desgarrado por las
revoluciones, hecho trizas por el jacobinismo y la anarquía, y que antes
de perecer se entrega al dulce dominio de sus reyes históricos.' La
dictadura me ha traído la paz, y aunque me entristece el pisar mis
iniciativas, caídas de mí como coronas marchitas y deshojadas, me
consuelo con la conservación de mi existencia dentro de una plácida
esclavitud" (pp. 48-49). The temporary dictatorship affords Calpena a
respite from passion. The passage of time is in itself healing. Calpena
comes to share in the life of the countryside, developing an interest in a
reality (the health of Maltrana's children, representing the future of
Spain) outside his selfish, fevered imaginings. His deliberate preference
for *El sí de las niñas* over the Romantic *El trovador* is a measure of his
progress toward socially useful goals. By the end of the novel, Calpena
has begun to expel from his mind the symbol of his Romantic delusion,
Aura. Not only has Calpena attained a greater equilibrium in himself
than he had before possessed, but the struggle between generations has
also been overcome, as Calpena is reconciled with and accepts the
authority of the mother against whom he had rebelled in *Mendizábal*.

But for Fernando Calpena to have an assured position in the world,
and for a true reconciliation to take place between the past (Pilar) and
the present and future (Fernando), Pilar must first put her own house
in order, by confessing her adultery and Calpena's existence to her
jealously suspicious husband Felipe. To settle her affairs, Pilar in her
private life follows a course of action that like Calpena's passage to

health, again parallels Costa's program for the regeneration of Spain. First, a cataclysm compels the abandonment of all pretense. Second, past misdeeds and present defects must be humbly acknowledged: Pilar, like the Spain of 1898, must totally renounce the lie to which she has clung for decades. Third, an intermediary must be sought to diagnose her complaint and to establish the new direction of her life. The intermediaries chosen—and Galdós uses Costa's term *cirujano*—are not poets or politicians but practical men, the banker Salamanca and the lawyer Cortina. Pilar's submission to Cortina is total, in order that the revolution in her life may be complete: "Para llegar a esto, dije a Cortina que aceptaré los procedimientos que él determine, imponiéndome cuantos sacrificios sean necesarios, los cuales estimo como una operación quirúrgica, con dolores transitorios. Venga todo lo que quiera. Hago en mí una revolución; destruyo lo pasado y fundo un régimen nuevo" (p. 189). The coincidence with Costa is intentional. Valvanera seeks the results of the *operación quirúrgica*. Echoing Costa's plea to padlock the Cid's tomb, she demands that Pilar abandon her false literary vision of life, her "Romanticism": "No ceso de pedirte que *encierres con cien llaves tu romanticismo,* todo ese imaginar insano que debes a las lecturas continuas, al hábito de vivir dentro del misterio, a esa fatalidad de tener drama oculto, vida de novela por dentro" (p. 222; my italics).

Galdós's optimism for Spain's future is evident in the denouement to Pilar's "drama." The "surgical operation" is entirely successful. Dragons, when exposed to the light of day, cease to terrify. Pilar's emotional nightmare, like Calpena's, was no more than the distorted apprehension of a fevered mind. In "real life," however, no "Romantic" drama need occur.[35] Truth brings its own surprises. Felipe, far from being a tyrant, proves to be a saintly, loving man, whom Pilar can now respect, even love. Her self-imposed torments of twenty years were the product of her sickly imagination. She and Felipe had lived a wasted life of "equivocación," each unaware of the true nature of the other. Similarly, in the years preceding 1898, the reality of Spain had been obscured by the fears and lies of politicians and professional patriots.

Calpena and Pilar, fictional representatives of different generations of Spaniards, both accept an imposed discipline to recover from the grave moral disorders with which they are afflicted. In his treatment of history, Galdós further emphasizes the need for direction, for leadership. Thus, Don Beltrán laments that Spain lacks guidance, lacks the rule of a leader with overall vision: "Verdad que la desorganización del Gobierno es causa de que ninguno de nuestros Generales tenga en su mano los elementos precisos para combatir con éxito. Córdoba con su talento macho, Oráa con su pericia, Espartero con su bizarría, no han podido realizar más que hazañas aisladas: no vemos resultados de conjunto, y ello consiste en que no hay cabeza que administre y gobierne" (p. 247). Leadership, not ideology, is the quality admired by Galdós. Thus, in the Carlist camp, Cabrera is "un caudillo de verdad," prevented from winning the war by the incapacity of his monarch.

Such Spanish vices as military indiscipline and the petty *pronunciamientos* that produce merely surface changes are only symptoms of the lack of true leadership. For a true revolution to take place in Spain, the supreme ambition of a Napoleon or a Cromwell (one of Costa's "heroes") is needed: "te diré que seguirá funcionando la máquina de los pronunciamientos; que no habrá revoluciones temibles, porque el pueblo es un buenazo, a quien se engaña con colorines y palabras vacías; que tendremos disturbios, cambiazos y trapisondas, todo sin grandeza, pues no hay elementos de grandeza, y las ambiciones son de corto vuelo. Redúcense a obtener el mando, y a que los triunfadores imiten a los vencidos en sus desaciertos y mezquindades. No late en la raza la ambición suprema de un Cromwell o un Napoleón. Todo es rivalidad de comadres y envidias de caciques" (p. 268).

Danger to Spain, however, does not only lie in the absence of a dictator or "iron surgeon"; the race itself cannot survive if agriculture is neglected. Calpena, echoing the Regenerationists' concern for the rural life of Spain, admires the industry of the enlightened squire Maltrana and portrays the happiness of the country family. However, if natural leaders abandon the peasantry, the nation will perish: "El día en que se queden solos en el campo los pobres colonos y cultivadores de la tierra, vendrá la consunción nacional" (p. 34). Symptoms of racial decline are evident, even in the Maltrana family. The children are sickly, the girls ill prepared by their education to face the "podredumbre del cuerpo social." Sounding an alarmist note, Galdós fears that the race itself, now decadent, is pushed to suicide:

Pues para mí no hay mayor confusión que esta descendencia menguada y enfermiza, siendo Maltrana un hombrachón vigoroso, que se precia de no haber padecido en su vida ni un dolor de cabeza, y Valvanera una mujer saludable y fuerte, aunque algo seca de carnes. Será una manifestación aislada, como otras mil que vemos, del cansancio y pesimismo de la raza española, que indómita en su decadencia, dice: "Antes que me conquiste el extranjero, quiero morirme. Me acabaré, en parte por consunción, en parte suicidándome con la espada siniestra de las guerras civiles." Si tuviéramos buenas estadísticas, se vería que ahora muere más juventud que antes. ¿Y qué me dices de la facilidad con que los chicos y chicas que han sufrido algún desengaño siguen las huellas del joven Werther? ¿Pues y la guerra civil, esta sangría continua, esta prisa que se dan unos y otros a fusilar rehenes y prisioneros, como si cobraran de la tierra o del negro abismo un tanto por cadáver? ¿No es esto, en la vida española una instintiva querencia del aniquilamiento? (pp. 38-39)

Vergara (October-November 1899) treats the final stages (from October 1837 to August 1839) of the Carlist War in the North of Spain. Much of the novel is devoted to the tedious account of Calpena's wanderings between Carlist and liberal lines. With the exception of two vividly presented scenes—the harangues by Espartero and Don Carlos of their respective troops—few historical events are recreated, a reflection of a war of skirmishes in which fatigue, not victories, decides the outcome of the struggle. Espartero, Zurbano, and Don Carlos are briefly sketched. Maroto, with his cunning and intermittent madness, is the only figure to come to life in Galdós's portrayal. Differences between Carlists and liberals are minor;[36] as in Unamuno's *Paz en la guerra* (1897), war itself, and not a specific ideology, is the enemy.

Novelistic action is slight. As an indication of the futility of war, Galdós repeats scenes from *Zumalacárregui*. Thus, Hillo, like Fago, is obliged to hear the confessions of soldiers about to be executed. Churi, a "monomaniac of love," pursues the same two Salomas desired by Fago in the earlier novel and, in the fury of passion, kills the woman he loves.

Calpena (a reformed Spain) has learned the lesson of experience. Serving, with deliberate refusal of any excess of zeal, as army officer, spy, and diplomatic go-between, Calpena now behaves with courtesy, dignity, and, above all, discretion. No longer the blind slave of passion, he observes and calculates consequences before acting. His mother's protective dictatorship (which had reduced him to the safe, but selfish, role of *muñequito*) is no longer necessary; his convalescence is sufficiently advanced that he can follow the dictates of his own will. But the will, the bemused Calpena ponders, also needs direction. Attracted

by the infectious "Romanticism" of his newfound friend Zoilo Arratia,
Calpena questions whether rational calculation is always the best guide
to conduct: "¿Es ley constante que las acciones muy estudiadas y
previstas resultan siempre bien? ¿Es seguro que los actos de impre-
meditación y de temeridad, comunmente tenidos por locuras y nece-
dades, enderezan siempre al mal? "[37]

Calpena now accepts limitations to man's efforts to control his fate.
Ideology is no guide to conduct: the Carlist Sabino Arratia and the
progresista Santiago Ibero are equally removed, in their simple-minded
intransigence, from the real needs of Spain. Chance also plays its part in
human affairs. (Maroto, despite his good intentions and energy, invokes
la suerte to explain his adherence to the losing side in the Carlist War.)
The will, when not directed by judgment, cannot always impose itself
on circumstances. Zoilo's determination attracts Calpena for a while
("Voy pensando, como tú, que querer es poder. Queramos y podre-
mos" p. 115); however, Zoilo's boundless ambition is ill directed and
rooted in amorous disappointment. His will, on the other hand, can be
more sensibly employed in the foundation of a family and the restoration of Aura to health.

More powerful than men's intellects and will is the force of life itself
which, willy-nilly, imposes its own solutions. Calpena acknowledges the
primacy of behavior over thought: "Según vivimos, así pensamos" (p.
37). Generals, politicians, and monarchs pursue their schemes and
ambitions. Far stronger than Carlist or liberal ideology, or the *amour
propre* of a Maroto or Espartero, however, is Spain's need for peace, for
a truce in the nightmare of war, for survival: "¿Qué quiere usted?
¿convertir a España en sepulcro de dos inmensos cadáveres? Pues
España no quiere eso: anhela vivir, y el obstinarse en que muera, en que
muramos todos, paréceme una terquedad salvaje" (p. 247).

The marked change in Aura Negretti, the bride of Zoilo, illustrates
the optimistic future awaiting Spain if energies are turned to peace
rather than to war. Reason was unable to cure Aura of her Romantic
sickness ("de esa locura de recordar lo muerto y esperar lo imposible,"
p. 133). Nature, however, imposes a solution, in the shape of a child.
Aura, now forced to concern herself with another, looking to the future
rather than to the past, is freed from self-torment, gaining thereby a
radiant physical and spiritual health: "El chiquillo era el médico, era
también el amo, y su existencia a todos imponía vida nueva y nueva
conducta" (p. 214).

Galdós's obsession with leadership continues in *Vergara*. Don Beltrán claims that Spain's future ruler will be drawn from those close to the soil of Spain: "Cuando la realeza falla, cuando la milicia es impotente, inepto el cleriguicio, incapaz la aristocracia, veamos, hombre, veamos si aparece algo grande y fuerte en medio del surco abierto en la tierra, allí por donde anda la reja del arado" (p. 62). The quality most admired by Beltrán is *energía*. He discovers this energy in *la voluntad férrea de un gran soldado,* in Cabrera, who will establish (as Costa advocated) a *protectorado,* a *dictadura.* Similarly, Espartero, who is treated in panegyrical terms throughout the novel, inspires his troops to heroic deeds: "Incansable, buscando siempre el primer puesto en el peligro, Espartero era el gran soldado, el caudillo que de su magnánimo corazón sacaba la increíble fuerza que a su gente infundía" (p. 117). "Electrizados por la presencia y la actitud arrogante del caudillo, los soldados avanzaban husmeando la victoria, gozándola antes de obtenerla" (p. 277). Maroto, also, with his energy and ruthlessness, is a true leader, able to impose his will on the pusillanimous Don Carlos.

Galdós's admiration is for the leadership of generals; he protests indiscipline within Spanish armies. Thus, Calpena justifies, although with anguish, Espartero's execution of rebellious troops. Similarly, the rising of Navarrese troops against Maroto[38] is a symptom of national sickness: "Era la enfermedad histórica de la Nación, la protesta armada . . . dolencia que con el tiempo había de corromper la sangre nacional" (pp. 301-2).

As in the two previous novels, Galdós's treatment of history is cursory in *Montes de Oca* (March-April 1900). With the exception of a novelized account of the hours preceding Montes de Oca's execution, the events of 1840 and 1841 (risings in many cities, María Cristina's abdication, Espartero's assumption of the Regency) receive only passing mention. Social and economic history (the appearance of new wealth, changes in social customs, technological progress, fashions) are treated at much greater length. "Official" history (that of the *Gaceta*) is dismissed as a web of lies and clichés, a fiction from which a few grains of truth can with difficulty be seized: "esa historia falsificada que elaboran diariamente los Gobiernos con ideas muertas y palabrería de mazacote, historia indigesta, destinada al olvido. Otra cosa será cuando no haya tanta distancia entre la psicología de Reyes o gobernantes y los moldes de la *Gaceta:* entonces tendremos la real historia escrita al día.

Pero es muy dudoso que este tiempo llegue; resignémonos a una vida de ficciones, y a recoger los granitos de verdad que a duras penas extrae la observación del fárrago indigerible de la literatura oficial."[39]

Galdós's disillusionment with "history" is accompanied by an equal distrust of programs of "reform." He thus launches in *Montes de Oca* a bitter and barely disguised attack on the Regenerationist movement with which he had sympathized but a few months earlier. By the spring of 1900, Silvela's "Ministry of Regeneration" had quite obviously failed in its promise to give a new direction to Spanish life. Furthermore, Costa's program for summary reform by now seemed utopian and rhetorical, little more than a modern expression of a centuries-old *arbitrismo*. The Unión Nacional (founded in January 1900) was as selfish in defense of the narrow self-interest of its constituency (businessmen who opposed the Villaverde budget) as were the parties of the Restoration. A movement that called for massive public investment and yet organized a taxpayers' strike smacked of hypocrisy. Also, Costa's calls for decentralization became associated in the public mind with the disturbances in Barcelona in late 1899. The demands of Catalans for regional autonomy aroused suspicion and fear in the rest of Spain.

Regeneración had already served as a catchword for the "reformers" of the 1840s. Galdós therefore had a ready-made vehicle for attacking the practicality of similar reforms advocated sixty years later. Thus, the unemployed office-worker José del Milagro holds that a few decrees of the *Gaceta*—the equivalent of Costa's *política sumarísima*—will suffice to bring to Spain prosperity and education. Milagro's program is identical in its general outlines to that of Costa: "Yo emplearía las tres cuartas partes del presupuesto de guerra en fomentar la riqueza pública, y por cada fusil que suprimiera, plantaría un árbol, y en vez de regimientos, pondría Sociedades de Amigos del País, y los cuarteles se convertirían en Universidades" (pp. 50-51). Milagro propounds his own imbecilic version of Costa's hydraulic policy, a plan to convert La Mancha into a second Garden of Eden by means of artesian wells:

Toda la noche, hasta la avanzada hora en que terminó la tertulia, estuvo el buen Milagro dándose un tono fenomenal, ora llevando a gloriosa regeneración los graves asuntos nacionales, ora los manchegos. Las esperanzas optimistas, los risueños programas afluían de su boca como un fresco manantial inagotable, que fecundando toda la tierra, la poblaba de venturas. Las extensas plantaciones de arbolado darían a la

Mancha frescura y sombra, y la desecación de las lagunas de Ruidera aumentaría en muchos miles de fanegas los terrenos laborables. Con una administración proba y activa y unos cuantos *toques de Gaceta,* el país de D. Quijote sería un edén, y vendrían en tropel a establecerse en él los extranjeros, cargados de capitales (pp. 127-28).

A cataclysm (and Galdós is now satirizing the Regenerationist claim, which he had himself accepted in *La estafeta romántica,* that the defeat of 1898 would galvanize Spanish energies) will, the coffee-house pundits proclaim, lead to regeneration: "¿Qué saldría del cataclismo? Pues la regeneración grande y sólida, un Estado potente, costumbres europeas y una civilización de nueva planta" (p. 146).

A leader (Manuel Cortina) will prepare the reforms that, like Costa's, will transform industry, commerce, education, and finances: "Hombres como D. Manuel son los que han de regenerarnos. Prepara reformas en todos los ramos, en minas, en policía, en caminos vecinales, y sobre todo, en Instrucción pública, que es el *barómetro,* ya lo saben ustedes, *el barómetro de la civilización de los pueblos.* Con esto, y el buen gobierno de la Hacienda y las economías, la riqueza pública y privada tomará gran desarrollo. Un buen Gobierno trae la confianza, y la confianza trae la riqueza, el curso de los capitales, la circulación del numerario" (pp. 117-18).

For Galdós, such programs are obviously purely rhetorical. Immediately following the above-quoted panegyric of Cortina's projects, Rafaela del Milagro points out with harsh common sense that the proffered panaceas are merely the device of politicians to obtain and conserve power: "—Esas son tonadillas, D. Gerardo—dijo Rafaelita burlándose con gracia del rígido funcionario,—tonadillas que nos cantan todos mientras tienen la sartén por el mango. Pero como al fin resulta que lo que es buen Gobierno aquí no lo hay nunca, tampoco tenemos confianza, y todo se queda en música: música de himnos, música de discursos, y en tanto el dinero no parece . . . que es a lo que vamos" (p. 118).

The fundamental defect of the Regenerationists (of 1900 as well as of 1841) is their belief that radical reform will come without effort. They mistake the symbol (words, projects, the trappings of "revolutionary" change) for reality.[40] The *progresistas* are most easily satisfied by appearances. The *moderados,* more practical, look to their own interests: "Los caballeros del Progreso, aferrados a la política sentimental, todo lo resolvían con himnos, abrazos y banderolas; los otros iban un poco más al bulto" (p. 70). The sentimental attachment to symbols is exemplified in *Montes de Oca* in Santiago Ibero. Ibero, emotional, naive, and puerile, is incapable of critical examination of the political abstractions and journalistic clichés which he mindlessly mouths and which he mistakes for "thought": "Era un rudo soldado incapaz de filosofar sobre cosas públicas, un monomaniaco del patriotismo, que no entendía bien las razones contrarias a la breve fórmula de su demencia" (p. 47).

The mistaken identification of symbols with reality is not the only Spanish defect diagnosed by Galdós. A related disease of Spaniards is Quixotry, which Galdós defines as an inability to recognize one's self-interest, an unwarranted intrusion into the affairs of others, and an incapacity to assess correctly the external world. Santiago Ibero becomes the quixotic, and unwanted, defender of Rafaela's morality. Bruno Carrasco sacrifices family happiness to set right the ills of Spain: "pensando en la falta que haría en la Corte su presencia para deshacer tantos agravios entre pueblo y Monarquía, y resolver tanto litigio hispánico, ultramarino y europeo" (p. 139). While the Manchegan Carrasco confidently expects to reform Madrid, the *madrileño* José del Milagro, blindly unaware of his abandoned daughters' prostitution, believes with a confidence equally inane that his "honest" (and totally ineffective) administration will make La Mancha bloom.

Fictitious models are bad guides to life. The Romantic drama and the *novela de entregas* inspire the conspiracies of both *progresistas* and *moderados*. Montes de Oca, poet, dreamer, Romantic, pays with his life for his *desconocimiento de la realidad*. Inveighing against political troubadours (whose ideal of government, Galdós laments, is to be sought in literary manuals rather than in reality), Galdós points out the disproportion between Montes de Oca's ideal (María Cristina) and reality, a reality that is always to be preferred to the dreams of poets: "Valía más el Quijote que la dama, y era ella menos ideal de lo que la suponía el ofuscado caballero. Si en la imaginación de éste ahechaba perlas, a la vista de todo el mundo ahechaba trigo candeal superior la buena de Aldonza Lorenzo" (p. 253). Appeals to patriotic sacrifice become, by repetition, a literary mannerism, masking, as in 1898, a national instinct to destruction: "Las tiradas de prosa poética, y el amaneramiento trágico ya no hacían temblar a nadie; el abuso de las aventuras heróicas llevaba rápidamente al país a una degeneración epiléptica, y lo que antes creíamos sacrificio por los ideales, no era más que instinto de suicidio y monomanía de la muerte" (p. 244).

Furthermore, Spanish Quixotry and "Romanticism" are not disinterested; beneath high-sounding phrases lurk personal ambitions. The struggles of the Carlist War, the grandiloquent slogans of the *cristinos,* conceal the rival aspirations of liberal generals; José del Milagro and Bruno Carrasco seek not only justice but also jobs. The contradictions of Spanish Quixotry are nowhere more apparent than in Santiago Ibero, the incarnation of the virtues and vices of a Spain without education and without judgment. Devoted to the cause of liberal Spain, he trusts that the war will continue long enough for his promotion to general's rank. Idealistically worshiping his distant love, Gracia de Castro-Amézaga, he seduces the willing Rafaela del Milagro. His liberal rationalism bears little relation to his behavior. In love, and without the stimulus of war, he is superstitious and prey to nightmares. With a hypocrisy all the more dangerous for being unconscious, he demands that Rafaela cloak her actions in phrases of Romantic love. He tyrannically proclaims himself the protector of Rafaela's virtue. Her resistance to the prying of the self-appointed redeemer provokes his brutality and physical violence.

Galdós's affirmation of values based on life, on experience, rather than on ideology, is evident in his forceful portrayal of Rafaela del Milagro. Rafaela, separated from her brutal husband, sees clearly into the hypocrisies of a society that offers her neither moral nor material support. Life has taught her to be a *materialista;* she has observed the fortunes made by war-profiteers and purchasers of clerical lands. Santiago Ibero, her seducer, mouths the abstractions of morality. Rafaela shocks him with her frank admission that she has used him as much as he used her. Refusing to submit to the "ideological" role that Ibero seeks to impose on her, she demands that her own "reality" be accepted. She is, as Ibero is finally forced to admit, a *woman,* not a *doll.* She alone sees clearly that the attempt to regenerate Spain by governmental decree is only an exercise in rhetoric and that Santiago's attempts to protect her virtue are merely a further form of slavery. For Rafaela, the political liberties proclaimed by the *progresistas* are empty words, for they touch neither the inequitable distribution of wealth nor divorce (two questions equally absent from the programs of Spanish political parties in 1900): "¿Con qué libertad?   ¿Y para qué sirve esa libertad? Para escribir en los papeles mil disparates, para insultar a los ministros y no dejarles gobernar; libertad para los que alborotan, y entre tanto el pobre, pobre se queda, y los ricos se hacen más ricos, y nosotras las mujeres seguimos esclavas" (p. 115).

The Spain of *Montes de Oca* is inhabited by fools and hypocrites, a nation of public and private treasons. Real problems (of financial and sexual slavery) receive no attention in a land where self-appointed redeemers pursue impractical ideals. The leader—Galdós's obsession in previous *episodios*—now receives only passing mention. Espartero, Galdós remarks, enjoyed the good will and enthusiasm of the nation. His failure to create lasting institutions is left for treatment in a later work: "No ha existido en España popularidad semejante, tanto más hermosa cuanto eran más efectivos los méritos que la justificaban. ¡Qué caminito para fundar algo grande y duradero! Ya se irá viendo, a medida que vaya clareándose el balance histórico, lo que España debió a Espartero, y lo que Espartero quedó a deber a España. Esta pobre vieja siempre sale perdiendo en todas las cuentas" (p. 73).

The historical events recreated in *Los Ayacuchos* (May-June, 1900)—a lengthy, and at times tedious, novel—are few: the education of the young princesses, the attack on the royal palace in October 1841, the execution of Diego de León, and Espartero's crushing of the Barcelona rising in the closing months of 1842. The dominant forces in the corrupt politics of the period are *caciquismo* and *compadrazgo;* cynical *moderados* await their turn in office, the certain consequence of the incompetence of *progresista* rule. Changes in social customs, briefly mentioned, include the vogue for Andalusia and the ostentation of the new rich. Economic motives receive more acknowledgment than in previous *episodios:* English and Catalan interests struggle to protect their respective textile industries; liberal industrialists become conservatives at the possibility of a social revolution; the intrigues of Spanish politicians are financed by the gold of France and England.

Los Ayacuchos was written during months when the failure of Silvela's "Ministry of Regeneration" to heal national divisions was obvious. Bickering in the Cortes and the opposition of the Unión Nacional had delayed passage of the Villaverde budget until March 1900. To protest the new taxes, the Unión Nacional organized a shopkeepers' strike in Madrid on May 10 and provoked at the same time serious street disturbances in Valencia, Barcelona, Segovia, Sevilla, and Cádiz. Strong governmental policies (which included the suspension of constitutional guarantees in June) led to the collapse of the taxpayers' strike and the flight of the leading members of the Unión Nacional. A graver problem, that of Catalonia, proved more intractable. Separatist sentiment had been strong in Catalonia since the previous fall, when a state of war had been declared in Barcelona (October to December 1899) to force recalcitrant businessmen to pay their taxes. In early May 1900, Eduardo Dato, the reformist minister of the interior, hoping to capitalize on his recent social legislation protecting the rights of factory workers, toured Catalonia. Noisy hostile manifestations against his presence in Barcelona, Manresa, Tarrasa, and Reus demonstrated the strength of Catalan feeling against the Spanish government.

Galdós's attack in *Los Ayacuchos* on political divisiveness and his call for strong government obviously reflect the Spanish situation of early 1900. For Galdós, the infatuation of Spanish politicians with rhetoric and their imitation of foreign political systems indicate their distance from the reality of Spain. The opposition of *progresista* politicians to their leader Espartero (and in 1900 Silvela and Sagasta found control of their respective parties equally impossible) leads Galdós to question the sanity of Spanish politicians: "¿Pero aquí están todos dementes? ¿Es esto la metrópoli de una nación o el patio de un manicomio? "[41] Espartero's weakness as a ruler, his tolerance of those working for his downfall, provoke Galdós's scorn. Similarly, Van Halen's failure to suppress dissent in Barcelona led to worse disorders: "Nuestro Capitán General no está, como diría cualquier periódico, a la altura de las circunstancias. . . . No ha muchos días subió a Montjuich, desde dónde truena con timidez e inoportunidad: tronando antes con fuerza, se habrían evitado tantos desastres" (p. 271).

It is in his treatment of Catalonia that Galdós most obviously applies to the past the judgment of a *madrileño* of 1900. Galdós's lack of comprehension for Catalan separatism was in any case long-standing.[42] There are, Calpena implies, "good" and "bad" Catalans. The "good" Catalans are exemplified in the inhabitants of Sitges, courteous in their treatment of strangers and contented with their lot in life (see *Los Ayacuchos*, p. 89). Similarly, the lower classes of Barcelona can be divided into patriotic defenders of the nation and criminals who corrupt the dutiful by their attacks on property (see *Los Ayacuchos*, pp. 255-56). The Barcelona rising of 1842 merits Calpena's total contempt.

Catalan complaints (the destruction of their textile industry by English competition, forced military service)—the same complaints as were leveled in late 1899 and early 1900—are dismissed as without foundation. Not only is there no basis for the Catalan rebellion, but their leaders also lack moral integrity, for, Calpena deduces, they are obviously in the pay of French and *cristino* gold. The dregs of the populace take part in the rebellion; the rapid succession of juntas, and the presence in them of humble businessmen and artisans (Costa's *clases productoras?*), prove their incapacity for self-rule. The Barcelona rising—and Galdós's portrayal of Espartero's dilemma would equally fit Silvela's situation in 1900 in the face of the agitation in Barcelona—undermines Espartero's rule and with it the chance of an orderly succession of government in Spain. Repression of the revolt would end Espartero's popularity; toleration of the disturbances would signify his powerlessness to control events.

Political divisions, the incessant criticism of the government, are for Calpena a form of madness. The remedy for Spanish discord will be found when Spaniards abandon their tendency to see political questions in terms of angels and demons (a further example of that simplified abstract thought that Galdós had already denounced in *Vergara* and *Montes de Oca*), when they accept self-discipline and agreed modes of behavior in both political and social life:

Seamos menos exclusivos en nuestras apreciaciones, y no abramos un foso tan profundo entre las dos familias. Diré a usted que conozco a no pocos moderados que son personas excelentes, y todos conocemos a más de cuatro liberales sin ningún escrúpulo. . . . No debemos despreciar, tratándose de política, las formas, amigo mío, las socorridas formas, necesarias en este arte más quizás que en ningún otro; formas pido a los hombres en lo que escriben, en lo que decretan, en lo que hacen; formas en el trato político como en el social, y sin formas, las ideas más bellas y fecundas resultan enormes tonterías (pp. 94-95).

Fernando Calpena, now the calm contemplator of the political and social scene, has little in common with the ardent revolutionary and Romantic of *Mendizábal*. The apparently smug representative of the ruling class (he refers to himself as *señorito pudiente* and future *gentilhomme campagnard*), he takes pride in his friendship with bankers and generals. He is devoted above all else to the care of his mother. His earlier passion for Aura Negretti he casually dismisses as "juveniles amores de que no quiero acordarme" (p. 92). His lack of ardor extends to all spheres of life: his letters to Demetria (his fiancée) are stilted literary essays; in politics, he reserves judgment, affirming that private affairs must take precedence over national concerns.

Like Galdós's ideal leader, Calpena reveals a grasp of reality and a capacity for taking decisive, even arbitrary, action. Rather than railing futilely against the prevailing immorality, Calpena adapts easily to an age of *caciquismo* rather than of chivalry. He feigns religious belief when circumstances so demand; he lies to friend and foe alike; he kidnaps Santiago Ibero from the monastery where he is studying for the priesthood. Twice Calpena declares that the end justifies the means,[43] thus: "se han de juzgar los hechos por los beneficios que producen, y no es justo que maldigamos los medios cuando bendecimos los fines" (p. 293).

Apart from the passing mention in *Bodas reales* of the marriages of Calpena and Santiago Ibero to Demetria and Gracia, *Los Ayacuchos* represents the final stage of Calpena's evolution in the third series of *episodios*. Calpena has now reached that ideal combination of the will and intelligence that Spain should choose as its goal. Cured of his Romantic frenzy,[44] he no longer needs the benevolent dictatorship of his mother. Calpena is now able to act, both for himself and for others.

Although Calpena's action—the rescue of Santiago Ibero (the redemption of a sick Spain)—is presented in terms of knight-errantry,[45] Calpena has not rejected the hard lessons of experience established in earlier novels. His intervention represents self-interest (the pleasing of his fiancée, the preservation of the health of his future sister-in-law). His ruthlessness in carrying out his task illustrates the authoritarian measures that Galdós believes a morale-shattered and divided nation needs. Above all, the reformed Calpena, unlike the young Romantic of *Mendizábal* or the Quixotes of *Montes de Oca*, acts after deliberation and by choice. No longer reacting mindlessly to circumstances, Calpena assesses reality with detachment and chooses the appropriate means to attain his ends. Furthermore, Calpena now has self-knowledge and can treat the roles (*señorito pudiente*, knight errant, Romantic) he essays with irony. The mind is in control; however quixotic his actions may appear, Calpena is not the slave of his emotions or of abstract systems of thought. His final adventure brings into play those qualities that Galdós desires for a future Spain cured of its Romantic sickness: the mature judgment and strong will which, when working in harmony, act forcefully for the good of individual and nation.

Historical events are discussed at much greater length in *Bodas reales* (September-October 1900) than in the preceding *episodios*. Galdós treats such outstanding issues as Espartero's fall from power, Narváez's dictatorship, and the diplomatic maneuverings of foreign powers to secure suitable marital partners for the young princesses. He also scornfully evokes the qualities of lesser figures, whose defects resume those of the nation: the childishness and petty ambitions of generals whose ill-conceived *pronunciamientos* convert Spain into a madhouse, the puerile Romanticism of the Galician rebel Solís, the tumultuous disorder of the *Congreso,* the empty rhetoric of the prime minister López, the cynicism of González Brabo, and the manipulation of Spanish public opinion by *manos oscuras.* Social history merits Galdós's attention. Thus, he recreates the life of the popular quarters of the south of Madrid, comments on the vogue for opera, discusses the replacement of Romanticism by a languid *sentimentalismo bobo,* works into the text contemporary catchwords and phrases (which mark the absence of thought in politicians, journalists, and coffee-house pundits), and refers to the fortunes being made by monopolistic speculators.

As in previous *episodios,* disorder provokes Galdós's anger. Opportunistic politicians bring down their own leaders; generals rebel against established authority; and provincial cities claim to dictate national policy. For Galdós, the continuation of Espartero in power was, despite his manifest incompetence, preferable by far to the disorder and corruption inherent in the overthrow of authority: "Aun admitiendo que su gobierno no fuera el más acertado, y sus errores muchos y garrafales, ¿no valían menos diez y seis meses de mal gobierno que todo aquel delirio, que aquel ejemplo, escuela y norma de otros mil desórdenes de la desmoralización y podredumbre de la política por más de medio siglo? "[46]

Galdós's admiration for strong government leads him, in his portrayal of the unsavory Narváez, to complain not so much of Narváez's authoritarianism and roughshod suppression of dissent—qualities of a certain efficacy in a nation lacking leadership—but rather of Narváez's ignorance of history and of the art of government, of the absence in him of any far-reaching plans for the future development of Spain ("ideas que la llevasen a fines gloriosos y a una existencia fecunda," p.

37). Although Narváez, with his intellectual incapacity, was only "la mitad de un gran dictador," he merits, by his brutal exercise of command, the leading position in the Spanish pantheon of "ilustraciones chicas" or "eminencias enanas" (p. 38).

The gravest defect in the national character is, for Galdós, infatuation with words. Empty rhetoric (*palabrería*) is the substitute in Spain for will-power and rectitude. The mouthing of high-sounding ideals masks the pettiness and vulgarity of political and military ambitions ("la necesidad de alimentarse medianamente, la persecución de un cocido y de unas sopas de ajo," p. 45). The abuse of politics to serve private ends, the cynically hypocritical divorce between the altruistic language of political discourse and the sordid reality such language conceals, have created in Spain a legacy of corruption for generations to come, a vicious enslaving of national life, in which principles themselves are robbed of all meaning: "Entre todos hicieron de la vida política una ocupación profesional y socorrida, entorpeciendo y aprisionando el vivir elemental de la Nación, trabajo, libertad, inteligencia, tendidas de un confín a otro las mallas del favoritismo, para que ningún latido de actividad se les escapase. Captaron en su tela de araña la generación propia y las venideras, y corrompieron todo un reinado, desconceptuando personas y desacreditando principios; y las aguas donde todos debíamos beber las revolvieron y enturbiaron, dejándolas tan sucias que ya tienen para un rato las generaciones que se esfuerzan en aclararlas" (p. 50).

Attacks on political corruption, laments at the lack of established authority, and the realization that political abstractions have little in common with reality were postures common enough among the Regenerationists following the defeat of 1898. In *Bodas reales*, however, Galdós suggests that Costa's program is as removed from reality, as rhetorical, as the policies of the governments of the Restoration and Regency. Thus, the cynical politicians of the 1840s appeal for national change by offering the same programs and using the same words as those of Costa. *Moderados* and *progresistas* alike take as their catchword *regeneración;* González Brabo's plea for "Menos política y más administración" and his call for a government of reconciliation, to be composed of all *buenos españoles,* antedate similar demands by Costa and Silvela. The keystone of Costa's program, his hydraulic policy, is satirized in the claim of the *arbitristas* of the 1840s that the climate of Spain can be changed by afforestation: "y ello tiene por objeto estudiar y dirigir la replantación de arbolado, para que llueva más y no tengamos tanta sequía" (p. 289). That Galdós's attack is leveled at Costa, and not merely at possible abuse of his theories by politicians, is indicated by Galdós's contemptuous dismissal of self-appointed regenerators and reference to Zaragoza, the headquarters of Costa's movement: "marcharon a Zaragoza, sin acordarse de que esta ciudad es y será siempre la primera de España en no admitir ciertas bromas, y en su aversión a dejarse regenerar por el primero que llega" (p. 29).

The Regeneration that Spain needs will not, if the experience of *Bodas reales* is to serve as guide, be imposed from above by ill-educated generals or cynical politicians. Furthermore, the aping of foreign political systems, and consequent neglect of Spanish reality, wastes national energies. One minor character in the novel echoes the calls of Don Beltrán (in *La Campaña del Maestrazgo*) and Calpena (in *Los Ayacuchos*) for a change in manners. He pleads that a reform in Spanish life at the base—in social customs, in the fashion in which Spaniards treat one another—would be a better means to the "civilizing" of Spain: "Pero aquí hemos querido empezar el edificio por el tejado, dejando para lo último los cimientos, y los cimientos son las costumbres, los modales, la buena educación" (p. 135).

Galdós's fundamental pessimism, should his solutions not be applied, is most evident in his account of the vicissitudes of the Carrasco family. Doña Leandra, like the Princess Isabel of *Los Ayacuchos,* is at the outset of the novel full of good health, joyfully sharing in the life of the people. Foreshadowing, however, the unhappy marriage of Isabel, her healthy instincts are thwarted by outside pressures. Out of place in the Madrid she hates, far from La Mancha, which she adores, she degenerates, like a Spain diverted from healthful goals, into paralysis and madness. The fate of the Carrascos serves as a cautionary tale to those Spaniards who lose sight of their true interests in an insane obsession with national politics. Carrasco neglects wife, property, and honor to conspire and pontificate in cafés and casino, his lack of sense reflected in the deformed political catchphrases he imbecilically mouths. He can discourse at length on the royal marriages; he has less time for his own daughters' behavior. Doña Leandra justly castigates a rhetorical patriotism that replaces concern for family: "¿A qué hablas tú de patriotismo, si el primer patriotismo no es ser buen padre y tú no lo eres? " (p. 319).

In sarcastic contrast to the celebrations of "official" Spain, Doña

Leandra's death takes place on the day of the royal wedding. The closing lines of *Bodas reales,* a description of the wedding decorations, strikingly express Galdós's black vision of the present and future dishonor of Spain: "todo estaba oscuro, solitario; sólo vieron el triste desarme de los palitroques y aparejos de madera, lienzos desgarrados y sucios por el suelo, y las paredes de todos los edificios nacionales señaladas por feísimos y repugnantes manchurrones de aceite. Parecían manchas que no habían de quitarse nunca" (p. 355).

In the final chapter of *Bodas reales,* Galdós refers to the fate of Fernando Calpena and Santiago Ibero. Both had, unlike Carrasco, learned to cultivate private affairs and abandon the will-o'-the-wisp of national glory. They are, at the end of the novel, happily married and parents. Their "happiness," however, is Galdós's final sarcasm in the third series of *episodios nacionales,* the expression of his fundamental pessimism with regard to the future of Spain. It is not in Spain that the two enlightened "heroes" can find bliss, for they flee the intrigues of their native land to live in France. Galdós conveys, indeed, by refusing to illustrate in a Spanish context the blessings that will flow from the practice of the teachings of the *episodios,* his own lack of faith in the remedies he propounds.

Chapter Three

The Fourth Series of
Episodios Nacionales, 1902-1907

Galdós completed *Bodas reales* in October 1900. It was not until a year and a half later, in March 1902, that Galdós began composition of a fourth series of *episodios*, treating Spanish history between 1848 and the September Revolution of 1868. The new *episodios* reveal a slackening of Galdós's interest: the novelistic intrigues are less complex and well knit; the teaching repeats in large measure that of the third series; the novels were written at a much slower pace, the final novel of the series being completed only in May 1907. Save for the last two novels of the series (*Prim* and *La de los tristes destinos*), for which Galdós was able to draw on memories of his youth in the Madrid of the 1860s, few historical events or figures are recreated in any detail. The treatment of history in the fourth series is, indeed, skimpy to the point of casualness. Galdós himself confessed to a journalist how wearisome the task of fitting historical events to a novelistic intrigue had become: "Yo había hecho bastante de este trabajo, que al principio me agradaba y ahora me molesta. No puede usted figurarse lo difícil y desesperante que es para el escritor colocar forzosamente dentro del asunto novelesco la ringla de fechas y los sucedidos históricos de un episodio."[1]

The decreased interest shown by Galdós in the fourth series reflects not only a personal tedium with his self-assigned task but also the changed circumstances of Spain; 1898, 1899, and even the early months of 1900 had been years of crisis, of defeat, and of hopes for a radical change in national structure. By way of contrast, the period between October 1900 and May 1907 was one of drift, of lack of direction in Spanish life. The Regenerationist movement had become one more ineffective and corrupt pressure group; the Catalan problem proved as insoluble as ever; both Conservative and Liberal parties were without agreed leadership or policy and were rent by personal hostilities.

THE HISTORICAL BACKGROUND 1900-1907

Parliamentary majorities in Spain were not the expression of the wishes of the electorate; they were the artificial creation of the government to whom the monarch granted the dissolution of the Cortes. The numerous changes of government in the period reflected neither shifts in public opinion nor the vitality of Spain's rulers but rather the absence of clear-cut leadership within the traditional parties.[2] Thus, between October 1900 and January 1907, there were thirteen changes of prime minister.

Spain's political leaders were ill fitted to give a new direction to national energies. They had made their careers in the corrupt atmosphere of Regency politics; their policies had led to the Disaster of 1898; their age and experience had left them with a fundamental skepticism, as Fernández Almagro has commented:

Bajo un signo de renovación,—impuesto por la necesidad de persistir,—nacen y crecen los españoles de este período, aleccionados por un duro escarmiento contra la presunción *juris tantum* que el desastre colonial vino a desmentir. España tenía todo, según los padres, y los hijos comenzaron a ver que faltaba todo, empezando por el Estado, razón de lo demás: Administración, Ejército, Enseñanza, Industria . . . Mal podrían crear nueva y mejor realidad los que gastaron fe y esperanza, participando del Poder bajo la regencia de Doña María Cristina: Sagasta, en primer término. Diferente por la motivación y el uso, en cada caso, forma el escepticismo una escala que va de Silvela a Montero Ríos.[3]

The Liberal party lacked both accepted leadership and an agreed policy. Their leader, Sagasta, aged and without understanding of the new situation prevailing in Spain, was no longer able to impose his authority within the Liberal party. Even before Sagasta's death (January 1903), the Liberals were split by the personal antipathies of Canalejas and Moret, who each hoped to succeed to the party leadership. In May 1902 Canalejas, disgusted with Sagasta's double-dealing in secretly consulting with the Vatican on the proposed *Ley de Asociaciones* and out of step with the majority of his party in social matters (Canalejas believed the state should intervene in economic and labor questions), resigned his ministerial position. During the summer of 1902, Canalejas was warmly received by the Republicans, whose cause he now appeared to favor. In late 1902 the energetic Maura defected to

Silvela's Conservatives. When the Liberals returned to power in 1905, Montero Ríos and Moret displayed greater energy in jockeying for power than in producing administrative reforms. It was Moret's attempt to replace, by underhand means, López Domínguez in office in November 1906 which led to the return of Conservative rule.

The Conservative party, led by dissenters from the Restoration political settlement, offered greater hope for reform than did the Liberals. The Conservatives were also, however, divided by the rivalries of aspirants for the party leadership. Silvela's gifts did not include that of forceful command. His ambitious plans for the reorganization of Spain were opposed by Villaverde's determination to balance the Spanish budget. After Silvela's self-imposed departure from the political scene, both Villaverde and Maura vied for control of the Conservative party. Maura's arrogance—he proposed to revolutionize the nation "rápidamente, radicalmente, brutalmente"—alienated many, as also did the far-reaching nature of the reforms that he advocated (the fundamental reform of local administration, the elimination of a corrupt political system based on *caciquismo,* the reorganization of the navy). It was not until 1907 that Maura could rule Spain without challenge from within his own party.

Hopes for change from outside the traditional political structure were quickly doomed. Maura Gamazo has described the rapid degeneration of the Regenerationist movement into one more corrupt political pressure group: "bastaron dos años para que el movimiento regenerador, obra de la masa neutra, quedase reducido al grupito beligerante de la Unión nacional, tan poco escrupuloso en maniobras y combinaciones como el más desacreditado de los gremios históricos."[4] Costa himself, who had previously declared that Spain's problems could not be solved by change of political constitution, joined the ineffective and divided Republican party in 1902. The association of the various republican groupings into the *Unión Republicana* (February 1903) under the leadership of Salmerón was but short-lived. In the same year, streetfighting broke out in Valencia between the partisans of Blasco Ibáñez and those of Rodrigo Soriano, the two Republican "bosses" of the city.

The army had last decisively intervened in Spanish politics in December 1874, when Martínez Campos's coup had restored the Bourbon monarchy. From 1898 onwards, however, the fear of a military coup (which would impose dictatorship) was ever-present in governing circles in Spain. Fernández Almagro has alluded to the fears expressed by Silvela to his intimates: "El jefe del gobierno, en ambiente más íntimo, pudo aludir al fantasma que desde el 98 por lo menos, no dejó un solo día de rondar la actualidad política: la Dictadura" (p. 35).

In November 1905, some two hundred army officers sacked the offices of two Barcelona journals, the weekly *Cu-cut* and the daily *La Veu de Catalunya:* the attack was motivated above all by the support that the journals had given to the Catalanist cause in the municipal elections of that month. The captains-general of Barcelona, Madrid, and Sevilla, as well as garrisons all over Spain, supported the action of the Barcelona officers. The organ of the army, *El Ejército Español,* expressed its approval of the attack, resurrecting the nineteenth-century claim that the army is the incarnation of patriotic opinion: "Las autoridades, que debieron poner coto a la vergonzosa propaganda, no lo hacían. Su pasividad era criminal; era como una especie de complicidad con los malvados. Era preciso cortar de raíz la planta maldita. Y para ello nadie más obligado que el Ejército, que es la encarnación sublime y augusta de la Patria."[5]

The government, should it have persisted in its intention of punishing the Barcelona officers, was faced with the almost inevitable prospect of a military coup d'etat. Under the combined pressures of the military and the monarchy, Montero Ríos was replaced as prime minister by Moret. In 1906 Moret obtained passage of the *Ley de jurisdicciones,* which reserved to military courts the trial of any offenses against the army, police, or nation. The army now formed a state within the state. For Fernández Almagro, approval of the *Ley de jurisdicciones* revealed not only the militaristic nature of the monarchy but also the total impotence of Spanish liberalism: "En votación minimal—183 contra 11,—se aprobó la ley de Jurisdicciones: 20 de marzo de 1906, fecha importante, en cuanto marcó inequívocamente el carácter militarista de la monarquía y la impotencia absoluta de los liberales históricos" (p. 88).

Alfonso XIII assumed power as constitutional monarch in May 1902. At his first cabinet meeting he insisted on his constitutional right to grant honors and titles. Alfonso's education had included a strong military component;[6] as monarch, he saw to the advancement of officers loyal to himself in person. Liberal opinion of the period accused the king (and his military supporters) of interference in the political life of the nation beyond the role allotted to him by the constitution. Thus, Alfonso was held responsible for the resignation of Silvela in 1903,[7] the settlement of the Bilbao miners' strike of 1903 on the miners' terms, the resignation of Maura in 1904 (in opposition to Alfonso's insistence that Polavieja be appointed minister of war), and the dismissal of the López Dom ínguez ministry in November 1906.

Despite the fears expressed by Liberals and Republicans of the renewal of the *obstáculos tradicionales,* supporters of Alfonso could justify his ready use of the royal prerogative: the Spanish Cortes and party system were notoriously unrepresentative; the lack of established leadership in the traditional parties warranted the frequent changes of prime minister in this period.[8]

The major problem faced by the governments of the period 1900-1907 was the resurgence of the religious question. Anticlerical feeling had been strong in Spain throughout the nineteenth century. After the defeat of 1898, many priests and members of religious orders returned to Spain from the former overseas possessions; anticlerical Spaniards accused the clergy of responsibility for the rising in the Philippines against Spanish rule.

At the same time, there was the example in France of the vigorous anticlerical policy of Waldeck-Rousseau and Loubet. The Combes ministry of 1902 suppressed most religious congregations, removing their right to operate schools and to dispose of property. By November 1904 Combes had broken diplomatic relations between France and the papacy. Many French friars and nuns emigrated to Spain in flight from the Combes legislation, thereby exacerbating Spanish anticlerical feeling.

In late 1900 Liberals and Republicans began a violent campaign against what they termed "clerical reaction." The virulence of the campaign reflected above all the bankruptcy of Liberal policies, a wish, even if subconscious, to distract national energies and attention from the obvious inability of the Liberals to develop any program for fundamental change in Spain.[9]

The ostensible reasons for Liberal fears of clericalism were isolated Carlist risings in the fall of 1900; the projected marriage of Princess Mercedes to the Neapolitan prince Don Carlos (whose father had briefly served in the Carlist army); an administrative decree (the "Order of Vadillo") refusing recognition to civil marriages unless the priest of the parish had declared beforehand that the spouses were not members of his congregation; and the scandal caused by an article by the royal tutor, the priest José Fernández Montaña, advocating government in accordance with the "política de Dios y gobierno de Cristo."

Not only were many liberals hostile to the Church; certain sectors of Catholic opinion were rigidly opposed to liberalism. Representative of this intransigent attitude is the article by the priest Martiartu in Ramón Nocedal's journal *El Siglo Futuro,* defending the thesis that "liberalism is a sin": "Los católicos forman un campo y los liberales otro; campos opuestos, entre los cuales no caben confusiones ni conciliación. El liberalismo abomina de la doctrina católica, y los católicos abominamos del liberalismo. No se trata de una lucha de hombres contra hombres, sino de doctrina contra doctrina, de principio contra principio, de la verdad contra el error, del cielo contra el infierno. A un lado, los fieles de Cristo; a otro, los imitadores de Lucifer."[10]

Anticlerical agitation continued throughout 1901, the "año anticlerical" for many historians. In early January the leading Liberal newspapers of Madrid campaigned against "Jesuitism."[11] Galdós's drama *Electra,* performed for the first time on January 30, became the rallying point for anticlerical feeling. Its performances in Madrid and other Spanish cities were accompanied by riots and violent press campaigns in defense of or attacking its thesis, to wit, that the clergy can exercise a destructive influence on family life and will use any means to obtain dominance over the souls of others. In February violent riots (including the burning of convents) accompanied the wedding of Princess Mercedes and the trial in the Supreme Court of the Adelaida Ubao case.[12]

In September 1901 the Liberal government promulgated the *Ley de Asociaciones,* requiring that all religious orders register with the state within the space of six months, in accordance with a nonenforced law of 1887. Furthermore, the government decreed that products manufactured by religious orders for sale be taxed. Romanones, as minister of public instruction, limited the power of the clergy in education, requiring that religious schools obey the same regulations for hygiene and educational standards as state schools. In December 1901 changes in the Concordat were proposed, including a reduction of the clerical budget and resolution of the vexed question of the third religious order permitted by law.[13] Sagasta, however, to the disgust of his more anticlerical ministers, carried out secret negotiations with the Vatican. The anticlerical legislation was never enforced; Canalejas, who proclaimed "Hay que dar batalla al clericalismo," abandoned the cabinet in

May 1902 in protest against Sagasta's evasiveness on the religious question.

Anticlerical campaigns and mob violence were constant features of the following years. Maura's attempt to woo right-wing support by his nomination in early 1904 to the diocese of Valencia of the former archbishop of Manila (who was accused by liberals of complicity in the surrender of Manila to the United States) led to rabidly hostile press attacks. Canalejas's article in *El Liberal* exemplifies the extravagance of anticlerical sentiment in this matter: "el nombramiento del padre Nozaleda es una provocación inaudita, un ultraje a los sentimientos liberales del país, que en modo alguno puede tolerarse. Es la continuación de una política reaccionaria, clerical, la persistencia en una obra de retroceso intelectual y moral."[14]

Anticlerical feeling, with counterattacks by the Church protesting "persecution," again came to a head in late 1906, when the Liberal ministry of López Domínguez attempted to resurrect the proposed legislation of 1901. In August, Romanones exempted those contracting civil marriage from any religious declaration (a decree annulled the following year by Maura); furthermore, educational establishments were not allowed to function without authorization, a measure aimed at Church schools.[15] The most violent campaigns centered, however, around Canalejas's proposal for a new *Ley de Asociaciones*, to be enforced by the Spanish government without prior consultation with the Vatican. It was, indeed, the failure to impose the *Ley de Asociaciones* that led to Galdós's conversion to Republicanism, as he announced in a letter of early April 1907 to the editor of *El Liberal:* "tiempo hacía que mis sentimientos monárquicos estaban amortiguados; se extinguieron absolutamente cuando la ley de Asociaciones planteó en pobres términos el capital problema español; cuando vimos claramente que el régimen se obstinaba en fundamentar su existencia en la petrificación teocrática. Después de esto, que implicaba la cesión parcial de la soberanía, no quedaba ya ninguna esperanza. ¡Adiós ensueños de regeneración, adiós anhelos de laicismo y cultura! El término de aquella controversia sobre la ley Dávila, fue condenarnos a vivir adormecidos en el regazo frailuno, fue añadir a las innumerables tiranías que padecemos el aterrador caciquismo eclesiástico."[16]

Neither the Villaverde Conservatives (obsessed with balancing the Spanish budget) nor the Liberals (committed to laissez-faire economics)

had any solution for the social question that, with the religious problem, dominated public attention in the early years of the twentieth
century. Thus, the Liberal program of 1902, emphasizing economic
freedom, showed little comprehension of modern industrial society; its
avowed aim was to protect both the individual worker and the "sacred
liberty of capital."[17]

From 1901 onwards, strikes demanding a nine-hour working day and
improvements in wages and working conditions became common in
Spain. The first general strike in Europe took place in Barcelona, in
February 1902. The strike, under anarchist leadership (it was opposed
by Pablo Iglesias and the Socialists) led to bloody battles with the Civil
Guard and the declaration of a state of war in Barcelona. In the same
year, there were strikes by miners in Bilbao, Asturias, and La Unión, by
longshoremen in Málaga, by bakers in San Sebastián, and by agricultural
workers in Andalusia and Valencia. In the following year, fifteen
thousand striking miners erected barricades in Bilbao; their demands
were accepted after the intervention of the captain-general of the
region.

Strikes often took on political overtones. In August 1903 strikers
assaulted the town hall and law courts of Alcalá del Valle; accusations
that imprisoned strikers had been tortured exercised European and
Spanish left-wing opinion for the following year. Similarly, protests
against local taxes on food led to widespread riots at the end of 1906.

The violence associated with unsolved social problems was above all
evident in Catalonia, which suffered more than other regions of Spain
from the loss of overseas markets and where anarchists possessed some
strength in the labor movement. An anarchist attempted to assassinate
Maura on the occasion of the royal visit to Barcelona in 1904. Bomb
attacks in public places were frequent in Barcelona throughout the
period. Twenty-three people were killed and a hundred wounded by a
bomb hurled by Mateo Morral (a young anarchist teacher employed by
the Escuela Moderna of Barcelona) at the royal wedding procession in
May 1906.

Spanish agriculture suffered even more than did industry. In 1905 a
severe drought caused the failure of the harvest in Andalusia. Many
farm workers were forced to emigrate to Argentina. Famine conditions
prevailed in Andalusia, Galicia, and León. Fernández Almagro describes
the hunger in the south of Spain in 1905: "Parecía hacerse endémico el
del hambre en Andalucía. Falta de trabajo, escasez de lluvias, primavera

dramática. En Sevilla, Córdoba, Málaga . . . El hambre, indistintamente, postró o irritó pueblos enteros: Alternaron la amenaza de arrasar comarcas y la sumisión por la limosna. Representativo episodio el de los braceros de Cártama, marchando sobre Málaga, con ademán iracundo, para luego, disgregados, mendigar en la ciudad. Juntas de socorros, concentración de guardia civil para asegurar el orden . . . Se emprenderían obras públicas a fin de conjurar el paro, ofreció preocupado el gobierno, pero el problema reaparecía" (p. 60).

Not only was Catalonia afflicted by industrial problems (the loss of overseas markets, demands by workers for minimal working conditions, the endemic violence of anarcho-syndicalist attacks), Catalonia had also removed itself from the Liberal-Conservative political alignment of the rest of Spain. The elections of 1901 were fought in Catalonia between the *Lliga Regionalista,* which demanded the implantation of the *Bases de Manresa,* and the Radical Republicans of Alejandro Lerroux, who advocated a centralized republic and opposed Catalan autonomy. Although Lerroux received the covert support of the government of Sagasta, the *Lliga* swept the elections. Maura, on the occasion of the royal visit to Barcelona in 1904, made numerous concessions to Catalanist demands, in an attempt to draw the *Lliga* into the mainstream of Spanish political life. However, the military assault on two Barcelona journals in 1905 and the passage in the Cortes of the *Ley de jurisdicciones,* which was strongly opposed in Catalonia, united the divided Catalan movements. The newly formed *Solidaridad Catalana* swept the elections of 1907, winning forty-one of the forty-four seats occupied by Catalan deputies in the Cortes.

The inability of the government to suppress violence in Barcelona—numerous terrorist attacks occurred just before the elections—explains in part the triumph of *Solidaridad Catalana.* Indeed, the party with "centralizing" tendencies (Lerroux's Radical Republicans) openly exhorted to violence. Here is the extravagant call to destroy a "decadent civilization" which Lerroux published in *La Rebeldía* on September 1, 1906:

Jóvenes bárbaros de hoy, entrad a saco en la civilización decadente y miserable de este país sin ventura; destruid sus templos, acabad con sus dioses, alzad el velo a las novicias y elevadlas a la categoría de madres para civilizar la especie; penetrad en los registros de la propiedad y haced hogueras con sus papeles para que el fuego purifique la infame organización social; entrad en los hogares humildes y levantad las legiones de proletarios para que el mundo tiemble ante sus jueces despiertos. . . . No os detengáis ni ante los altares ni ante los sepulcros. . . . Luchad, matad, morid (Quoted by Fernández Almagro, p. 104).

Catalan separatism awakened echoes beyond the boundaries of Catalonia. Catalanists visited the *Liga Foral* of Guipúzcoa in July 1906 to teach tactics to Basque nationalists. The *Solidaridad Catalana* also lent its support to the *Centre Regionalista Valencià,* a union of Valencian Carlists and Republicans which, under the leadership of Rodrigo Soriano, was locked in a bitter struggle with Blasco Ibáñez's Republican following.

After the defeats of 1898, most Spaniards regarded matters of foreign policy with apathy and disillusionment. However, the jostling of European powers to obtain control of the disintegrating Moroccan Empire touched Spanish interests closely. The instability of Spanish governments in the early years of the reign of Alfonso XIII prevented the signing of favorable treaties negotiated with the French. French and Spanish spheres of influence were defined in the Treaty of Algeciras in January 1906, but the risings in Morocco in 1908 left most of its provisions a dead letter and involved Spain in the foreign adventure she had wished to avoid.

Spain, isolated in the war with the United States, sought to build up its relations with other European powers during this period. The personable Alfonso made a favorable impression during royal visits to France, Germany, Austria, and Great Britain. Foreign monarchs, however, alleging fears of anarchist attacks, refused to enter Spain, save for brief forays from the safety of visiting warships. Spanish sympathies for foreign powers reflected political orientation: the parties of the right turned to Berlin and Vienna for inspiration, the parties of the left to Paris and Rome. Liberal sympathies were with Great Britain; the anglophile Segismundo Moret was prime minister when the engagement was announced between Alfonso and Princess Ena of Battenberg, the niece of Edward VIII. Despite the increasing rapprochement between Spain and Great Britain during this period, distrust of Great Britain existed in many sections of the Spanish population. Thus, when hemophilia appeared in the royal offspring, the suspicion existed that Alfonso had been imposed upon by the perfidious English.

THE IDEOLOGY OF THE FOURTH SERIES

Regeneration, so important a theme of the third series of *episodios*, scarcely receives attention in the fourth series. Costa's call for an "iron surgeon" no longer interests Galdós. Thus, while Fajardo longs in vain for the rule of a great man who will combine the qualities of a Caesar, a Cromwell, and a Bonaparte, his longing reflects petulance with the mediocrity of Spain's rulers, not belief in the virtues of dictatorship. The sickness of Spain is in any case, as the priest Merino and Jerónimo Ansúrez pessimistically agree, beyond the skills of any "doctor." Unlike Fernando Calpena, Aura Negretti, and Santiago Ibero, the novelistic characters of the fourth series afflicted with the "Romantic" malady are granted neither an imposed solution nor protected convalescence. Responsibility for cure now rests with the individual alone.

While awareness of rural poverty is strong in the fourth series, Costa's ambitious proposals to Europeanize and to foment the material prosperity of Spain are reduced to a delirium in the mind of the semiconscious O'Donnell, who confesses the impossibility of creating a modern nation out of "este cementerio de la Quijotería y de la Inquisición."[18] Indeed, Spanish folly is perhaps not to be cured by English measures, for the medicine is to the Spaniard worse than the disease: "la medicina que intenta curar estos males, que son la vida misma, es peor y más dolorosa que la enfermedad" (*O'Donnell,* p. 134). Only with Galdós's renewed involvement in the political life of the nation, with his conversion to Republicanism in 1907, does he enthusiastically advocate contact with Europe which, he lyrically proclaims in *La de los tristes destinos,* will serve to clear the air of Spain and bring in fresh ideas.

In the third series of *episodios,* Galdós had sought to define the strengths and weaknesses of the national character and to indicate the way to national and individual well-being. In the fourth series of *episodios,* however, his concern, almost to the point of obsession, is above all with one contemporary problem: the religious question. In novel after novel of the series, Galdós attacks the role of the Church in Spanish life. The Church, he claims (ostensibly discussing clerical manipulations in the reign of Isabel II), is a political institution; it controls governments and the most trivial of appointments; the papal nuncio has more power in Spain than a dictator. Catholic political "thought," with its ready-made answers, is a facile avoidance of real problems. A

Catholic politician, Cándido Nocedal, is portrayed as an amiable cynic. Religious devotion is professed by hypocrites to further their material interests. The Church serves the interests of the ruling class. Religion, a moneylender's wife holds, has the social utility of preventing the poor from protesting their place in society: "fomentemos también la religión, de la que nace la conformidad del pobre con la pobreza. ¿Para qué pagamos tanto clérigo, y tanto obispo y tanto capellán, si no es para que enseñen a los míseros la resignación, y les hagan ver que mientras más sufran aquí, más fácilmente ganarán el Cielo? "[19]

It is not only the political role of the Church that attracts Galdós's scorn. The convent is an unhappy prison for those who, without vocation, are trapped within its walls. Miracles are either a deliberate deceit of those who are credulous, as are the stigmata of Sor Patrocinio, or the hallucination of those under stress. Church ceremonies can be barbaric rituals (the defrocking of the priest Merino) or mere theater (the histrionic activities at executions of the Brothers of Peace and Charity). The clergy are often personally unworthy; hence the detailed treatment in two novels of Merino, who plotted regicide while exercising his clerical functions.

As in the thesis novels of his early years, Galdós laments the lack of charity and spirituality in the Spanish Church. Such Catholic practices as confession, set prayers, and priestly intervention are unnecessary for a truly spiritual life. Devotion to religious images is symptomatic of the absence of true religious faith in Spain: "Oye, Pepe: ¿No te parece que sobre todas las estupideces humanas está la de adorar a esos santos de palo, más sacrílegos aún cuando los visten ridículamente? ¿No crees que un pueblo que adora esas figuras y en ellas pone toda su fe, no tiene verdadera religión, aunque los curas lo arreglen diciendo que es un símbolo lo que nos mandan adorar entre velas? "[20]

Fanatical religious attitudes are an integral part of the national temperament. Inside each Spaniard lies a friar or executioner. The Spanish language lends itself to mockery, not to the expression of charity or meekness: "Dentro de cada español, por mucho que presuma de cultura, hay un sayón o un fraile. La lengua que hablamos se presta como ninguna al escarnio, a la burla, y a todo lo que no es caridad ni mansedumbre."[21]

In *La de los tristes destinos*, Galdós uses the religious question to measure the commitment to change of the revolutionaries of 1868. The refusal of the revolutionary leaders to consider the possibility of civil marriage–Galdós obviously had in mind Romanones's controversial decree of August 1906 easing the difficulties placed in the way of civil marriage; the decree was abrogated by the Maura government in March 1907–provokes Galdós's scorn: "Ya ves: todavía creen que eso del casarse es cosa del Papa. . . . La Revolución que traen quedará, pienso yo, en un juego de militares."[22] In the same novel, written at the time of Galdós's conversion to Republicanism, a conversion motivated almost entirely by his disappointment at the failure of the Liberal government to pursue a strong anticlerical policy, Galdós accuses Spanish Liberals of religious fanaticism: "Sí, hijo mío: el fanatismo tiene aquí tanta fuerza, que aunque parezca vencido, pronto se rehace y vuelve a fastidiarnos a todos. Los más liberales creen en el Infierno, adoran las imágenes de palo, y mandan a sus hijos a los colegios de curas" (*La de los tristes destinos,* p. 308).

The social question receives comment in the first two *episodios* of the fourth series–*Las tormentas del 48* and *Narváez*–in which Galdós notes the miseries of Spanish rural life. Starving peasants eke out a bare existence, always at the mercy of the vagaries of nature and the extortions of moneylenders and tax collectors. Spanish institutions exploit and offer no assistance to those engaged in the harsh struggle for survival. There is no escape, through God, the devil, or mankind, from the all-pervasive poverty: "Por encima, un Dios que mira y calla y no suelta mosca, y por debajo un Diablo que si uno quiere venderse a él, no da ni para zapatos; tacaño el de arriba, tacaño el de abajo, y los hombres que están en medio, más tacaños todavía" (*Narváez,* p. 57). In 1904, in *O'Donnell,* Galdós again remarks on the sufferings of the peasantry. Narváez shoots agrarian rebels whose only crime is hunger. Teresa Villaescusa observes with compassion the harsh lot of the inhabitants of the Castilian countryside, condemned to poverty, premature aging, and exploitation: "Ni amenidad, ni frescura, ni risueños prados veía . . . . Las mujeres vestidas con justillo, y con verdes o negros refajos, atraían su atención. Sentía piedad de verlas desmedradas, consumidas prematuramente por las inclemencias de la naturaleza en suelo tan duro y trabajoso. Las que aún eran jóvenes tenían rugosa la piel. Bajo las huecas sayas asomaban negras piernas enflaquecidas. . . . Todo lo vio y admiró Teresa, ardiendo en piedad de aquella desdichada gente que tan mal vivía, esclava del terruno, y juguete de la desdeñosa autoridad de los poderosos de las ciudades" (*O'Donnell*, p. 213). In *Prim*, Galdós remarks in passing on the irrelevance of political changes to those engaged in a struggle with nature for survival: " ¡Pobre gente! Para ellos no había más *obstáculos tradicionales* que la nieve y ventisca, la miseria y el bajo precio del carbón."[23]

Hans Hinterhäuser has commented that Galdós treats the social question from the perspective of an outside observer.[24] Certainly, Galdós, save for his implicit condemnation of the exploitation of the peasantry by the organs of the state, offers no solution to the agrarian problem. Galdós's timidity is most apparent in his treatment of the first social revolution in Spain, the peasant rising in Loja in 1861. Writing in a time of Andalusian famine, Galdós guardedly observes that the rising was premature and, with singular evasiveness, that agrarian strife is but one further symptom of the natural madness of Spaniards: "o los españoles son locos sueltos en el manicomio de su propia casa, o tontos *a nativitate.*"[25]

Galdós is equally aware of urban poverty. In *O'Donnell,* he acknowledges that civil servants often earn less than shoe-shine boys; the family protected by Santiuste is dying of starvation. In *La revolución de julio,* Galdós declares that hunger is the driving force behind Spanish revolutions. Barbaric exploitation by Spain's ruling classes explains the occasional outbursts of popular violence: "Nadie ve las víctimas obscuras que inmoló la ambición de los poderosos, ni los atropellos que se suceden en el seno recatado de una paz artificiosa, sostenida por la fuerza bruta dominante, y todos se horrorizan de que la fuerza oprimida y dominada se sacuda un día y, aprovechando un descuido del domador, tome venganza en horas breves de los ultrajes y castigos de siglos largos" (*La revolución de julio,* p. 252). But, for Galdós, remedies to the social problem are to be sought in individual effort, not in political action. Political revolution, which changes only externals, merely distracts the poor from their humble labors. With compassion, Galdós notes that the poor dream of constitutional change, not of improving their sad lot: "Y después de pasarse largos días y noches en tan peligrosas andanzas, volvería cada cual a sus obligaciones. El uno seguiría fabricando obleas y lacre; el otro, jeringas, y el tercero vendiendo sanguijuelas, para ganar un triste cocido y vivir estrechamente entre afanes y miserias. Todo lo soñaban, menos llegar a ser ricos, o al menos, vivir con desahogo" (*La revolución de julio,* p. 290).

Monarchical institutions are not attacked in the fourth series of *episodios*. Even in *La de los tristes destinos,* written at the time of Galdós's adherence to Republicanism, the British monarchy is praised and Fajardo postulates an ideal monarchy in which the king resumes the aspirations of an entire nation, not merely those of a clique. Accusations leveled against Alfonso XIII in the early years of his reign—that he relied too heavily on a small group of palace advisers, that he interfered in the political life of the nation, that his education was overinfluenced by clerical interests—are reflected in Galdós's charges against his predecessors. Thus, Isabel II is criticized for her willingness to be manipulated by a *camarilla;* the sterile theological training that the future Alfonso XII received is attacked.

The leading foreign question with which the Spanish government, if not the generally apathetic public of Spain, was concerned in the early years of the twentieth century was that of Morocco. Negotiations with other European powers were brought to a conclusion in 1904, just before the composition of *Aita Tettauen.* In this novel, as also in *La vuelta al mundo en la Numancia,* Galdós warns strongly against Spanish involvement in foreign adventures. Wars in pursuit of patriotic glory are futile and serve only to divert national energies from more urgent tasks at home. Spain sought in Morocco (in the "Romantic War" of 1859) what she already possessed at home. True "conquest" is in any case impossible, for Spaniards are unwilling to adapt themselves to the ways of thought of others.

The regional question, which so agitated Spanish public opinion in the years in question, receives but passing mention, when Narváez testily protests the rival claims of Catalonia and the Basque Provinces for special privileges: "¿Pero esto es España o la ermita de San Jarando que hay en mi tierra, donde cada sacristán no pide más que para su santico? Ea, caballeros, yo estoy aquí para mirar por el Padre Eterno, que es la Nación, y no por los santos catalanes o vascongados" (*Narváez,* p. 146).

Linked to the dismissal of regional claims is Galdós's support of the role of the army (the defender of national unity) in Spanish life. Echoing nineteenth-century Spanish liberal theory, Galdós claims that, in a context of national maladministration, military uprisings can be justified as a reaction against corruption: "Los militares se sublevan cuando la Nación no puede aguantar ya más atropellos, inmoralidades y corrupciones, y en estos casos el brazo militar triunfa, sencillamente porque debe triunfar" (*La revolución de julio*, p. 97). Again, in the final novel of the series, *La de los tristes destinos*, after the notorious *Ley de jurisdicciones* had become law in Spain, Galdós defends military intervention to prevent either reaction or excessive license (and here he is in all probability taking issue with Catalan agitation):

"Siempre que ha venido la asfixia, o sea la reacción, el Ejército ha dado entrada a los aires salutíferos, y cuando los excesos de la Libertad han puesto en peligro la paz de la Nación . . . .
—Claro, ha restablecido el orden, el buen temple interior. Por esto, no debemos juzgar con rigor excesivo las sediciones militares, por que ellas fueron y serán aún por algún tiempo el remedio insano de una insanidad mucho más peligrosa y mortífera" (*La de los tristes destinos*, pp. 107-8).

Comments directed at the contemporary political situation form only part of Galdós's teaching in the fourth series of *episodios nacionales*. As in the third series, Galdós attacks time and again the two major defects of Spaniards: their mistaken belief in the efficacy of words and Romantic evasion of reality. Fajardo, Lucila before her marriage, Baldomero Galán, Santiuste, and the young Santiago Ibero are all afflicted with a Romanticism, or Quixotry, which distorts their perception of reality. Their tempestuous loves, dark melancholies, random violence, pursuit of illusions, and attempts to force life to conform to literary models make individual happiness impossible and are dangerous to society.

Much more than in the third series, Galdós is now keenly interested in examining the nature of an individual's Romanticism. The Romantic drive, as presented by Galdós, would in modern terms be described as neurotic. Here is the description by Galdós—himself as much an *investigador de almas* as were the obsessed Gracián and Fajardo—of Bartolomé Gracián, who is perpetually discontented with reality:

—Es un soñador, que no se conforma con la realidad, y busca siempre lo que está detrás de lo visible.
—Y detrás de lo visible, ¿qué se encuentra? . . .
—Se encuentra . . . lo que se busca . . . una imagen que al encarar con ella nos dice: "no soy lo que quieres . . . . Lo que quieres viene detrás . . . ." Y así sucesivamente hasta lo infinito . . . .

—Pues el que persiste en buscar lo que no encuentra, o es un loco, o necio de solemnidad.

—Es un descontento, un ambicioso, un investigador de almas. Puedes creerlo: el tal Gracián me interesa y deseo tratarle (*La revolución de julio*, p. 151).

The Romantic impulse has no direct relationship with objects. It is an *efusión—efusión patriótica, efusión amorosa, efusión popular, efusión estética*—which emanates from within the individual and is projected capriciously onto the outside world. The *efusión* is a sickness, a combination of a reaching out to a world that has no real existence and an inner anxiety: "padecí la *efusión estética*, un mal terrible, Manolo, un mal que consiste en adorar lo que suponemos privado de existencia real; un mal que es amor y miedo" (*La de los tristes destinos*, p. 98). The impulse is always the same; only the object changes. Thus, Santiuste's *efusión patriótica* is converted almost immediately into *efusión amorosa*. On a national plane, ideologies and heroes provide convenient focal points for the yearnings of individuals. Thus, Prim serves as a symbol of the varied hopes and illusions of many: "En las cabezas grandes y chicas ardían hogueras. Las llamaradas capitales *Prim, Libertad*, se subdividían en ilusiones y esperanzas de variados matices: Prim y Libertad serían muy pronto Paz, Ilustración, Progreso, Riqueza, Bienestar" (*Prim*, p. 233). Similarly, revolutionary action itself, in the period covered by the fourth series of *episodios*, is theatrical, a mask for individual discontent and a sordid search for governmental jobs. A true revolution, one in which individual aspirations and the needs of Spain are in harmony, has not yet taken place in Spain.

Spaniards suffering from the Romantic sickness are blinded both to self and to outside world. They are caught in self-imposed traps—excessive idealism, the deceit of rhetoric, *efusiones*—which conceal, and yet prevent any escape from, a fundamental emptiness of the soul. Skepticism, the denial of all idealism, is merely the reverse side of the coin and is equally destructive. Thus, many of the characters of the third series of *episodios* reappear in the fourth series as *escarmentados*, conformists who, interested only in financial and social security, make a cult of appearances and are fundamentally unhappy. The refusal to accept goodness where it exists is a further form of blindness. Thus, Galdós scathingly attacks the cynicism of the corrupt *unionista* Tarfe:

"El romanticismo, ya pasado de moda en el Teatro, no había dejado ni una chispa de fuego en las almas glaciales de los señoritos de la clase media" (*La de los tristes destinos,* p. 333). ("Romanticism," in the above example, does not have the pejorative implications of earlier *episodios;* in this case, it represents the recognition by Galdós, now politically involved, of the possibility of political idealism and his rejection of the values of the Revolution of 1868 and of the Restoration.)

Individuals seeking an escape from self-imposed limitations receive no help from the society of 1868 or preceding years. The society portrayed in the fourth series of *episodios*—like that perhaps of the early years of the reign of Alfonso XIII in Galdós's eyes—is one of opportunism, lack of direction, conformity with the status quo, gray mediocrity. Often blind, beset by the pressures of Church and hypocritical society to conform, the individual must indeed, as Fajardo recognizes, forge his own values, however difficult this may prove to be.

Savagely attacking escapist Romantic dreams, disgusted with a conformist society, Galdós no longer offers the easy imposed solutions of the third series of *episodios.* There is no leader to save Spain; there is no *desconocida* to arrange a safe prosperity for the descendants of a Fernando Calpena or of the older Santiago Ibero. Neither will the historical process (subject to chance, as the imagined histories of *Confusio* illustrate) bring to Spain a solution for her problems, for these, Galdós now increasingly suggests, are to be explained by national temperament and racial atavism.

The revolutionaries who carried out the Revolutions of 1854 and 1868 were either deluded or corrupt. The Revolutions themselves produced—and Galdós is here in agreement with the attacks by Silvela, Costa, and others on the fictional nature of nineteenth-century Spanish institutions—only superficial changes. A fundamental revolution is, nevertheless, needed if the nation's ills are to be cured. This revolution will come, however, not by governmental decree or the rhetoric of a political caste but rather from changes within the wills and minds of individual Spaniards.

Spaniards, or at least those who participated in the political life of the nation in the nineteenth century, lack two qualities: will-power and judgment. Will-power is needed if Spaniards are to work steadfastly toward goals conducive to their material and emotional well-being and to overcome temporary set-backs; judgment is required for a wise choice of goals and the means to attain them. Will-power and judgment are not given; they are gradually developed in life. Patience and effort are needed to conserve achievements; experience is a far better guide to conduct than are books. The exemplary cases of María Ignacia and Teresa Villaescusa (who both, despite their unpromising family backgrounds and initial uncertainties, create a sure domestic happiness) illustrate what can be accomplished by determination and awareness. Santiuste *(Confusio)*, on the other hand, is the sad illustration of the consequences of self-centered projections and the cult of an "idealism" born of books and political rhetoric.

Galdós's message is not, as critics have suggested, one of conciliation. (There is no conciliation between Spaniard and Moor, between politician and worker, between Church and nonbeliever, between the cynical Tarfe and the trusting Santiago Ibero.) Rather, Galdós advocates a middle path which, avoiding both extremes of Romantic evasion and sterile conformism, transcends the values of contemporary society to lead Spaniards to a better life. Galdós rejects the possibility of an immediate amelioration of Spanish society. He nevertheless illustrates through certain of his characters the path to individual happiness, a happiness that will serve as a model for the revolution in values needed by the nation. This individual salvation is found not in politics but in love. First Virginia del Socobio and the mechanic Leoncio Ansúrez, and later Teresa Villaescusa and the young Santiago Ibero, reject—flamboyantly and totally—the conventions of a corrupt society. The values that they embrace are not imposed on them by others but arise from their intimate being. Their choice of independence is not "Romantic" in the pejorative sense which Galdós applies so frequently to the term; rather, the young lovers must struggle to survive in a harsh world. Not dreams and projections, but courage, hard work, sacrifice, trust, and the ability to profit from experience allow love, and happiness, to grow.

The message of the fourth series is optimistic, for Galdós affirms the possibility of personal happiness. Rebellion against hypocrisy and conformity leads to knowledge of self and society; when such awareness is accompanied by sustained effort, individual liberation is possible. The triumph of love in these novels is more than a convention of fiction; it indicates a vital reshaping of personal destiny, that fundamental revolution which Spain, as a society, still awaited.

In *Las tormentas del 48* (March-April 1902) Galdós portrays a corrupt society in terms readily applicable to the Spain of his own day. The Spain of 1848 is without ideals; social injustice is rampant; a powerful Church extends its control into all sectors of Spain's political and economic life. The narrator of these novelistic "confessions" typifies a society without values and without inner force: the young and callow García Fajardo, a former theological student, is bookish, given to fantasy, precocious, unstable, of hasty temper, and an ardent womanizer. Fajardo, possessing neither will nor goals of his own, fits easily into all environments.[26] His total flexibility makes him as willing to join the exploiting classes—by accepting an arranged marriage with the ugly and ignorant María Ignacia de Emparán—as he was previously to befriend the downtrodden. An intellectual who plays with ideas, he is unable to commit himself to any cause or person. Thus, love itself is no more to him than a game; he finds the overpowering passion of Antoñita bothersome and prefers to woo an Eufrasia who rejects his demands.

In keeping with the lack of transcendental values of the society portrayed, no events of historical importance are recreated in *Las tormentas*. The liberal papacy of Pius IX, the coming of the French Republic, and the abortive Spanish revolution of March 1848 (which is dismissed by Fajardo as "vanidad, interés de personas") receives little more than passing mention. The future democratic leader Nicolás Rivero and the insane priest Martín Merino (who was later to attempt the assassination of Queen Isabel) appear but briefly in the novel.

Galdós's concern is above all in the portrayal of a society, a society that is totally corrupt and has no values beyond a selfish and purely immediate expediency. Moneylenders and speculators grow rich; an honest civil servant loses his position for attempting to do his duty. The fixed religious and social creeds of Fajardo's saintly mother represent an earlier morality that has no understanding of the hypocrisies of the society of 1848, in which the usurer is praised for his devotion to work, the seminarian is sensual, and Romantic adventure is parodied. Money and social status are now the only goals of those who once were capable of passion. Thus, the independent Rafaela del Milagro of *Montes de Oca* has found her "oasis" in marriage with *Don Frenético* and now hypocritically cultivates the true power in Spain, the nuns. Her advice to Fajardo is that he abandon his dreams and accept "reality": "Déjese de andar por las nubes, y bájese a la realidad."[27] The "reality" she advocates, however, is one of spiritual and emotional impoverishment.

Similarly, the daughter of Bruno Carrasco, Eufrasia, now "muy escarmentada," has found, not happiness, but a mediocre tranquillity with an ailing husband, Saturnito del Socobio. She has learned the lesson of experience. Renouncing her passionate past, abhorring all mystery, she carefully plots her rise in society. As Fajardo's "eminente maestra del vivir," she offers friendship, not love, which she now considers to be *mentira*. Wealth and comfort are now the principal aims of her life: "No soy vanidosa; me gustan las comodidades, la riqueza, que nos hacen alegre y fácil la vida; me gusta poseer los bienes positivos, vengan como vinieren" (p. 278).

Galdós's treatment in *Las tormentas* of the Church and its followers could only add fuel to the anticlerical campaign being waged at the time of its composition (1901 had been the year of *Electra* and of numerous anticlerical riots; the *Ley de Asociaciones* was under consideration in early 1902). The Church is portrayed in *Las tormentas* as a political organization. Foreign diplomatic interests are concerned in the election of Pius IX; the political role of the Church in the Italy of the 1840s is stressed; the theory of a liberal papacy—and here Galdós is using a "Catholic" argument to challenge the contemporary *integrista* claim that liberalism was a sin—is expounded at length. Throughout the novel, "Catholics" are depicted in an unflattering manner. The priest of Sigüenza is barbaric and exploits his parishioners; Fajardo's saintly mother is simple-minded; his sister, the nun Sor Catalina, speaks with "formulillas hipócritas." Nuns intervene in worldly affairs; hypocrites feign loyalty to the Church to further their own social ambitions; a speculator and usurer can confidently expect to purchase a papal title. The clergy, according to a moneylender's wife, are paid to prevent the poor from protesting their place in society: "fomentemos también la religión, de la que nace la conformidad del pobre con la pobreza. ¿Para qué pagamos tanto clérigo, y tanto obispo y tanto capellán, si no es para que enseñen a los míseros la resignación, y les hagan ver que mientras más sufran aquí, más fácilmente ganarán el Cielo? " (p. 302) The hypocritical wealthy followers of the Church avidly purchase Church lands placed on the market by Mendizábal's *desamortización*. This property will—and Galdós's remarks are aimed at the financial power of the Church in 1902[28] —in the course of time return to the Church: " ¡Cómo que también están afanando lo que fue de frailes y monjas! . . . Claro que luego volverán las aguas a su nivel; los que vivan mucho verán cómo se forma una nueva aristocracia de la cepa de esos ricachos, y cómo recobrará el clero lo suyo, no sé por qué medios, pero ello ha de ser" (pp. 151-52).

The social problem, so evident in the Spain of early 1902 (numerous strikes had taken place throughout 1901; the first general strike in Europe was that of Barcelona in February 1902), is also reflected in *Las tormentas*. Fajardo perceives the miseries of Spanish rural life. The peasants of Atienza are dying of hunger, their only recourse the charity of individuals. Village *señoritos* behave with brutal ignorance: "nunca he visto señoritos de pueblo más arrimados a la cola de la barbarie, ni gaznápiros más enfadosos con sus alardes de fuerza bruta y su desprecio de toda ilustración" (p. 15). Socialism lurks behind the European revolutions of 1848, a socialism that scares men of property: "Es la voz poderosa del Socialismo, la nueva idea que viene pujante contra la propiedad, contra el monopolio, contra los privilegios de la riqueza, más irritantes que los de los blasones" (p. 253). Fajardo questions a social system that can so richly and arbitrarily reward him while peasants and workers are starving: "¿Qué organismo social es éste, fundado en la desigualdad y en la injusticia, que ciegamente reparte en tan absurdo modo los bienes de la tierra? " (p. 290) Fajardo flirts briefly with the theories of Saint-Simon, Fourier, Owen, and Lamennais. His vision of socialism is, however, superficial and purely external. His claim that wealth belongs to the workers is no more than the transitory enthu-siasm of an unstable novelistic character and is far from representative of the views of Galdós:[29] "La riqueza pertenece a los *trabajadores,* que la crean, la sostienen y aquilatan, y todo el que en sus manos ávidas la retenga, al amparo de un Estado despótico, detenta la propiedad, por no decir que la roba" (p. 291).

In *Narváez* (July-August 1902) Galdós bitterly attributes to the Spain of 1848 the restrictions of the society of his own day. Individuals are trapped, unable to free themselves from the poles of resentful resignation or fitful, ill-considered attempts at superficial change. Re-strictions are in part self-imposed: individuals blindly use empty ideo-logical abstractions to conceal personal ambitions; they set for them-selves such selfishly limited aims (mere material survival, social "advancement") that happiness is impossible; prey to a corrosive skepticism, they are unable to commit themselves to any cause of benefit to both individual and society; they lack, indeed, that combination of the will and judgment that Galdós had advocated in the third series of *episodios*. Restrictions also come from outside the individual: Spanish institutions, in the hands of fools and exploiters, are hostile to all dissidents; the Church not only is a political organization but also controls the "thought" of its adherents; nature itself in Spain is the enemy of man.

Despite Fajardo's claim that personal life is more important than public affairs, more attention is given in *Narváez* to historical figures and events than in *Las tormentas del 48*. Two figures are treated at great length: Narváez and Queen Isabel. The defects of Narváez are many (he is nervous, impatient, childishly ill tempered, grossly brutal, and envious): nevertheless, he possesses for Fajardo both will and intelligence, although these two qualities do not function in harmony. Significantly (if only as a measure of Galdós's inability to formulate alternative solutions to Spain's problems), Narváez is encouraged by Fajardo to continue in his task of "strong man" of Spain. Queen Isabel—and the analysis of her qualities and defects is perhaps in part directed at the young King Alfonso, who had assumed his constitutional duties in May 1902—is "la síntesis del españolismo," well intentioned but ignorant, relying on feeling rather than on reason. As an indication to his contemporaries that clericalism can be successfully fought, Galdós evokes at length the clerical conspiracy that produced the short-lived *ministerio relámpago* and Narváez's immediate and forceful resumption of power.

The Spain ruled by Narváez ("rector de un manicomio") is, like that of 1902, without grandeur or transcendental values. The Spanish ruling classes are little more than bandits; the government and its cliques of hangers-on are corrupt. The numerous conspiracies properly belong to comic opera; the history of the period is a *folletín tonto*. Galdós harshly comments on the sterility of this Spain "at peace": "La Historia de Españo, mientras hubo guerra, es una Historia que pone los pelos de punta; pero la que en la paz escriben ahora estos danzantes no se pone los pelos de ninguna manera, porque es una historia calva, que gasta peluca."[30]

A selfish disregard for the well-being of the nation is not limited to the governing circles of Madrid. Galdós, in words that obviously refer to the regionalist movements of his own day, has Narváez, when beset by rival claims of Catalan and Basque interests for special privileges, testily exclaim: "¿Pero esto es España o la ermita de *San Jarando* que hay en mi tierra, donde cada sacristán no pide más que para su santico? Ea, caballeros, yo estoy aquí para mirar por el Padre Eterno, que es la Nación, y no por los santos catalanes o vascongados" (p. 146).

Continuing the anticlerical attacks of *Las tormentas del 48*, Galdós harshly criticizes the political role of the Church in Spain. It is the papal nuncio, and not Narváez, who decides whether or not Sor Patrocinio can be expelled;[31] clerical conspirators place sufficient pressure (and blackmail is hinted) on the queen to overthrow the government;[32] the papacy, with the support of such allies as Spain, engages in a conventional war to establish papal power over its Italian dominions (María Ignacia's apt comment is that Christ had no need of artillery); Donoso Cortés's defense of the Church is dismissed by Fajardo as the vainest rhetoric.

It is not only the political role of the Church, however, which is condemned in *Narváez*. Galdós, in a return to the views expressed nearly thirty years earlier in such novels as *Doña Perfecta* and *La familia de León Roch*, criticizes, through the progressive skepticism of María Ignacia, many Catholic practices. María Ignacia would suppress all convents. She prefers, during the rosary, to formulate her own prayers. She believes that a married woman should confess only to her husband. She complains about the impertinent questions asked by priestly confessors. In her attack on devotion to religious images, she questions whether true religion exists in Spain: "Oye, Pepe: ¿no te parece que sobre todas las estupideces humanas está la de adorar a esos santos de palo, más sacrílegos aún cuando los visten ridículamente? ¿No crees que un pueblo que adora esas figuras y en ellas pone toda su fe, no tiene verdadera religión, aunque los curas lo arreglen diciendo que es un símbolo lo que nos mandan adorar entre velas?" (p. 126)

In his treatment of the "social question," Galdós portrays the harsh conditions under which country dwellers struggle to exist. Peasants lose their crops through hail storms and drought; farmers are overwhelmed by taxes and rarely escape the clutches of moneylenders; poor laborers live a life of slaves. In Atienza, the weavers are unemployed, the girls without a possibility of education. The peasantry, engaged in an intense struggle for survival, is more closely linked to the eternal life of Spain ("la Historia") than to "la Civilización" (the purely superficial "progress" of the nineteenth century): "¡El campo, el monte, el río, la cabaña! No es sólo la égloga lo que en tan amplios términos se encuentra, sino también el poema inmenso de la lucha por el vivir con mayores esfuerzos aquí que en las ciudades, y el cuadro integral de nuestra raza, más enlazada con la Historia que con la Civilización, enorme cantera de virtudes y de rutinas que componen el ser inmenso de esta nacionalidad" (p. 36).

Institutions (national and local) and their representatives (politicians, the clergy, court officials) oppress and exploit the peasantry:

El mundo es malo de por sí, y ésta nuestra tierra de España tan sembrada y rodeada está de males, que no puede vivir en ella quien no se deje poner trabas en manos y pies, dogales en el pescuezo, que al modo de cordeles son las tantísimas leyes con que nos aprieta el maldito Gobierno, y lazos los arbitrios en que nos cogen para comernos tantos sayones que llamamos jefe político, alcalde, obispo, escribano, procurador síndico, repartidor de derramas, cura párroco, fiel de fechos, guardia civil, ejecutor y toda la taifa que mangonea por arriba y por abajo, sin que uno se pueda zafar (pp. 54-55).

Institutions (the monarchy, constitutions, the judicial system, religion, conventional learning) are without relevance to those engaged in the harsh struggle for survival. Neither God, the devil, nor man will, Jerónimo Ansúrez declares, offer help to the individual, who can survive only by declaring his independence of all social bonds:

Somos todos indómitos, y aborrecemos leyes, y renegamos del arreglo que han traído al mundo los reyes por un lado, los patriotas por otros, con malditas constituciones que de nada sirven, y libertad que a nadie liberta, religión que a nadie redime, castigos que no enmiendan a nadie, civilización que no instruye, y libros que no se sabe lo que son, porque éste los alaba y el otro los vitupera. Por encima, un Dios que mira y calla y no suelta mosca, y por debajo un Diablo que si uno quiere venderse a él, no da ni para zapatos: tacaño el de arriba, tacaño el de abajo, y los hombres que están en medio, más tacaño todavía (p. 57).

Ansúrez's pessimism results from his harsh experience of Spanish life. A similar fundamental skepticism, which acts as an inner barrier to any sustained search for happiness, possesses characters representative of the middle and upper classes. Eufrasia, for example, in her determination to bite rather than be bitten, is unable to find happiness as she coldly calculates her progress in society. She will not drop her mask of prudence even in the company of her lover; neither will she commit herself to one man, for Fajardo is forced to share her favors with others.

Skeptical of all belief, the characters of *Narváez* can give themselves only to the most passing of passions. Passion, not ideology, governs conduct: "El mundo, según Eufrasia, se gobierna por pasiones, no por ideas, y éstas no influyen sino cuando son apasionadas" (p. 219). Narváez and Fajardo agree that Liberty and other abstractions escape definition. Abstract goals are personal dreams, nothing more: "que en usted, como en mí, todo es un sentimiento, un deseo, una soñación y nada más" (p. 251). Passion, not thought, determines Fajardo's ideology; thus, it is his maniacal search for Lucila which provokes the temporary resurrection of his revolutionary love for the people.

Passions arise from the inner needs of the individual; the objects of passionate desire are never perceived in their reality. Thus, the abulic Fajardo, acknowledging that he is an "artist" with neither art nor goal, recognizes that his cult of Lucila is an *efusión estética* or *efusión popular;* his sickness is "la *efusión de lo ideal,* de lo desconocido, de lo que debiendo existir no existe" (p. 292). Similarly, the queen's malady is an *efusión popular,* a reliance on sentiment unaccompanied by the will (which would lead to sustained action) or judgment (the rational assessment of reality).

Fajardo's imperfect contact with reality is reflected in his approach to history. Refusing the practical María Ignacia's suggestion that he merely relate what he sees and hears, he seeks to go beyond gossip, rumor, and innuendo (his only sources of information in the clouded atmosphere of the Spain of Narváez) to compose an ideal history, formed of two elements: *el pueblo* and *el trono.* The projected history will contain more than the narration of the deeds and sentiments of Spain's rulers and people. For the deluded Fajardo, his history will go beyond observable reality to capture an abstraction, the "soul of Spain": "la del Ser Español, la del Alma Española . . . como una diosa, mujer real y al propio tiempo divina, de perfecta hermosura" (p. 289).

Fajardo is now, indeed, as skeptical of "history" as are the novelistic characters of altruistic goals. Fleeing the present (a Spain in which mediocrities struggle for survival and in which personal authenticity is buried in the lies and fictions of a corrupt society) and pursuing an abstraction as illusory as those liberal dogmas elsewhere decried by

Galdós, Fajardo in *Narváez* postulates an "eternal" reality of Spanish life. Thus, establishing links with the past of Spain (and hence, by implication, with Galdós's own time), Fajardo relates the feudal manner in which he and his bride are received in Atienza, describes the superstitions of country dwellers, and suggests, through the crazed imagination of the erudite D. Ventura Miedes, that the elemental "people" has persisted unchanged over the centuries. The elemental "people" is symbolized in the Ansúrez family[33] which, nomadic, rebellious, and "Celtiberian," use their varied talents to survive in the harshest of physical and social environments. The primitive soul of Spain ("el alma ibera, el alma española") is, for the insane Miedes and the equally deluded Fajardo, represented by the only woman of the family, Lucila, with her "absolute proportions" and her pagan beauty.

Fajardo, with his sickly *efusiones* and flight from historical reality into a mythical past, and Eufrasia, whose bitter skepticism makes all happiness impossible, serve as models of what is to be avoided if healthier attitudes are to prevail in Spain. Fajardo's wife, María Ignacia, on the other hand, has her feet firmly grounded in reality. Like the Aura Negretti of the third series of *episodios*, María Ignacia is transformed by matrimony. Increasingly confident, escaping the artificialities and limitations imposed on her by her superficial parents, she now reveals hidden zones of the spirit. She is tenderly loving, expresses herself with clarity, forms firm independent judgments on her family and on the Church, and is able to give of herself in her charitable concern for the starving peasants of Atienza and in her unselfish care for her husband. The true foundation of the family, she persuades Fajardo to work, as a remedy for his despair. She refuses to be unhappy. Her aim is to raise and educate her children: "Ya sabes que mi gloria es tener muchos hijos y poder criarlos gordos y sanos, y educarlos después para que sean hombres de mérito, o mujeres de su casa. Es mi ambición y no tengo otra" (p. 256). She is sufficiently sure of herself to place stability of the family over any possible jealousy she might feel over her husband's amorous involvement with Eufrasia: "aplicando al caso una filosofía suya, soberana, elevadísima, que en rigor no puede admitirse más que estableciendo ley conyugal distinta para cada sexo" (p. 224).

Under her influence, García Fajardo (now the Marqués de Beramendi) is more than the vainly frivolous figure of *Las tormentas del 48*. His *memorias* are now written in a direct manner, without the pretentious imitation of the styles of others so noticeable in the preceding novel. He can adapt to different social settings, but nevertheless has increasingly an identity, a judgment, of his own. His growing respect and love for his wife make him a figure to be taken seriously. Even when, like the Fernando Calpena of the third series of *episodios,* he falls prey to a black depression and is consumed by Romantic madness (his desperate search for the "ideal" Lucila), he now has an element of stability in his life, his love for his family: "Conviéneme declarar que ni en mis delirios ni en mis sedaciones me ha faltado el cariño a mi mujer y a mi chiquillo, sentimiento de un orden reposado, compuesto de deber y amor, y que ha llegado a parecerme armonizable con mis ensueños" (p. 213).

In *Los duendes de la camarilla* (February-March 1903), as in the two previous *episodios,* Galdós attacks clericalism and refers, in passing, to Spain's social problems. Spaniards face two forms of slavery: that imposed by society (pressures to conform, clerical control of thought and behavior) and that proceeding from within the individual (the maniacal pursuit of "Romantic." i.e., false goals). Galdós's teaching is that of the third series of *episodios:* passions and "Romantic" fantasies distort our perception of reality and our behavior; "Romantic" passion destroys both individual and society; work and the passage of time heal. There is, however, no "iron surgeon" capable of curing the sickness of Spanish society; the remedy must come from within the individual.

The action of *Los duendes de la camarilla* takes place between November 1850 and February 2, 1852 (the day of Lucila's wedding and also of Merino's attempted assassination of Queen Isabel). Apart from a presentation of Merino (who serves as confessor to Domiciana) and Domiciana's description of Sor Patrocinio, there is little or no treatment of historical events and figures. The role of the military (on whom *progresista* hopes for a return to power depend) is reduced to that of the hotheaded Bartolomé Gracián, who in his simple-minded selfishness identifies Spain's liberty and military power: "No hay España sin Libertad, y no hay Libertad sin Ejército."[34]

Dominating the lives of the characters, both fictitious and historical, is the power of the Church. The nuns influence appointments in the royal household and in the civil service; they receive large sums of money from Queen Isabel. The power of Sor Patrocinio, one character remarks, is greater than that of Narváez. Prim complains—in words unconsciously prophetic of the early years of the twentieth century—that "nos están llenando la nación de frailes y monjas" (p. 251). Not only does the Church meddle in Spanish politics, it is also used in its turn by hypocrites seeking employment or advancement. Thus, the unemployed Centurión hysterically expresses his willingness to abase himself before the Church: "A eso voy yo, como una fiera, y no me contentaré con asistir a procesiones, sino que a todas horas saldré por la calle con mi cirio, rezando el rosario, para que me oigan, para que se enteren, para ser alguien en la comparsa social; para que no me llamen *Don Nadie*, y poder comer, poder vivir . . . Díganme dónde están la última monja y el último capuchino para ir a besarles el borde de las estameñas pardas y la suela de la sandalia sucia" (pp. 105-6). Sor Patrocinio, as described by Domiciana, is vengeful and deceitful; her stigmata are false. The nuns, it is hinted (and the charge would add fuel to anticlerical accusations of the early 1900s), are unchaste, for the devil reputed to visit the convent is a friar in disguise. The "morality" of the nuns is flexible. They teach that the end justifies the means: "Lo que en ti o en mí, que somos tan poco y no valemos para nada, sería bárbaro, pecaminoso, y hasta sacrílego, en otras personas, llamadas a empresas altas por méritos de su caletre y de su voluntad, puede ser bueno, necesario y hasta indispensable" (p. 59).

Lucila, on the other hand, lays claim to a greater understanding of Christian truth than those more closely connected with the Church.[35] She thus, in her simplicity, protests that good and evil do not depend on social position: "Yo, Domiciana, pienso siempre por derecho; creo que lo que es malo en mí, malo ha de ser en las reinas y emperatrices" (p. 59). Furthermore, Lucila recognizes that Sor Patrocinio never provides favors in a disinterested manner: "Si concede un favor a tal o cual persona, es a cambio de otro favor, o de que la adoren como a los santos" (p. 53). For Lucila, the nuns' behavior is contrary to Christian teaching: "Lo cristiano es favorecer al prójimo sin pedirle nada" (p. 54).

The unhappiness of convent life, for those who have no vocation, is stressed in the account of the sufferings of Domiciana, who is freed from the cloister only by insanity. The imperfections of the secular priesthood are also indicated in the evocation of the historical Merino. Merino, insane, contemptuous of theology, obsessed by the difficulties of collecting debts owed to him as a moneylender, meditating the murder of the queen, nevertheless hears confessions and, on the morning of the attempted regicide, says mass.

In contrast to the artificial, conformist society imposed by the nuns stands the authentic passion and total honesty of Lucila. Lucila is not the mythological creation of García Fajardo's and Miedes's insane dreams. She is a woman, talkative, entertaining, tender, and almost maternal in her care for her lover, the fugitive Bartolomé Gracián. Her manner of loving is, however, disordered, "Romantic":[36] "En proporción de su desgracia estaba el origen de ella: amor tempestuoso, irregular, semejante a un soberano desorden de los elementos; si amó a Tolomín con ternura cuando le vio y conoció fugitivo y condenado a muerte, locamente le amó después, teniéndole a su lado en lastimosa invalidez y acechado por cazadores de hombres" (p. 29).

Although for Galdós passion is preferable to the slavery and hypocrisy of a theocratically controlled society, Lucila nonetheless lacks judgment in her choice of lover and in her total fixation on the unworthy object of her love. As in the case of Fernando Calpena's obsession with Aura Negretti, her Romantic "love" is a form of madness. Thus, when Gracián disappears, Lucila becomes deliriously ill and plots the killing of her rival Domiciana. Her bitterness turns to melancholy. For months, she vacillates between temporary relief from her suffering and the return of her suicidal black passion.

Time, however, heals. The absence of Domiciana from Madrid provides rest and, gradually, recovery: "¡Qué descanso no verla más ni saber nada de ella! Así cayendo irían sobre su memoria esas capas de polvo que traen el lento olvidar, la renovación pausada de las ideas. De este modo se llega, por gradación suave, a ver y apreciar el reverso de las cosas" (p. 218).

Although her Romantic passion is still strong in her, Lucila, however reluctantly, takes the first steps of her passage to emotional health. Thus, without enthusiasm, she agrees to marry the rich farmer Vicente Halconero. She shows the beginnings of a mature judgment in her acceptance of him for his goodness and tenderness, rather than for the more obviously seductive features of a Bartolomé Gracián: "Lucila vio en él un marido de tipo paternal, y creyó firmemente que reinaría en su corazón por la bondad y el tutelar cariño" (p. 240).

As in *Narváez,* calls for abstract ideals are merely the distorted expression of personal ambitions or torments. Gracián's defense of

Liberty cloaks his desire for rapid promotion. Merino's dream of the rule of Peace and Justice is inspired by his inability to collect the money owed to him. Lucila's craving for a cataclysm, for the reign of Justice, masks her craving for vengeance.

Work at a useful task—Don Beltrán's remedy in the third series of *episodios* for the ills of Spain—is again proclaimed in *Los duendes de la camarilla.* Domiciana, with her sly hypocrisy, is a less admirable character than Lucila. Through Domiciana, however, Galdós contrasts the sterility of nuns' lives with the greater opportunities to serve neighbor and self outside the convent. Domiciana, neurotic to the point of insanity as a nun, is far happier in the outside world, dwelling with her family and occupying herself usefully in the preparation of cosmetic and pharmaceutical products: "Ansiaba morar con los suyos, ver gente, ocuparse en menesteres gratos, lucidos, y de eficacia inmediata para la vida" (p. 37). "Yo no aspiro a gobernar a nadie, sino a ser útil a unos cuantos, y a emplear mis días en un trabajo modesto que a mí me sostenga y me dé mejor y más cómoda vida" (p. 70). "Me gusta trabajar, hacer cosas; me gusta vender, me gusta cobrar" (p. 75).

The social problem looms in the background of the novel. Jerónimo Ansúrez and the priest Merino complain in their frustration of the exploitation and unjust distribution of wealth in Spain: "Loco es en España el que fíe del trabajo para vivir a gusto, que de su sudor no ha de sacar más que afanes, y ser el hazmereir de los que manipulan con lo trabajado. Tres oficios no más hay en España que labren riqueza, y son éstos: bandido, usurero, y tratante en negros para las Indias" (p. 290). "Pues mientras los cortesanos se hartan en banquetes, el pueblo cena pan seco, y por no tener para carbón, que vale, como sabéis, a catorce reales, no puede ni calentar agua para hacer unas tristes sopas" (p. 291).

In their bitterness, Merino and Ansúrez deny that Spain can find salvation in a leader (Costa's "iron surgeon"). For Merino, the savior of Spain (the "Messiah") must unite the qualities of Moses, Numa, Caesar Augustus, Cyrus, Semiramis, and Alexander. Ansúrez, with greater pessimism, holds that a "doctor" uniting all imaginable talents would be insufficient to heal the sickness of Spain: "Pienso—dijo el *celtibero,*—que al hombre, remediador de los males de España, o sea médico de esta enferma nación, no podemos imaginarlo reuniendo en un sujeto a todos los talentos del mundo, pues aún sería poco material para formar el gran seso que aquí necesitamos" (p. 293).

In *La revolución de julio* (September 1903-March 1904), Galdós treats two historical events at length: the defrocking and execution of the priest Merino in February 1852 and the Revolution of 1854. In this bitter novel Galdós goes beyond his previous anticlericalism to attack an intolerance that lies in the heart of every Spaniard. Repeating Costa's emotion-laden charge that the liberal "revolutions" of the nineteenth century produced merely surface changes,[37] Galdós dismisses the Revolution of 1854 as "comic opera." The poor misguidedly struggle for a political revolution that will produce no change in their lot; fundamental problems of hunger and exploitation remain ignored; Spaniards, avoiding reality, seek immediate "Romantic" solutions to their problems and convert life into "theater." Nevertheless, despite his harsh portrayal of the frustration of popular hopes in 1854, Galdós offers hope for a future Spain. A true revolution is needed. The Spanish "sickness" may be the prerequisite to future health. Individual revolt against the hypocrisy and conformism of Spanish society is possible.

In his description of the degradation of Merino, Galdós attacks, as in previous novels, the lack of spirituality and charity in Spanish "religion." Merino's thoughts as he said mass were, according to popular repute, directed toward a woman friend, not toward God. The defrocking, portrayed in detail, is a barbaric ceremony that inspires in Fajardo, if not in the participating ecclesiastics, a compassion for the demented priest. The spiritual assistance offered by the Brothers of Peace and Charity (and rejected by Merino) is a grotesque theatrical "program." Galdós's heavily sarcastic treatment is worthy of a Blasco Ibáñez: "don Martín no dejó de *guasearse* de la Justicia, del verdugo, de los clérigos asistentes y de los respetables Hermanos de la Paz y Caridad. Todo este interesante personal se veía defraudado en el ejercicio de sus caritativas funciones; por los suelos estaba el programa patibulario, pues el reo faltaba descaradamente a sus obligaciones de tal, negándose a llorar, a besuquear la estampa, y a dejar caer su cabeza sobre el pecho con desmayo que anticipaba la inacción de la muerte."[38]

The execution itself recalls the Inquisition and, presumably in its savage theatricality, a "fiesta de caníbales." Galdós's criticism now extends beyond the role of the Church. For Fajardo, there is a friar or executioner in each Spaniard (compare Macías Picavea's well-known dictum: " ¡Frailes por dentro; jacobinos por fuera! "). The Spanish language itself lends itself to the mockery of others, not to charity or meekness: "sostuve que somos un país bárbaro, donde la justicia toma formas de Inquisición, y los escarmientos de pena capital visos de fiesta de caníbales. Dentro de cada español, por mucho que presuma de cultura, hay un sayón o un fraile. La lengua que hablamos se presta como ninguna al escarnio, a la burla, y a todo lo que no es caridad ni mansedumbre" (p. 19).

The liberal Revolution of 1854 is but a further example of a national fondness for theater. Spanish politics and society are a branch of comedy: "la política, que también es ya comedia pura, de enredo muchas veces, otras de figurón" (p. 33). The Battle of Vicálvaro is a theatrical function, an inglorious comic revolution, decided by the "compadrazgo disimulado" of the two "opposed" branches of the army. The Manifesto of Manzanares fails to concern the disabused Fajardo; similarly, O'Donnell's harangue is cynically dismissed as "picos y flautas . . . los tópicos de siempre" (p. 177). "Professional" patriots and "poetas y escritores sin juicio" join the revolutionary forces; self-interest is the only motive of those who lead and support the revolution. Only externals, as Costa had charged in his attack on the myths of nineteenth-century Spanish liberalism, are changed by the July Revolution. The power of the *caciques* and their allies remains intact:

Todo es pequeño, en conjunto. Relativa grandeza o mediana talla veo en la obra del pueblo sacrificándose por renovar el ambiente político de los señoretes y cacicones que vivimos en alta esfera. Menguados son los políticos, y no muy grandes los militares que han movido este zipizape. Pobre y casera es esta revolución, que no mudará más que los externos chirimbolos de la existencia, y sólo pondrá la mano en el figurón nacional, en el cartón de su rostro, en sus afeites y postizos, sin atreverse a tocar ni con un dedo la figura real que el maniquí representa y suple a los ojos de la ciega muchedumbre (p. 325).

Spanish theatricality, although this time in the form of "tragedy," is also to be found in the lower classes of society, who man the barricades in a spontaneous outburst of hatred and hope: "Veía, por fin, una página histórica, interesante, dramática, producida en el tiempo, sin estudio, por espontáneo brote en el cerebro y en la voluntad de millares de hombres, que el día anterior ignoraban que iban a ser histriones de una teatralidad tan bella" (p. 251).

Writing with obvious anger, Galdós protests that the poor sacrifice lives and humble possessions for abstractions, for a constitution and rights which they do not understand and which have no practical consequence in their lives: "¿Y por qué lucha esta gente? Por ésta o la otra Constitución que no conocen, por derechos vagos que no entienden, o por idolatría fetichista de hombres y principios, cuyas ventajas en la práctica no han de disfrutar jamás" (p. 275). The ideals for which the downtrodden fight are no more than empty words: "aquel ideal de pura soñación" (p. 289), "un ideal político que entendían como la escritura chinesca" (p. 297). After their heroic sacrifice for a meaningless cause, the poor will return to their sad daily tasks, their lot unchanged: "Y después de pasarse largos días y noches en tan peligrosas andanzas, volvería cada cual a sus obligaciones. El uno seguiría fabricando obleas y lacre; el otro, jeringas, y el tercero vendiendo sanguijuelas, para ganar un triste cocido y vivir estrechamente entre afanes y miserias. Todo lo soñaban, menos llegar a ser ricos, o al menos, vivir con desahogo" (p. 290).

Such is the perpetual misadministration of Spanish public life that revolution provides the Spanish people with hope of escape. They thus embrace joyously during insurrections: "En estas expansiones populares, el abrazo entre desconocidos es el signo externo del cordial regocijo, de la esperanza que toda insurrección despierta en el sufrido pueblo español, mal gobernado siempre" (p. 180).

But behind the popular enthusiasm lurks hunger. Sebo, the police agent, will perform any task to feed his family ("El pobre mal comido dice a todo que sí," p. 134). It is hunger, and not political ideals, that provides the motivating forces for revolutions: "Los pueblos desgraciados se enamoran de lo nuevo . . . Y si en esos seres desgraciados están en mayoría los hambrientos, el entusiasmo por las revoluciones es delirio . . . La verdadera opinión, el verdadero *sentimiento público,* es el hambre" (p. 157).

The popular classes are exploited by the rich and powerful, who make the laws for their own interest. The ruling classes are, indeed, for Virginia little more than bandits (p. 161). Fajardo bitterly protests those who blame the people for temporary revolutionary excesses. Rather, it is governmental repression that is to blame for occasional popular outbursts:

¡Y las culpas de esta brutal plebe nadie las atenuará con el recuerdo de las horribles violaciones de toda ley moral y cristiana que se contienen en el gobierno regular de las sociedades; nadie verá la inmensa barbarie que encierra el régimen burocrático, expoliador del ciudadano y martirizador de pobres y ricos; nadie se acordará del sinnúmero de verdugos que constituyen la familia oficial, y cuya única misión es oprimir, vejar, expoliar y apurar la paciencia, la sangre y el bolsillo de tantos miles de españoles que sufren y callan! ... Nadie se fijará en el crimen lento, hipócrita, metodizado, de la acción gobernante, mientras que salta a la vista el crimen desnudo, instantáneo, de unas gavillas de insensatos que asaltan, queman, matan, sin respetar haciendas ni vidas. Nadie ve las víctimas obscuras que inmoló la ambición de los poderosos, ni los atropellos que se suceden en el seno recatado de una paz artificiosa, sostenida por la fuerza bruta dominante, y todos se horrorizan de que la fuerza oprimida y dominada se sacuda un día y, aprovechando un descuido del domador, tome venganza en horas breves de los ultrajes y castigos de siglos largos (pp. 251-52).

Obviously directing his remarks at the present, Galdós protests that no real revolution has taken place as yet in Spain. Spain has still to find its new form. A true revolution is needed to end the slow stagnation of Spanish life:

España no necesita de la acción consolidadora del tiempo, porque no tiene nada que consolidar; necesita de la acción destructora, porque sus grandes necesidades son destructivas. Las revoluciones, que en otras partes desequilibran la existencia, aquí la entonan. ¿Por qué? Porque nuestra existencia es en cierto modo transitoria, algo que no puede definirse bien. Yo la veo como si el ser nacional estuviera muriendo y naciendo al mismo tiempo. Ni acaba de morirse ni acaba de nacer.... Digo que el ser nacional está en todo este siglo muriendo y naciendo. Los hombres públicos y cuantos de política se ocupan, incluso los militares, sepultan y al propio tiempo vivifican.... La nación quiere mudanzas y revoluciones, para que el nacer sea fijo y se acabe el morir.....
—Ahora entiendo, porque ... como dijo el otro: los pueblos no mueren. —Se modifican, se refunden. España no ha encontrado el molde nuevo. Para dar con él, tiene que pasar todavía por difíciles probaturas, y sufrir mil quebrantos que la harán renegar de sí misma y de los demás (pp. 145-46).

In the context of national suffering, military uprisings are the norm of Spanish life: "Los militares se sublevan cuando la Nación no puede aguantar ya más atropellos, inmoralidades y corrupciones, y en estos casos el brazo militar triunfa, sencillamente porque debe triunfar."[39]
Spaniards are in any case ill prepared by education and in attitude

for life in the modern world. In the topsy-turvy world of Spain, foreign inventions are readily assimilated, but Spaniards do not take the effort to learn and invent for themselves: "Pero no empiezan por el principio, que es instruirse y civilizarse, para después gozar. Dicen: *gocemos, y luego nos civilizaremos*" (p. 61). The education of women (as dominated by the Church in the early twentieth century as it was in 1854) is manifestly inadequate. Thus, the Socobio sisters have little knowledge of religion, arithmetic, geography, or history. Ignorant of weights and measures, they are ill equipped for domestic tasks: "No conocen nada de la vida; no se ha permitido que en sus espíritus, amañados para la elegancia, penetre parte alguna del prosaísmo con que tenemos que luchar" (p. 35).

Appearances (superficial constitutional changes, parades, and speeches) and a naive belief that the abstractions of liberal rhetoric represent reality delude the revolutionaries of 1854. The sickness that afflicts both nation and individuals is, for Galdós, "Romanticism," a Romanticism as dangerous in 1904 as it was in 1854.

A particularly virulent form of Romanticism is exemplified in Bartolomé Gracián. Gracián, with his destructive passions for women and insurrection, is a perturbing element in society. A dreamer, unhappy with reality, obviously neurotic in his compulsions, Gracián, like an unreconstructed Spain, is forever condemned to seek the impossible:

—Es un soñador, que no se conforma con la realidad, y busca siempre lo que está detrás de lo visible. . .
—Y detrás de lo visible, ¿qué se encuentra? . . .
—Se encuentra . . . lo que se busca . . . una imagen que al encarar con ella nos dice: "no soy lo que quieres. . . . Lo que quieres viene detrás. . . ." Y así sucesivamente hasta lo infinito. . . .
—Pues el que persiste en buscar lo que no encuentra, o es un loco, o necio de solemnidad.
—Es un descontento, un ambicioso, un investigador de almas. Puedes creerlo: el tal Gracián me interesa y deseo tratarle (p. 151).

Fajardo also has sickly "Romantic" tendencies. He suffers from melancholia and lethargy and is overcome by boredom with the pedestrian events he chronicles. He, like Gracián, seeks the extraordinary: "Mi fogosa curiosidad de lo anormal, de lo extraordinario, de lo que borra y destruye la vulgar semejanza de todas las cosas" (p. 6). Fajardo, like nineteenth-century Spain, is given to violence: he would have the boring Rementería assassinated; he kills Gracián without premeditation. He wishes a revolution to take place for his own private entertainment ("para mi solaz y entretenimiento," p. 64) and seeks, in his flight from everyday reality, the tragic greatness of revolutionary turmoil: "Revolución quiero y necesito: revolución en los cerebros y en los corazones, revolución arriba y abajo, dentro y fuera" (p. 64).

Just as the *pueblo* and revolutionaries risk their lives and humble possessions for illusory goals, so also does Fajardo live in a world of dreams. He is superstitious, believing hidden celestial or demonic divinities protect him. His faith in Lucila (whom he has seen but twice) is "theological" and in his exaltation he regards her as a celestial creature whose son was engendered by a Celtiberian god or, alternatively, by the genius of the Spanish nation. Referring frequently to Melpomene (the Muse of Tragedy), he sees the events of the Revolution not as reality but as scenes in a theatrical representation; the revolution itself is for him a comedy; all play roles, with Gracián's being that of "popular hero." Nevertheless, Fajardo is also caught up in the drama. Inspired by a "Romantic" sympathy for the *pueblo,* he fights—temporarily forgetting both family and spectator's role—for a cause that his intelligence has told him is without meaning.

Fajardo (Spain), like the Calpena of the third series of *episodios,* needs guidance if he is to recover from, or limit the effects of, his "sickness." Thus, his wife establishes a regime to control the fevered workings of his mind: methodical writing is permitted, as a form of therapy, but is limited to one and a half hours a day. Sickness, however, in nations and individuals, is perhaps the necessary prelude to healthy growth: "Tendremos, pues, enfermedad saludable, de esas que hacen crisis en el individuo, y promueven el crecimiento, la adquisición de fuerza nueva" (p. 175).

Fajardo's apparent flight from reality, his longing for beauty and greatness in private and public life (his *ansia de belleza* or *desarreglo estético*), is more than the *aspiración insana* that his wife believes. In a cynical society that provides neither hope nor a firm moral structure, Fajardo gropes for values that will guide the individual and, as a consequence, Spain. He acts forcefully (if unconsciously) to protect the healthy marriage of Lucila (by killing Gracián). He admires Virginia and Leoncio who do not play roles but are fully involved in their love for each other. Despising the pettiness of the revolutionaries of 1854, he longs for the rule of a great man, and awaits the rule of intelligence and will-power that will replace the mediocrity that surrounds him:

Y para que se me quite el mal gusto de boca que me dejan estas peleas por un puñado de garbanzos, miro hacia las ambiciones de un César, de un Cromwell, de un Bonaparte.

Desdeño las tintas medias, la clase media, el justo medio y hasta la moral media, ese punto de transacción o componenda entre lo bueno y lo malo. No me gusta nada que sea medio; me seduce más lo entero. Váyase mucho con Dios el buen sentido, y tráigame la sinrazón, el desenfreno de la inteligencia y de la voluntad (p. 228).

The Romanticism attacked by Galdós is that which converts life into literature and, in its pursuit of sterile and illusory goals, denies reality. Another form of Romanticism, however, meets with Galdós's approval: the abandonment of the hypocrisies of society in favor of authentic values that permit the individual growth and happiness. Virginia leaves her cold, wealthy husband to join the mechanic Leoncio Ansúrez ("el hombre que amo, con el que es primero y único amor mío"). Happy caring for the man she loves and esteems, she liberates from within herself a joy that was unable to find expression within the conventional bonds of society. In her new freedom, Virginia discovers a true spirituality, as she worships God with simplicity and devotion. Furthermore, liberation from false values not only gives inner strength but also leads to a knowledge of the outside world. Thus, Virginia learns the real nature of Spanish life, as she shares the poverty and nomadic wanderings of her lover.

The elopement shocks a society obsessed with the pursuit of material wealth. Initially, García Fajardo and his wife take the side of Virginia's parents and society. María Ignacia cannot comprehend the total rejection of societal values and the accompanying material satisfactions: "Yo concedo a las flaquezas humanas todo lo que se quiera; comprendo las pasiones repentinas, la ceguera de un momento, de un día; ¡pero fugarse así . . . condenarse a la deshonra para toda la vida, a la miseria! (p. 76)

But Fajardo, increasingly recognizing the inadequacy of the values of Spanish society to satisfy spiritual and emotional needs, reserves his opinion, preferring to leave the errant couple in freedom. True morality, he now postulates, is not to be sought in society but in the heart:

"Mientras esto se averigua, no atentemos a la libertad de nadie, y dejemos a cada pájaro en su nido. ¡La ley! . . . ¡la moral! Créeme a mí, mujer: si queremos dar con la moral y la ley, busquémoslas en nuestros corazones" (p. 114).

In *O'Donnell* (April-May 1904), Galdós continues his attack on the lack of moral values, cult of appearances, and religious superstition of Spanish society. Portraying, as in no other novel of the series, the harsh poverty of the lives of many Spaniards, Galdós still proposes individual, and not societal, solutions to the social problem: individual dedication to productive tasks, individual practice of charity. *O'Donnell* is also a novel of conciliation. Galdós attempts to reconcile the pressures of material needs and of societal demands with an idealism without which all hope of a better life for Spain is lost.

Although *O'Donnell* covers five years of Spanish history (1854-1859), the history treated in the novel receives little more than passing mention. The novel begins with the degraded parading of the sick police chief Chico by the Madrid mob in 1854. It briefly covers Serrano's shelling of the *Milicia Nacional,* the expulsion of the deputies from the Cortes, Narváez's execution of those who rebel from hunger, and the corrupt policies of the *Unión Liberal.* The novel ends with the return of the *Unión Liberal* to power in 1859.

The absence in Spain of moral values deeply concerns Galdós. Throughout the novel, "fallen women" symbolize Spanish moral corruption: prostitutes who howl insults at the invalid Chico, aristocrats whose liaisons are the subject of common gossip, Manuela Pez and Valeria Navascués with their easy "virtue," and Teresa Villaescusa, who in her generosity and selfish materialism incarnates the *Unión Liberal* ("la pasión del buen vivir y la pasión de repartir el bien humano"[40]). The flamboyance, false promises, and inability to carry out any task of lasting value of a whole generation of politicians and generals lead Galdós sarcastically to compare Spain's leaders with women of the streets: "los militares muy valientes, los paisanos muy retóricos; aquéllos echando el corazón por delante en los casos de guerra, éstos enjaretando discursos con perífrasis galanas o bravatas ampulosas, y cuando era llegada la ocasión de hacer algo de provecho, todos resultaban fallidos, y procedían como mujeres más o menos públicas" (p. 100).

The society portrayed by Galdós is obsessed by appearances (a further example of form masquerading as substance, the major feature of Regenerationist analyses of nineteenth-century Spain). Whereas Virginia del Socobio is banished from society for the crime of openly living her passion, her sister Valeria, sexually unfaithful and financially extravagant, enjoys the reputation of "virtue." Young bureaucrats are socially esteemed and sought as husbands, although their earnings are less than those of shoe-shine boys.[41] The aristocrat Aransis wastes his fortune as he strives to preserve an ostentatious social front. A colonel's widow (Manola Pez) and her daughter, obliged to dress well, live in greater poverty than do street vendors. Kept women must conceal their wealth, while every liberty is permitted to married women.

The Spanish moneyed classes avidly seek position and wealth (and Galdós describes in detail the elaborate banquets offered by the gourmet Rivas Guisando); the underlying poverty of Spain is, however, all-pervasive. Santiuste and the family he protects are dying of starvation. Beneath the political slogans of the agrarian rebels of El Arahal lies the simple demand for bread: "cien hombres fusilados por el delito de no haber almorzado, ni comido, ni cenado en muchos días" (p. 197). Teresa—and Galdós's summary of her reactions reveals a feeling for Castile akin to that of the so-called Generation of 1898—is deeply moved by the stark poverty of the Castilian countryside and the suffering of its inhabitants:

Miraba los pueblos pardos como el suelo, las mezquinas casas formando corrillo en torno a un petulante campanario. . . . Ni amenidad, ni frescura, ni risueños prados veía, y no obstante, todo le interesaba por ser suyo, y en todo ponía su cariño, como si hubiera nacido en aquellas casuchas tristes y jugado de niña en los egidos polvorosos. Las mujeres vestidas con justillo, y con verdes o negros refajos, atraían su atención. Sentía piedad de verlas desmedradas, consumidas prematuramente por las inclemencias de la naturaleza en suelo tan duro y trabajoso. Las que aún eran jóvenes tenían rugosa la piel. Bajo las huecas sayas asomaban negras piernas enflaquecidas. Los hombres, avellanados, zancudos, con su seriedad de hidalgos venidos a menos, parecían llorar grandezas perdidas. Todo lo vio y admiró Teresa, ardiendo en piedad de aquella desdichada gente que tan mal vivía, esclava del terruno, y juguete de la desde-ñosa autoridad de los poderosos de las ciudades. Por todo el camino, al través de las llanadas melancólicas, de las sierras calvas, de los montes graníticos, iba empapando su mente en esta compasión de la

España pobre, a solas, muy a solas, pues la persona que la acompañaba esparcía sus pensamientos por otras esferas (pp. 212-13).

As in previous novels of the fourth series, Galdós attacks Catholic beliefs and practices. The miraculous intervention of heaven in Spanish politics is described in heavily satirical terms:

Fue que un venerado Cristo que recibía culto en una de las más importantes iglesias del Reino, se afligió grandemente de que los pícaros gobernantes quisieran vender los bienes de Mano Muerta. Del gran sofoco y amargura que a Nuestro Señor causaban aquellas impiedades, rompió su divino cuerpo en sudor copioso de sangre. Aquí del asombro y pánico de toda la beatería de ambos sexos, que vio en el milagro sudorífico una tremenda conminación. ¡Lucidos estaban Espartero y O'Donnell y los que a entrambos ayudaron! ¡Vaya, que traernos una Revolución, y prometer con ella mayor cultura, libertades, bienestar y progresos, para salir luego con que sudaban los Cristos! La vergüenza sí que debió encender los rostros de O'Donnell y Espartero, hasta brotar la sangre por los poros. Por débiles y majagranzas que fuesen nuestros caudillos políticos, incapaces de poner a un mismo temple la voluntad y las ideas, la ignominia era en aquel caso tan grande, que hubieron de acordarse de su condición de hombres y de la confianza que había puesto en ellos un país tratado casi siempre como manada de carneros. El de Luchana y el de Lucena se apretaron un poco los pantalones. Y la Reina firmó, y Sor Patrocinio y unos cuantos capellanes y palaciegos salieron desterrados, con viento fresco; al buen Cristo se le curaron, por mano de santo, la fuerte calentura y angustiosos sudores que sufría, y no volvió a padecer tan molesto achaque (pp. 35-36).

A kept woman, Teresa Villaescusa, and not Catholic organizations, acts as the "angel" of charity to the starving Santiuste. The leading Catholic politician of the period, Cándido Nocedal, is treated, sympathetically, as a cynical turncoat.[42] The ready-made answers of Catholic politicians to all problems of government are dismissed with terse sarcasm: "Fácil es la política en que todo se arregla echando a Dios por delante: no es preciso argumentar mucho para esto, porque en el ultramontanismo todo está pensado ya. ¡Qué cómodo es tener la fuerza lógica hecha y acopiada para cuantos problemas de gobierno puedan ocurrir! " (p. 200)

In contrast with the sad and impoverished nation of 1854, Galdós offers a vision of a possible regenerated Spain of the future. O'Donnell, in the shadowland between consciousness and sleep, meditates a material program (which is almost identical to that of Costa) to reconstruct a nation that is at present no more than an *hospicio suelto.* The *Unión Liberal* will unite "lo útil, lo mejor, lo más inteligente" (p. 142). The money from the sale of Church lands will create a new landowning class and be employed to construct the roads, railways, ports, and canals that the new nation needs. Liberty and order will be conciliated, and, with the entry of foreign ideas, Spain will properly take her place among the ranks of European nations.

But O'Donnell's ambitious schemes, like those of twentieth-century regenerators, are only dreams. The very same reforms were as urgently awaited in 1904 as they had been fifty years earlier. O'Donnell recognizes the industriousness of Spanish workers; however, Spanish moral attitudes—a propensity to fantasy and the iron grip of intolerance and resistance to change—render his task impossible: "No hay manera de crear un país a la moderna sobre este cementerio de la Quijotería y de la Inquisición" (p. 142). In sadly exemplary manner, the wastrel Aransis resists all efforts by Fajardo to redeem his financial situation. Aransis, like Spain, fatuously considers that to be false to his nature (i. e., to his past), to abandon a fleeting amorous passion, is a greater madness than paying heed to his financial straits: "la medicina que intenta curar estos males, que son la vida misma, es peor y más dolorosa que la enfermedad" (p. 134).

A further impractical dreamer is Juan Santiuste, a starving journalist who is rescued from near-death by Teresa Villaescusa. Santiuste, enamored of Castelar, imitates the extravagant rhetoric of the democratic politician and professor. A prisoner of his own "lenguaje de vaporosa espiritualidad" (the idealism of which nonetheless moves Teresa to tears), he glimpses only in a dream his true need (and that of Spain), which is to devote himself to productive labor: "No pienses en destinos del Gobierno, que no son más que pan para hoy y hambre para mañana ... Métete en el comercio; compra y vende patatas, fruta, madera, cal, huevos, cualquier cosa; aprende un oficio; ponte a hacer cosas, a fabricar algo, jabón, ladrillos, clavos, peines, velas, relojes o demonios coronados ... el cuento es que ganes dinero" (p. 271). Fajardo also stresses the need to contribute constructively to society: "Una parte de nosotros no es nuestra, es de la totalidad, y a la totalidad hay que darla. ... El que no hace nada, absolutamente nada, debe desa-

parecer, o merece que le tasen los bienes que derrocha sin ventaja suya
ni de los demás" (p. 72).

The contradictions of Spanish society—unsure of itself, caught in a
web of corruption, but nonetheless with generous impulses—are expressed in the character of Teresa Villaescusa. At first frivolous and
unstable (she evades her situation by reading novels, by spurning her
many suitors, and by plunging into melancholia), she is nevertheless
aware of her nature. In character, she is both ignoble and generous. She
prostitutes her body for personal enrichment. She also, however, re-
nounces Aransis rather than interfere with his career, disinterestedly
helps the poor, and returns good for insult. Torn between her idealistic
love for Santiuste and her practical awareness that money is needed to
live, she with difficulty in the final chapter of the novel decides to sell
herself to Manolo Tarfe, the cynical representative of the *Unión
Liberal.*

As in previous novels, Galdós in *O'Donnell* attempts to guide Spaniards in their choice of values. Spaniards long for an ideal. The ideal
may be destructive or futile (Aransis's amorous passions, Santiuste's
vain rhetorical fancies); it may also lead, however, to action toward a
better society (Fajardo's commitment to absolute justice, Fajardo's and
Teresa's respect for the exemplary lovers, Virginia and Leoncio). To live
in society, Galdós suggests, some compromise is essential. The compromise may be hypocritical (Valeria's immorality disguised as the conduct
of a "good" wife), but it may also facilitate the survival of the "pure"
in a complex and imperfect real world. Thus, Fajardo uses his political
influence (conventional as opposed to absolute justice) to protect
Leoncio and Virginia. He forcibly intervenes (abandoning temporarily
his determination to respect the will of others) to save Aransis from his
follies. Similarly, Teresa, to do good works and feed the poor, chooses
to seek money from her lovers.

Both "idealists" and "materialists," however, have their role to play
in the regeneration of Spain. They can, when honestly motivated, learn
from one another. Teresa's prosaic advice spurs Santiuste to seek
employment as an apprentice mechanic. Santiuste's poetical inspiration
motivates Teresa to give serious consideration to changing a way of life
that is crushing to her spirit.

In *Aita Tettauen* (October 1904-January 1905), Galdós attacks a
facile patriotic enthusiasm (and the relevance to the Spanish-American

War is obvious) which leads Spaniards to rush into bellicose adventures that serve no national interest. Furthermore, his warning against a fruitless involvement in Moroccan affairs was directly pertinent to the diplomatic negotiations of 1904, through which Spain endeavored to obtain the agreement of other European powers in fixing the boundaries of the Spanish sphere of influence in the Moroccan Empire.[43] Continuing the line of thought of previous *episodios,* Galdós adduces a moral explanation for Spain's readiness to entangle herself in overseas adventures: the Spanish language lends itself too readily to hollow abstractions; Spanish abuse of rhetoric provokes enthusiasms for causes that have little to do with the real needs of Spain; Spaniards, with their almost unlimited capacity for self-delusion, have difficulty in perceiving reality. In place of a patriotism based on aggression, Galdós proposes an ideal of peace, of the devotion of Spanish energies to productive tasks inside Spain.

Aita Tettauen traces events between October 1859 (the preparations for the war with Morocco) and February 1860 (the "triumphant" entry of Spanish troops into Tetuán). Galdós evokes the great patriotic enthusiasm for the war, an enthusiasm that temporarily united all social classes and political parties but that he nevertheless qualifies as "childish." As in the War of 1898, brave Spanish soldiers are sacrificed as pawns in the schemes of politicians. For Galdós, the Moroccan War was inspired by O'Donnell's aping of Napoleon III's quest for "glory" and by the Spanish prime minister's need to divert attention from the financial scandals of his administration.

From the beginning of the novel, Galdós conveys his scorn for a Spanish readiness to pursue a military glory that brings the nation no benefit. He satirically summarizes the good Halconero's "patriotic" views: "El buen Halconero, que en patriótico fanatismo daba quince y raya a todos los españoles, pensaba que después de la guerra los laureles nos abrumarían. Probablemente, tras la campaña en Africa, vendrían otras marimorenas con diferentes naciones europeas o asiáticas, y de este continuo pelear resultaría mucha, muchísima gloria y poco dinero, porque los brazos abandonaban la cosecha del trigo por la de laureles. ¿Pero qué importaba? Con tal de ver a España tosiendo fuerte, escupiendo por el colmillo en el ruedo de las naciones europeas, nos allanaríamos a sustentarnos con piruétanos y tagarninas."[44] Two other "patriots" reveal an equal compulsion to abandon self-interest: Jerónimo Ansúrez, so clear-sighted in *Las tormentas del 48* on the ills of Spain, now feels "un vago renacer de grandezas atávicas" (p. 13); Leoncio Ansúrez ("como genuino celtibero") leaves wife and child to set off to war.

The reality of war is far from that dreamed by patriots and poets. Santiuste is revolted by the sight of the dead and wounded; hunger pangs extinguish in him the mental exaltation that had inspired him to write of patriotic glory. The war not only fails to serve Spain's interest, it is also a fratricidal struggle, for the Moor and Spaniard prove to be brothers, both in death and in attitude toward life. The Spaniards deludedly seek in Tetuán what they already have at home: "Pues hay allí naranjales tan hermosos, según dicen, como los de Murcia y Valencia" (p. 170). The conquest of Tetuán is in any case illusory. The true conquest would be by cunning, by a willingness to penetrate Moorish attitudes, and not by "batallitas vistosas . . . y con música" (p. 327).

In place of the rhetorical ideal of war, Galdós propounds an ideal of peace. Despite the occasional memory of past illusions, Lucila, now a plump matron of thirty with five children, devotes herself to the humble, but necessary, tasks of every day: "Empezaba el día, la rutina normal y fácil, el conjunto de menudas obligaciones que, al modo de tejidos de mimbres, forman el armadijo consistente de una existencia mediocre, honrada, sin luchas" (p. 43). Wisely, Lucila dismisses the conqueror Hernán Cortés as "un vago, un perdido" (p. 28). Similarly, Vicente Halconero's steadfast working of the land and refusal to be caught up in political strife represent a truly useful contribution to Spain. Significantly, Halconero's bellicose patriotic delirium is the prelude to his death:

Las tres serían cuando entregó a Dios su alma el bueno, el honrado, el sencillo labrador don Vicente Halconero, que jamás hizo mal a nadie, y a muchos bien sin tasa; varón de grande utilidad en la República, o por mejor decir, en el Reino, porque no devoraba porción ninguna del Tesoro Nacional, sino que creaba, con su labor de la tierra, nueva riqueza cada año. No aumentaba la confusión de opiniones, sino que tendía con su patriótica fe a simplificar las ideas, y a buscar la síntesis que pudiera traer a nuestro país positivas grandezas. Su trabajo agrícola era un beneficio para España, y otro su inocencia, virtud preciada contra la invasión de maliciosos. Fecundaba la tierra, fecundaba el ambiente (pp. 55-56).

El Nasiry hazards unconvincing reasons to explain why the Catalans should abandon commerce and industry to die in war:

Acudí a ilustrar al Príncipe diciéndole que esta tropa viene de un territorio hispano que se llama *La Catalonia,* país de hombres valientes, industriosos y comerciantes; país que está todo poblado de talleres donde labran variedad de cosas útiles, papel, telas, herramientas, vidrio y loza. Como expresara extrañeza de que los *catalonios* dejaran sus telares, alfarerías y fraguas para venir a una guerra en que morirían como moscas, le respondí que allí sobra gente para todo, y que los trabajadores pacíficos no temen interrumpir su faena para ayudar a los fogosos militares, pues los pueblos de Europa saben por experiencia que después de la guerra es más fecunda la paz, y mayor el bienestar de las naciones (p. 233).

Spaniards, Galdós claims, readily accept abstract ideals that bear little or no relation to their true situation or needs. Thus, the lame and ailing child Vicentito Halconero becomes seriously disturbed by his enthusiasm for soldiers and by Santiuste's heady rhetoric. His true need, however, like Spain's, is for tranquillity. To idealize military glory (as does Santiuste in the letters intended for the young Halconero) or history (as does El Nasiry to please his Moorish protector) is to corrupt. Such histories lie and deceive only those too naive to penetrate beneath the surface. Santiuste, when he defends ideals of national honor and the revival of the past glories of Spain, is no more than a storyteller; his impassioned rhetoric is dismissed by Galdós as "música," "trompetazos."

The Spanish language, Santiuste comes to realize, lends itself to a hollow and fatuous patriotism: "Nuestra lengua es una hoja bien afilada para cortar cabezas mahometanas, y un instrumento sonoro y retumbante para dar al viento las fatuidades y jactancias históricas" (p. 111). Words falsify ideas (and the ideas themselves often have little connection with reality): " ¡Glorias! ¿No es verdad, amigo mío, que muchas palabras de constante uso no son más que falsificaciones de las ideas? El lenguaje es el gran encubridor de las corruptelas del sentido moral, que desvían a la humanidad de sus verdaderos fines" (p. 103). High-sounding phrases confuse or mislead. A Moorish poet who stirs his audience to patriotic and religious frenzy is characterized as "este farsante" (p. 257). Santiuste's ardent apology of Christianity wins no converts. His extravagant declaration of love provokes Yohar to protest that he use simpler language to woo her: "Exprime tu corazón con verdad y sin tanto requilorio, y ansi te entenderé . . . Para decirme que so mujer bella y que penas por mí, no hay precisión de tanta cuenta de palabras vacías" (p. 309).

The empty phrases—patriotic, amorous, or Castelarine—reflect an emptiness of the soul, a blindness to and substitute for reality. For Santiuste, Africa is an illusion, a dream of felicity created to fill an inner void: "la grande ilusión de Africa: este manantial de felicidad era entonces abundante y puro, y en él encontraba el alma todos los consuelos que pudiera necesitar" (p. 66). The yearning for war is related to erotic illusion: "La guerra era mi novia, y yo el novio compuesto y lleno de esperanzas" (p. 102). The real world (the horrors of war) is, however, very different from that painted by poets: " ¡Ay! querido Pedro, ese mundo vivido en los libros, en páginas de verso y prosa, ¡cuán distinto es del mundo real! " (p. 102)

As Fajardo had recognized in previous *episodios,* passion is an impulse stemming from within, not from the assessment of reality. Santiuste, disillusioned by war, immediately transfers his dissatisfied longings to the figure of Lucila, his distant idol. In love, he again loses all contact with reality: "Conoces muy bien mis arrebatos y los terribles incendios que levanta en mí el fuego de amor . . . Mis pasiones son exaltadas, delirantes. Divinizo a la mujer amada, y llego a creer que solos ella y yo existimos en el universo" (p. 108). Confused and in a state of spiritual vacuum, neurotically compelled (like a nation responding to the call to war), Santiuste has no conscious control over his actions: "Una inquietud mecánica le movía: su voluntad se encaminaba hacia un fin abstracto, nebuloso, como las promesas de ultratumba" (p. 182). In a further flight from acceptance of responsibility, he attributes his "success"—the elopement with Yohar—to divine intervention: "En su viaje al Africa vio la inspiración del Cielo, o *el dedo de Dios,* como dicen los historiadores y los políticos cuando quieren dar calidad de cosa divina a sus majaderías pomposas" (p. 317).

As in previous novels, Galdós attacks the narrowness and hypocrisies of religious creeds. Bishops preach war and vengeance. Neither Santiuste nor the freethinking army chaplain Toribio Godino accept the intervention of God in worldly battles; miracles (such as the intervention of Saint James) are explained as the hallucinations of battle-crazed soldiers. God—and we are reminded of Unamuno's teaching in *Paz en la guerra*—is, indeed, indifferent to the wars of men: "La obra de Dios no ponía ninguna parte de sí en la guerra que nos asolaba: bosques y peñas, montes y colinas eran indiferentes a los combates entre hombres, y si algo decían, era *paz* y siempre *paz*" (p. 228). Moors and Jews have similar religious concepts to those of Christians: the *Koran* teaches compassion; the Jews receive Santiuste kindly (a kindness he repays by eloping with Yohar). The Moors follow their Holy Book and believe in one God. They, like Christian believers in Divine Providence, attribute their defeat in battle to Allah's punishment for their lack of faith and their neglect of religious practices. Just as compassionate men may be found in all three religions, so also are there fanatical Hebrews, Muslims, and Christians.

Ideology has little to do with conduct. Juan Santiuste, as *Juan el Pacificador,* preaches doctrines of peace and love. He makes no converts, however, and, in his demand that Yohar become a Christian, takes little heed of reality. Santiuste's "Christianity," indeed, is a mask for his amorous desires, which lead him to denounce priestly celibacy. The ending to the novel is ironic: Santiuste conquers *Yohar la blanca,* an apparent conquest of peace, while Spain conquers *Tetuán la blanca paloma,* a conquest of war. Both, however, will fail. Spaniards will refuse to assimilate themselves to Moorish ways and thus will never master Morocco; similarly, Santiuste refuses to consolidate his "conquest" by converting to Judaism.

Carlos VI en la Rápita (April-May 1905) is divided into two sections. In the first part, Santiuste continues his Moroccan adventures, witnessing the flight of the defeated Moors after the Battle of Was Rad. In the second part, after his return to Spain, he glimpses General Ortega and the Carlist princes after the abortive rising in La Rápita (1860). The Spanish invasion of Morocco and the Carlist rising were equally ill conceived and thus necessarily produce only disillusionment. The conquest of Tetuán is short-lived, its only practical consequence a temporary change of street names. (Spain ultimately accepted financial compensation—never paid—for the return to Morocco of the city; apart from that, she obtained only "glory" from the war.) The Carlist landing is a fatuous interlude in the history of Spain, ending in the comfortable treatment of the insignificant Montemolín and the execution of the unfortunate Ortega. Galdós's teaching repeats that of *Aita Tettauen:* that followers pay dearly for a leader's schemes and that *romanticismo,* such as that which inspired Ortega, is a form of madness.

In his criticism of Spanish attitudes, Galdós establishes facile, and overly literary, parallels between Spain and Morocco. The Spain penetrated by Santiuste strongly resembles Morocco in its desolation and in the superstition of its inhabitants. Slavery persists in Spain (Donata had been purchased by Juan Ruiz), and the archpriest of Ulldecona ("Arcipreste, Patriarca y Califa") has Moorish attitudes. The presence of a shared past is strong in both nations: just as Mazaltov in *Aita Tettauen* recreated the character of Celestina, so also does Juan Ruiz reproduce the figure of his medieval namesake.

As in the preceding novel, Galdós explores the relationship between individual, ideology, and the outside world. The mouthing of high-sounding ideals masks selfishness. This selfishness isolates from others and, being a form of blindness, makes fruitful activity in the world impossible. Reality is not changed by incantation or by "Romantic" projections. Observation and experience, not books, are truer guides to conduct.

Santiuste, now fittingly nicknamed *Confusio*, lacks—like Galdós's Spain—knowledge of self and outside world. Erotic fantasies and a facility with words provide him with but a tenuous identity. Thus, at the beginning of the novel, he is uncertain as to his name and religion. Santiuste's ideological claims bear little relationship to his behavior. He seeks a personal religious synthesis, yet demands that Yohar embrace Christianity; he professes nonviolence, but fights when provoked; he denounces Yohar's desire for wealth, but accepts money to compensate for her loss; he attacks her superstitious belief in *la suerte* yet sees the hand of Providence in their union. He lives by illusions, one of which at least (Santiuste's fatuous idea of exporting fruit or cultivating cotton in the Valley of Tetuán) pointedly resembles those of the Regenerationists of Galdós's day: "¿Verdad que me parezco a los políticos proyectómanos de mi patria, que amenizan los ocios de la oficina engrosando ilusiones, fabricando porvenires, o construyendo emporios con materiales de cifras mentirosas, y amañadas premisas de aptitudes falsas o de fertilidades de fantasía? [45]

Santiuste's blindness to self and to the outside world, and his mistaken reliance on the power of words, are fully realized in the initial episode of the novel, that relating his idyllic love for Yohar. For Santiuste, Yohar is always loving and tender, never depressed, always smiling. He has, indeed, created in his imagination a figure who bears little relation to the real woman with whom he lives. His lyrical attempts to persuade her to embrace a life of poetic poverty fail. He believes he conquers a fortress with his verbal skills, but each following day she again raises the walls of her own desires ("los mismos caprichos y tenaces deseos"). Despite Yohar's elopement with another, it is not until the close of the novel that Santiuste learns the lesson that others have an existence independent of his. Finally recognizing that his enthusiasm and superior arguments are insufficient to free Donata of her superstitions, he is forced to acknowledge that one cannot change another person: "No sé quien dijo que nadie entrega sus ideas para que le pongan otras. Lo que llamamos conversión no existe en la realidad; es siempre un engaño del catequizador o del catequizado" (p. 287).

In his portrayal of Santiuste's deluded behavior, Galdós invites Spaniards to examine cherished beliefs. For Galdós, concepts drawn from literature, dreams, or illusory "ideals" of honor, chivalry, and emulation of long-dead heroes deform perception of reality and lead to behavior ill in accord with circumstances. Santiuste, like the Spain that sold Tetuán to the Moors or the Spain of the *patrioteros* of 1898, deceives none but himself. Thus, his flamboyant pretense of outraged Spanish honor (when Yohar flees from him) is countered by a rabbi's reasonable observation that Gonzalo de Córdoba and the Cid have nothing to do with the matter, that the situation demands *cordura, agudeza* (p. 36). His initial refusal to accept compensation for Yohar is merely play-acting, the striking of a childishly heroic pose which has little correspondence to his real behavior. El Nasiry comments ironically on Santiuste's indignation: "Pues en esta tierra, para que te vayas enterando, poco tienen que hacer los Quijotes y Cides" (p. 40). Santiuste's self-deception, his ability to cloak the most ignoble action in fine-sounding words, leads him, indeed, to break his oath and to abuse the hospitality of a friend, when he attempts to steal a slave from El Nasiry's harem.

Santiuste's malady is an extreme form of Romanticism, a self-centered and bookish vision that prevents his perceiving with any exactitude the outside world. Forever ensnared (like a Spain seeking the glories of a phantom past) in the pursuit of his own projections, he is constantly and necessarily disappointed. His infatuation for Bab-el-lah, whom he has never seen, comes purely from within himself, as the terms he employs indicate: "fantasía loca," "mis románticos deseos," "mis románticos ensueños," "me acosté mecido por mi imaginación en vagorosas ilusiones, y soñé que en mí se reproducía la historia del Cautivo contado por Cervantes en el *Quijote*" (p. 91). Instability characterizes the Romantic lover; thus, Erhimo (also unseen) almost immediately replaces Bab-el-lah as the object of Santiuste's Romantic effusions; he selfishly sees himself as both happy lover and saver of a soul. Similarly, on his return to Spain, he creates yet another illusion, that of Lucila ("la ideal mujer"). A little later, Donata, whom he confuses at times with Erhimo, becomes for him "la expresión sintética de la hermosura de mujer, tal como yo la soñé, sin verla nunca realizada" (pp. 175-76).

Not only do Santiuste's bookish projections have little to do with reality, but his fertile imagination also makes him an easy prey to the manipulations of others. Thus, the Erhimo whom the prankster El Nasiry imposes on Santiuste is insane, ugly, toothless, and one-eyed; Santiuste's one Romantic "conquest", Donata, is epileptic and superstitious; she is, indeed, a "slave" of whom Juan Ruiz is happily rid and who has used Santiuste to further her own plans for escape; she will almost immediately abandon him for a rich priest. (See *La vuelta al mundo en la Numancia.*)

By way of contrast, two characters, Juan Ruiz and El Nasiry, see reality as it is and are thus able to exercise some measure of control over the world in which they live. Both lead healthy, joyous lives, helping others, serving in positions of authority. They base their lives on experience, on the observation of reality,[46] and against these two, the bookish, "idealistic" Santiuste is defenseless. Both El Nasiry and Juan Ruiz attempt, generously if unsuccessfully, to correct Santiuste's distorted vision of the world:

El Nasiry: "que no vives en la realidad, sino en el mundo de los ensueños tontos y falaces" (p. 106).

"No olvido, Juan, que tus amigos españoles te llaman *Confusio,* con lo que indican que está en tu naturaleza el confundir las cosas, sin que sepas remediarlo" (p. 83).

Juan Ruiz: "Eres un gran majadero, *Confusio;* eres un chiquillo sin conocimiento, esclavo de tu imaginación y de las mil vaciedades románticas que has sacado de los malditos libros" (p. 300).

The seven-month period that passed between completion of *Carlos VI en la Rápita* and the commencement of composition of *La vuelta al mundo en la Numancia* (January-March 1906) is indicative of Galdós's waning enthusiasm for the *episodios nacionales.*[47] *La vuelta al mundo* is perhaps the most superficial of the *episodios;* its intrigue is trivial in its simplicity (a father's search for his eloped daughter). Only two historical events are recreated: the peasants' rising in Loja in 1861 and the War in the Pacific of 1865 to 1866, a war of marginal importance in Spanish history. Galdós's conclusions are banal and moralizing: defects in the national character, not history, explain the arbitrary rule of *caciques,* agrarian unrest, and the instability of Spanish Americans. "Romanticism" leads Spaniards and Spanish Americans into foolish posturing and into the creation of problems (for nations and individuals) where none need exist.

In the year preceding the composition of *La vuelta del mundo,* wide sections of Andalusia had been afflicted with drought, massive unemployment, famine, and organized anarchistic agitation. For months, the famine received lengthy discussion in the Spanish press;[48] the search for remedies split the Liberal cabinet of Montero Ríos. Against this background of contemporary Andalusian starvation and unrest, Galdós treats with singular evasiveness the rising of Pérez del Alamo and the peasantry of Loja in 1861. Galdós's account of the rising (his only evocation in the *episodios* of an attempt at social revolution) is guarded, terse, and detached; the agrarian agitation is seen at second hand through the eyes of a bewildered sailor (Diego Ansúrez) whose concern, like that of Galdós, is to flee the struggle. Galdós is, indeed, manifestly unwilling to face social and economic problems that, for their solution, would demand radical structural changes in Spain. By way of contrast, his anticlericalism, his protests against political corruption and "Romanticism," touch only the surface of Spanish life.

To explain the agrarian strife in Loja, Galdós refers neither to historical nor to economic circumstances (both, conceivably, amenable to political solution). Instead, he presents the peasants' struggle in moral terms—fallen man living in the earthly Paradise—which preclude political solution. Loja is a second Garden of Eden. Hence, no rational explanation need be sought for the vicious social struggle taking place amid such wealth and fertility:

¿Por qué se peleaban los hombres en aquel delicioso terreno, en aquellos risueños valles fecundísimos que a todos brindaban sustento y

vida, con tanta abundancia que para los presentes sobraba, y aún se
podía prevenir y almacenar riqueza para los de otras regiones? . . . Las
lomas de secano se cubrían de olivos, almendros y vides lozanas; en las
vegas verdeaban los opulentos plantíos de trigo, cáñamo, y de cuanto
Dios ha criado para la industria, así como para el sustento de hombres y
animales . . . Si los que en aquella tierra nacieron podían decir que
habitaban en un nuevo Paraíso terrenal, ¿para qué se peleaban por el
mangoneo de Juan o Pedro, o por el reparto de los bienes de la
Naturaleza, que en tal abundancia concedían el suelo y el clima? [49]

Diego Ansúrez's conclusion—that Spaniards are either fools or madmen—strikingly evades all consideration of the social problem: "o los
españoles son locos sueltos en el manicomio de su propia casa, o tontos
a nativitate" (p. 31).

The oppressive rule of *caciques* is also presented in terms that
preclude immediate political action. *Caciquismo* is to be explained by
feudalism, atavism, and the "Spanish temperament":

Esta [la *Moderación*] no era más que un retoño de la insolencia señorial
en el suelo y ambiente contemporáneos; el feudalismo del siglo XIV,
redivivo con el afeite de artificios legales, constitucionales y dogmáticos, que muchos hombres del día emplean para pintarrajear sus viejas
caras medioevales, y ocultar la crueldad y fieros apetitos de sus bárbaros
caracteres. . . . Sin duda aquel noble señor y su familia obedecían a un
impulso atávico, inconsciente, y creían cumplir una misión social redu-
ciendo a los inferiores a servil obediencia. . . . Los perifollos eran
códigos, leyes, reglamentos, programas y discursos que no alteraban la
condición arbitraria, inquisitorial y frailuna del hispano temperamento
(pp. 16-17).

Galdós passes no judgment on the efforts of the peasant secret
society to obtain adequate wages for day laborers ("la terrible lucha del
pueblo con el feudalismo" p. 23). His comment on Pérez del Alamo is
guarded to an extreme. He notes only that the revolt was premature
and—obscurely—that Pérez del Alamo's "idea" would bear fruit at a
later date: "Representó una idea que en su tiempo se tuvo por delirio.
Otros tiempos traerían la razón de aquella sinrazón" (p. 47).

Toward the end of the novel, Galdós returns to the theme of the
common ownership of property, in his description of the earthly
Paradise of Tahiti: "Todo era de todos, del pueblo, que en la enramada
frondosa tenía sus bien provistas despensas . . . El propio comunismo

vieron" (p. 283). Tahiti, however, offers no model for the organization of Spanish society and is merely a curiosity; the island life itself, Galdós notes, was being corrupted by civilization.

Galdós is on more familiar ideological ground in his treatment of the war with Chile and Peru (1865-1866). Like the Moroccan War, the war served no political, military, or commercial end of Spain. It was provoked in part by a puerile imitation of the French cult of glory and in part by the ineptitude of Spanish emissaries who acted without clear orders from the government in Madrid. The Spanish sailors do their duty faithfully, suffering in a futile cause absence from home, casualties, and sickness. Even the heroism of Méndez Núñez in bombarding El Callao is a vain gesture, for he disobeyed orders from Madrid to withdraw. The only consequences of his "heroism," Galdós notes, was to delay reconciliation between Spain and her former colonies for a further twenty-five years.

The parallels between Spanish conduct in the War of the Pacific and her sacrifices in the more recent war with Cuban separatists are too obvious not to have been intentional. In both wars, Spain was diplomatically isolated; peoples closely linked by blood and culture engaged in a vicious struggle; vacillating Madrid politicians had announced no clearly defined aims; brave men gave their lives for a cause that was no concern of Spain. Galdós's comment on Spanish intervention in the Pacific War was equally applicable to the Cuban struggle: "Los españoles no querían ser la buena madre, sino la madrastra de América" (p. 142).

The novelistic intrigue—Diego Ansúrez's quest for his daughter Mara, who has fled with the Peruvian Belisario Chacón—symbolizes the uneasy relationship between Spain and her former colonies. It is the parent's harsh inflexibility and lack of perception that caused the daughter to rebel. The Peruvian Belisario is also to blame, for he refused to state his intentions clearly. The sailor Binondo, whose own daughter died of grief after he had cut short her courtship, expresses Galdós's teaching, an affirmation of the right to independence of Spanish America: "Padres, antes que dejar morir a vuestras hijas, dejad que se vayan con sus novios" (p. 106). Spain's sense of loss at the alienation of her former subjects is expressed in Diego's frenzied search for his lost daughter; at the end of the novel, father and daughter are reunited; the family quarrel is at an end.

While Galdós hopes for future good relations between Spain and the American republics, he views Spanish America in as pessimistic a light as he does Spain. Spanish customs and attitudes are continued in the Americas. Thus, Spaniards feel at home in Lima, for the unfortunate traits of the mother country (pride, violence, corruption) exist in exaggerated form there: "La fiereza española, todo lo grande de la raza y todo lo violento y vicioso adherido a lo grande, permanecían escritos allí en cosas y personas, con más vivos caracteres que los que aún conserva en su propio rostro la madre común" (p. 139). Like Spain, the American republics engage in wars and civil strife. Demagogic leaders stir the mob to an unthinking rhetorical patriotism: "Este patriotismo gordo y populachero es excelente cosa para ornamentar las banderas revolucionarias en los países de sangre española" (p. 158). At war, both Spain and Peru pursue the same "fantasma de la gloria"; both nations invoke for success in battle the saints and the Virgin.

Galdós had, of course, never visited Spanish America. His view of the New World is as literary as the visions of those whose *desconocimiento de la realidad* he had so harshly attacked in earlier *episodios*. The American continent is for Galdós an exotic land. He evokes the wildness of the passage through the Straits of Magellan, the animal-like savages of Patagonia, and the feverish visions of early colonizers and conquerors. A sick sailor dreams of vast buried treasure. The delirious Ansúrez has a *modernista* vision of his daughter's fate: she will dwell in a palace amid great wealth, her wants catered to by five hundred servants of varied hues.

Spanish pride, the Spanish search for glory, and the Spanish tendency to dream are only facets of "Romanticism." In *La vuelta al mundo*, as in so many earlier novels, Galdós declares "Romanticism" to be the fundamental defect of Spaniards, a "Romanticism" that in this novel finds expression in histrionic gestures, in the concealment of intent, and in the choice of a hard rather than a straightforward path. The Spanish bombardment of El Callao is "una función de . . . romanticismo" (p. 257); Mara, who in Peru becomes an "antiespañola furibunda," is, like so many of those who rebel against the mother country, suffering from *romanticismo* (in this case, the inability to recognize one's origins or impulses). The poet Belisario is "un romántico". Rather than obtaining the hand of Mara without difficulty by frankly stating his circumstances, he instead chose the tortuous path of illusion: "Lo poético era meterse por el camino más largo y más difícil, manteniendo la ilusión, que es la salsa de que se alimentan las almas románticas" (p. 78). Romantic souls, furthermore, are Romantic only when it so suits them. Belisario is "Romantic" in his poetry and in his courtship; in the elopement, however, he willingly bribes to steal Mara away. Diego Ansúrez, at first bewildered by a *romanticismo* that he cannot understand, realizes that his own rage at Belisario's proposed marriage was also theatrical, "Romantic." Romanticism, indeed, only interferes with the process of life, contributing nothing of benefit.

History plays a much greater role in *Prim* (July-October 1906) than in previous *episodios* of the fourth series. Galdós recreates scenes from his own youth in Madrid. He portrays the preparations for the revolution that would in time give birth to the political system still prevailing in 1906. With a greater optimism than that shown in the preceding *episodios*, Galdós reveals a Spain fitfully preparing to break with the oppressive and corrupt system that was smothering the national spirit. Galdós also examines Spanish perceptions of the nature of revolutionary change. As in previous novels, he attacks the psychological need of Spaniards to embody their aspirations in a person or symbol, the excessive Spanish devotion to abstract ideals, and the Spanish propensity to illusion.

The Madrid described by Galdós is that of his student years. Santiago Ibero, like the youthful Galdós, enjoys wandering the streets of Madrid in solitary observation: "Y ved al hombre en Madrid, brujuleando en las calles, gozando de esa forma de soledad que consiste en andar entre el gentío sin conocer a nadie, observando cosas y personas, y tomando el tiento por de fuera al populoso mundo en que había caído."[50] Santiago Ibero witnesses the same scenes as did the young Galdós: the changing of the guard, the Night of San Daniel (when troops dispersed rioting students), the royal procession. The influence of Castelar, with his "música oratoria," is mentioned. The *Ateneo*, which Galdós had frequented almost daily, and its members are described with respect: "Era la gran logia de la inteligencia que había venido a desbancar las antiguas, ya desacreditadas, como generadoras de la acción iracunda, inconsciente. Por su carácter de cantón neutral, o de templo libre y tolerante, donde cambian todos los dogmas filosóficos, literarios y científicos, fue llamado el Ateneo la *Holanda española*. En aquella Holanda se refugiaba la libre conciencia: lo demás del ser español quedaba fuera del vulgarísimo zaguán del 22 de la calle de la Montera" (p. 123).

Most of the novel is devoted to Prim's repeated attempts to carry out the revolution. In the background, popular discontent simmers; ministries are changed at the whim of a queen manipulated by Sor Patrocinio and Padre Claret; Isabel, generous yet fickle and superstitious, has now lost the confidence of the people who once adored her. After evocations of Prim's attempted risings and the wanderings of his followers across Spain, the novel culminates in an account of the rebellion of the sergeants of the Barracks of San Gil (1866) and of the smashing of the revolt by the energetic conduct of O'Donnell and Serrano.

Prim is the only historical figure of the fourth series of *episodios* to be presented in heroic terms. Like such heroes of the third series as Mendizábal and Cabrera, he possesses good and bad qualities: he has intelligence and foresight ("más avisado y perspicaz que todos sus contemporáneos"); he is also bad-tempered, nervous, impatient, and impulsive. The indefatigable soul of numerous conspiracies, he is a new knight-errant, as Galdós only half ironically observes in his description of Prim's escape after the abortive rising in Valencia: "Allá iba en un barco roto, sin víveres ni abrigo, valiente, inflexible, temerario. Resucitaba en nuestro tiempo la andante caballería, desnudándola del arnés mohoso y vistiéndola de las nuevas armas resplandecientes que van forjando los siglos" (p. 185).

Prim's role as revolutionary hero reflects more than his individual qualities. Spaniards, Galdós observes with fascination, need in times of distress a symbol on whom to center their aspirations. Thus, for Teresa Villaescusa, condemned to live with a balding and hypocritical bureaucrat, Prim represents her personal freedom; for the spiritualist Ramón Lagier, Prim is "un enviado de Dios"; for the idealistic Santiago Ibero, Prim is "la encarnación de un pueblo que lucha por desatarse de ligaduras cuyos nudos estaban endurecidos por los siglos" (p. 173). For the revolutionaries, each adapting the simple slogan "Prim, Libertad" to fit his heart's desire, Prim is the harbinger of the perfect society: "Nadie durmió aquella noche; nadie pudo eximirse del delirio expectante, del presumir y anticipar el suceso futuro, que todavía era un enigma. En las cabezas grandes y chicas ardían hogueras. Las llamaradas capitales *Prim, Libertad,* se subdividían en ilusiones y esperanzas de variados matices: Prim y Libertad serían muy pronto Paz, Ilustración, Progreso, Riqueza, Bienestar" (p. 233).

From the beginning of the novel Galdós stresses the gap between illusion and reality. The ingenuous Santiago Ibero believes that Prim will restore in Mexico the Spanish Empire; in reality, the expedition was intended only to collect debts and was manipulated by French interests. Similarly, with the benefit of hindsight, Galdós attacks the vague and rhetorical nature of the revolutionary program. Spaniards, in their excessive devotion to abstract ideals, lose sight of personal, practical interests. Thus, the credulous businessman Rivas Chaves (like the Don Alonso of the third series of *episodios*) sacrifices wealth, family life, and enthusiasm in the service of a *progresista* cause which will produce no fundamental change in Spain: "Y la Causa era, en suma, un ideal fantástico y verboso, un *Progreso* de fines indecisos y aplicaciones no muy claras, una revolución que tan sólo cambiaría hombres y nombres, y remediaría tan sólo una parte de los males externos de la Nación" (p. 286). The revolution, Galdós insinuates, will serve only the interests of a minority. A large part of the nation—the rural peasantry— is unaffected by political changes: " ¡Pobre gente! Para ellos no había más *obstáculos tradicionales* que la nieve y ventisca, la miseria y el bajo precio del carbón" (p. 251).

Galdós, however, never doubts the need for the revolution. While admitting the possible simplicity of mind of those afflicted with the *candor progresista* (a term that Galdós attributes to the sarcasm of Restoration oligarchs), Galdós, in his assessment of the major event of his youth, justifies the sacrifices made by the *progresistas*. The Revolution freed the nation from paralyzing, atavistic bonds. Those who followed Prim represented the youth, the life, the optimism of the nation:

Admirable cosa era que, gozando de tantos bienes domésticos, mujer buena y hermosa, lindos, inteligentes hijuelos, floreciente negocio comercial, todo esto y su reposo y su tiempo y sus ganancias, lo sacrificase Chaves en altares idolátricos de la política. O eran aquellos tiempos de mayor inocencia, de mayor virilidad. De todo habría seguramente. Ello es que, sin el llamado *candor progresista* de que tanta burla han hecho los oligarcas de poco acá, no se habría limpiado esta vieja Nación de algunas herrumbres atávicas que la tenían paralizada y como muerta. Si héroes anónimos hubo siempre en nuestras epopeyas guerreras, también los hubo en los dramas políticos; héroes de abnegación no menos grandes que los que arriesgaron la vida y el honor militar. Chaves fue de los más esclarecidos patriotas, más candorosos mártires por la idea, que martirio y candor parecen la misma cosa, y el hombre se dejó ir a su ruina y descrédito por secundar valerosamente las ideas de libertad y justicia que sintetizaba en cuatro letras el sugestivo nombre de Prim. Prim era la luz de la patria, la dignidad del Estado, la igualdad ante la ley, la paz y la cultura de la Nación. Y tal maña se habían dado la España caduca y el dinastismo ciego y servil, que Prim, condenado a muerte después de la sublevación del 3 de Enero, perso- nificaba todo lo que la raza poseía de virilidad, juventud y ansia de vivir (pp. 304-5).

As in previous novels, Galdós warns strongly against those who live solely in a world of illusion. The case of Santiuste sadly illustrates the fate of those who lose contact with reality. Santiuste, now prematurely aged, without interest in women, and answering only to the name *Confusio,* is writing the logical history of Spain ("la verdad lógica y esencialmente estética"), the history of Spain not as it is but as it should be. Real history, that of Spain's sordid political manipulations, is dismissed by *Confusio* (and also in part by the unstable Fajardo) as *Historia ilógica y artificial* (p. 113). Rather than study Spanish life with all its imperfections, *Confusio* takes refuge in an ideal universe of the spirit: "Yo escribo para el Universo, para los espíritus elevados en quienes mora el pensamiento total" (p. 294). *Confusio*'s impracticality, verbalism, and blindness to the real world represent in extreme form national defects which, for Galdós, a reconstructed Spain must shun.

Galdós also attacks excessive idealism in the leading character of the novel, Santiago Ibero. Santiago Ibero is of disturbed mind, the conse- quence of an illness in his formative years which left him, depending on viewpoint, either simple-minded or insane. Santiago Ibero (like Spain) is, despite his courage and love of adventure, incapable of independent thought. Like Don Quixote (and his actions in the early chapters parallel those of Cervantes's character), he sees life through a veil of literature. Living in the imaginary world of tales of the conquistadores, he callowly believes that Prim will emulate the deeds of Cortés.[51] In Madrid, his ingenuousness leads Juanito Maltrana to welcome him as the last of the Romantics: "Eres el último romántico . . . porque ya no hay románticos" (p. 31). Obsessed with performing great deeds, lacking knowledge of the world as it is, he wastes his energies in the pursuit of the impossible: "Que no has podido hacer lo grande, porque el mundo no está para eso, ni lo chico ni nada, porque toda la fuerza se te ha ido en querer cosas imposibles" (p. 171).

Not only does Santiago Ibero have a faulty perception of reality but he also, like the followers of Prim, has a psychological need to place a blind faith in a leader or teacher. Thus, falling under the influence of the spiritualist Ramón Lagier, Santiago learns to talk with the spirits and to practice a Christianity divorced from Catholic dogma. Santiago's confidence, like that of the *progresistas,* is simple and total. He believes that his thoughts and feelings form part of a universal thought: "Sé que mi pensamiento es parte del pensamiento total, y que un querer mío o un sentimiento mí o no están aislados del sentir y del querer que envuelven toda esa masa de mundos vivos" (p. 262). Like the Spanish people in search of a revolution or a perfect society, Santiago childishly holds that whatever we desire must necessarily exist: "Mi maestro me ha dicho que en el mundo existe siempre lo que deseamos. Es cuestión de buscarlo bien" (p. 264).

The revolution was inspired, however, by more than the deluded, if generous, beliefs of Santiago Ibero and his ilk. In the person of Teresa Villaescusa, Galdós portrays a Spain that is painfully awakening to consciousness of its situation. Sick, exploited by her mother, brutalized by her lover (whom she unwittingly betrays), Teresa suffers inner torments as she uncertainly seeks a new path in life. Teresa (Spain) is gradually coming to awareness of herself, of her own moral degradation. The need to cast off the past is now paramount; the manner in which this may be done, however, is not yet clear.

In the final novel of the fourth series of *episodios nacionales, La de los tristes destinos* (January-May 1907), Galdós reaches conclusions similar to those of the third series. Spaniards must avoid two extremes: "Romantic illusion" (self-centered, unable to perceive the outside world) and passive acceptance of societal values (which stifle individual possibilities of growth and happiness and equally involve a failure to judge the outside world). Instead, Galdós advocates the clear-sighted assessment of present circumstances and the working toward practical goals conducive to personal happiness. This ideal combination of the exercise of the individual will and judgment, of steadfast labor toward a worthwhile future, is symbolized in the novel in the union of Santiago Ibero and Teresa Villaescusa.

La de los triestes destinos is the lengthiest novel of the fourth series and the one most densely packed with history. Treating the period between the execution of the sergeants of San Gil (June 1866) and the triumph of the Revolution in September 1868, Galdós vividly recreates the life of the émigrés in Paris, the abortive revolutionary expedition to Ansó, Prim's direction of the revolution from London, Prim's voyage to Cádiz, the proclamation of national sovereignty, the Battle of Alcolea, the reception of the revolution in Madrid, and Queen Isabel's departure from Spain.

Brief, but lively, portraits of numerous prominent figures are given. Thus, Sagasta, living in poverty in Paris, is summarized in the cautious advice that he proffers Santiago: "En este mundo no hay nada peor que las prisas . . . Si corremos tras de las cosas, encontramos siempre las peores. Las buenas, créanlo ustedes, vienen a nosotros."[52] Ruiz Zorrilla, on the other hand, is willful and bitter: "Era un hombre voluntarioso, contumaz, carácter forjado en los odios candentes del bando progresista, nutrido con los amargores del retraimiento, que fue como un destierro para la vida pública, y como un largo ejercicio en el arte de la conspiración" (p. 257).

Galdós's judgment of the Revolution of 1868, made with the hindsight of 1907, is pessimistic. The sufferings and the sacrifices of the conspirators, their enthusiasm for the cause of Liberty and Honor, will bring no fundamental change in Spain. The principal goal of many of the rebels is, as in previous revolutions, to obtain governmental employment: "La inmensa grey desheredada del Progreso y Democracia aprestábanse a invadir los nacionales comederos" (p. 374). Symbolic of the Revolution is the drunken Manuela Pez (who had prostituted self and daughter) who proclaims herself "la honra de España." Santiago Ibero, rapidly disillusioned, recognizes (like the Regenerationists three decades later) that the revolutionary changes are no more than superficial: "—Ahora veo todo lo vulgar, todo lo indecente y chabacano de esta revolución que ustedes han hecho—dijo Ibero con negro pesimismo.— ¡Inmensa y ruidosa mentira! La misma *Gaceta* con emblemas distintos. . . . Palabras van, palabras vienen. Los españoles cambian los nombres de sus vicios" (p. 334). Significantly, Santiago and Teresa choose to live in France, not in the Spain of the Revolution of 1868.[53]

The totality of Galdós's rejection of the Revolution of 1868 is at first sight surprising. In *Prim*, Galdós had balanced the qualities and the naiveté of the revolutionaries; he praised the contribution of the Revolution in freeing Spain from the dead weight of the past. In *La de los tristes destinos*, however, the Revolution is attacked (for its failure to produce fundamental change, for the timidity of its religious policy, for the corruption and self-seeking of the revolutionaries) in far harsher terms than the earlier novel would have suggested.

The unusually bitter treatment of the Revolution of 1868 reflects, I believe, Galdós's decision to work within the system for radical political and constitutional change, a decision made between October 1906 (the month of completion of *Prim*) and May 1907 (when *La de los tristes destinos* was finished). In these months, the Spanish political climate changed markedly. In late 1906 the religious question again polarized Spanish opinion: in August, Romanones authorized civil marriages without previous religious declarations; Dávila presented a project for a far-reaching *Ley de Asociaciones* which, the government intended, would be enacted without prior negotiation with the Vatican; Catholic bishops strongly protested what they interpreted as a new persecution. At the end of November, however, the Liberal anticlerical position was shattered in the *crisis del papelito*.[54] Moret replaced for a period of four days López Domínguez as prime minister. When Moret's position proved untenable, the aged Marqués de la Vega de Armijo headed a caretaker government until late January 1907, when the king invited Maura to form a ministry. As a result of Moret's double-dealing, the Liberal party was split into embittered factions; the government's anticlerical policy became a dead letter; the Conservatives under Maura were firmly entrenched in power (to follow policies that to many seemed to favor clerical interests); and King Alfonso came under savage attack (in Liberal quarters) for his "unconstitutional" interference in politics.

Galdós's newfound hostility to the Revolution of 1868 marks his reentry into the Spanish political scene. The Revolution, which had set in motion the chain of events that led to the Restoration settlement and, ultimately, to the "constitutional" rule of Alfonso XIII signified the corrupt past of Spain. Galdós's concern is now with present politics, with overturning the Restoration settlement. His reaction to the crisis of late 1906 and early 1907 was immediate. In March 1907 Galdós announced his conversion to Republicanism; in April he was elected to the Cortes as Republican deputy for Madrid. The avowed reason for his conversion was the failure of the government to enact a *Ley de Asociaciones*. In his political manifesto (the letter of April 6, 1907, to Alfredo Vicenti, the editor of *El Liberal*), Galdós demanded policies of Europeanization and a relentless war on *caciquismo* and *la barbarie clerical*.

Galdós's message in *La de los tristes destinos,* while not particularly novel, reflects above all the program and attitudes of the Republican party. His teaching represents, in the context of 1907, a call for political action. Thus, Galdós levels a barely veiled attack on the monarchy of the Restoration, assails Spanish leaders' timidity in tackling the religious question, expresses his admiration for the army, justifies military intervention in Spanish politics, and extols the virtues of opening Spain to European ideas.

Galdós does not openly plead the cause of the Republic in the novel;[55] instead, he criticizes the rule of Alfonso XIII by insinuations that would readily be understood by his contemporaries of 1907. From Canalejas's resignation in 1902 to the outrage provoked by the *crisis del papelito,* rumors were rife in liberal quarters that the young Alfonso XIII was swayed by improper palace influences to intervene unconstitutionally in the political sphere. In *La de los tristes destinos,* Galdós attacks the grossly superstitious Queen Isabel for her isolation from her people, an isolation created by her misplaced trust in a lying *camarilla.* The point is made more expressly by Fajardo, who demands that the king resume the aspirations of the whole nation, not merely those of a clique: "Un Rey es la cabeza, el corazón, el brazo del pueblo, y debe resumir en su ser las ideas, los anhelos y toda la energía de los millones de almas que componen el Reino" (p. 134). Liberals and Republicans had objected to the heavy theological component in the education of Alfonso XIII (Sagasta had, indeed, forced the dismissal in late 1901 of the royal tutor, the priest Fernández Montaña, for his ultramontane theories). Similarly, in *La de los tristes destinos,* Galdós attacks as an inadequate preparation for the throne the sterile theological education given to the future Alfonso XII.[56]

Galdós claimed that the failure of the Liberal government to pass a *Ley de Asociaciones* had decided his conversion to Republicanism. In *La de los tristes destinos,* Galdós uses the religious question as the test of commitment to genuine change on the part of the "revolutionaries." Serrano, interrogated by Lagier, will not involve the revolutionary cause in the question of civil matrimony (a matter of ardent polemic at the time of composition of the novel).[57] A revolution that would not act independently of the pope, Lagier realizes, is merely a game of army officers: "Ya ves: todavía creen que eso del casarse es cosa del Papa. . . . La Revolución que traen quedará, pienso yo, en un juego de militares. Como no vayan al bulto, no harán gran cosa" (p. 311). In words obviously aimed at the timidity of the Liberals of 1907, Galdós protests the interference of the Church in Spanish politics. He laments that Spanish liberals share the beliefs and behavior of Catholics: "Sí, hijo mío: el fanatismo tiene aquí tanta fuerza, que aunque parezca vencido, pronto se rehace y vuelve a fastidiarnos a todos. Los más liberales creen en el Infierno, adoran las imágenes de palo, y mandan a sus hijos a los colegios de curas. . . . No sé hasta dónde llegará esta revolución que hemos hecho con tanto trabajo. Avanzará un poco, hasta que al fanatismo se le hinchen las narices, y diga: 'Caballeros Prim y Serrano, de aquí no se pasa' " (p. 308).

Despite the cowardice of the revolutionary generals in religious questions, the army receives favorable portrayal in *La de los tristes destinos*. The courage of Spanish soldiers and their leaders is admired by Galdós. Even the conduct of Novaliches, who bravely defended a lost cause, provokes Galdós's respect: "La figura de Novaliches, dando el rostro a la impopularidad para defender lo irremisiblemente perdido, infundiendo a sus tropas un ficticio entusiasmo y peleando contra la Libertad hasta quedar fuera de combate, es digna del mayor respeto, y aun de admiración" (p. 325). In obvious recollection of the campaigns of 1898, Galdós caustically refers to the government's failure to provide adequate supplies to troops going to war: "La columna iba muy escasa de municiones; que en aquellos tiempos ya nuestros Gobiernos solían mandar los soldados a la guerra sin la conveniente provisión de pólvora y balas" (p. 186). *Confusio* and Fajardo, speaking for once without fantasy, defend the role of the military in preventing reaction or demagogic excess in Spain. Their arguments are exactly those used by the military in 1905 to justify their suppression of Catalanist agitation:

—Claramente hemos visto que la Fuerza pública, o sea Pueblo armado, obedeciendo a una fatal ley dinámica, ha sido el verdadero Poder moderador, por ineptitud de quien debía ejercerlo. Siempre que ha venido la asfixia, o sea la reacción, el Ejército ha dado entrada a los aires salutíferos, y cuando los excesos de la Libertad han puesto en peligro la paz de la Nación . . .
—Claro, ha restablecido el orden, el buen temple interior. Por esto, no debemos juzgar con rigor excesivo las sediciones militares, porque ellas fueron y *serán aún por algún tiempo* el remedio insano de una insanidad mucho más peligrosa y mortífera (pp. 107-8, my italics).

Galdós, of course, had no personal reasons for hostility to the Spanish army; his brother was captain-general of the Canary Islands. Praise of the army was, furthermore, a staple of Republican oratory in the early years of the twentieth century.[58] Without the benevolence of the military, chances of a Republican regime in Spain were nil; thus, Ruiz Zorrilla had devoted many years to organizing Republican conspiracies within the military. Nicolás Estévanez (Galdós's correspondent and the Republican "hero" of the fifth series of *episodios nacionales*) expressed, indeed, in 1909 the fear that the events of the Tragic Week would create a divorce between the people and the army.[59]

Galdós, in his Republican manifesto of April 1907, called for the Europeanization of Spain, for an opening to outside influences that would permit escape from the "asfixia nacional."[60] In similar terms, in *La de los tristes destinos*, Galdós sings the praises of the railroad to France, by means of which Spain is freed from isolation and receives the advantages of modern civilization: "Los inmensos beneficios que nos trajiste, ¡oh grande amigo y servidor nuestro, puerta del tráfico, llave de la industria, abertura de la ventilación universal, y respiradero por donde escapan los densos humos que aún flotan en el hispano cerebro! " (p. 65).

The remedies proposed by Galdós are not only political and Republican; as in previous *episodios*, he demands the moral reform of Spaniards. He attacks, as always, Romantic illusions and illustrates those qualities that will lead to personal happiness: the will, intelligence, experience, independence. Romantic dreamers attempt to impose personal fantasies on outside reality. Thus, Fajardo, recalling his infatuation with Lucila, confesses that his "love" was sickness, the worship of the nonexistent: "padecí la *efusión estética*, un mal terrible, Manolo, un mal que consiste en adorar lo que suponemos privado de existencia real; un mal que es amor y miedo" (p. 98). Similarly, Santiago Ibero pursues the dream of military and revolutionary glory (symbolized in Prim) and the dream of ideal love (Salomita Galán).

Galdós's positive teaching is exemplified in his portrayal of the love of Santiago Ibero and Teresa Villaescusa. (Love, indeed, represents on a personal plane that decisive reshaping of destiny which Galdós desired for Spain and which the Revolution of 1868 had manifestly failed to provide.) Both Santiago and Teresa have the intelligence to learn from experience. Thus, the dreamer Santiago, for whom Teresa initially represented no more than a passing conquest, gradually comes to value the calm happiness of life with Teresa. His living in the present rather than in the non world of the past or the future causes his fantasy of a distant Dulcinea (Salomita Galán) to recede: "El hombre vivía más en el presente que en el pasado azaroso y en el porvenir obscuro. Y es que el presente, cuando viene con fácil curso y libre de inquietudes, tiene una fuerza incontrastable. Es un constructor de vida que emplea los materiales más sólidos, desechando todo lo inconsistente, ilusorio y fantástico" (p. 155).

Teresa, the kept woman of previous *episodios,* in love has dignity and loses all egotism; her will power and intelligence ("su poderoso razonar, inspirado en la realidad de la vida," p. 165) enable her to place her love on a sure footing. She thus courageously and wisely encourages Santiago to put his twin illusions (military glory and ideal love) to the test of experience. Only when ignorance has cured Santiago of both madnesses can the two construct a full life together.

False societal values (the greed of the revolutionaries, the cynicism of the corrupt Tarfe) and the sickly pursuit of personal illusion (Fajardo) are equally inimical of love. Love, for Galdós, demands trust in another person and a true appreciation of the worth of the other. Happiness—and Galdós's lesson is equally applicable for the healthy development of Spanish society—is not given but is slowly won in the day-to-day struggles of life. Teresa and Santiago use their intelligence and will to forge a life in common. Happiness is the by-product, not the cause, of their efforts.

Their independence of society (and therefore of slavery to the values of others) contributes to their growth. Both Teresa and Santiago work for their living at humble manual tasks. They refuse to depend on the public purse or the recommendations of the powerful. Santiago accepts Lagier's teaching: that the internal and external causes which govern our lives cannot be known, and that we should guide our conduct by personal values which arise from our own experience (p. 309). Lagier's final teaching is surely that of Galdós: heroism (as an abstract ideal) is illusory and cannot be sought. Another form of heroism lies in the acceptance of an obscure life of humble labor and in the practice of virtue in accordance with personal conscience: "El heroísmo no se busca; se acepta y se practica cuando la ocasión nos lo trae, cuando nos vemos obligados a ser heróicos ... También en la vida obscura y laboriosa hay heroísmo; también hacer frente a los fanáticos y derrotarlos con el ejemplo de las virtudes que ellos no practican" (pp. 312-13).

Chapter Four

The Fifth Series of
Episodios Nacionales, 1907-1912

Antonio Maura, originally a dissident from Sagasta's Liberals and now unchallenged leader of the Conservative party, headed the Spanish government in January 1907. The reforms he promised were ambitious: the destruction of *caciquismo* (by the fundamental overhaul of local government), the reconstruction of the Spanish navy, and the resolution of the Catalan problem.

Maura had only partial success in carrying out his program. The ambitious project for the reform of municipal administration, introduced in the Cortes in October 1907, failed to become law. Not only did it affect the interests of *caciques* but it also, with its provisions for corporative representation, earned the distrust of Liberals and Republicans and divided the Catalan coalition. The rebuilding of the navy was voted, with the support of both Liberals and Republicans. The Catalan question remained insoluble; *Solidaridad Catalana* split into its component elements; Maura was successful in winning the close collaboration of Cambó, the leader of the right-wing *Lliga* (numerically the most important party of *Solidaridad Catalana*); in the 1908 elections, however, Republicans (Lerroux, Sol y Ortega) replaced in the Cortes deputies of *Solidaridad Catalana*.

Maura's downfall came as an aftermath to the *Semana trágica* (July 26 to August 1, 1909). Spanish intervention in June 1909 in the region surrounding Melilla to suppress insurgent Moroccan tribes led to the summoning of Catalan reservists. The Moroccan campaign was without popular support; it was widely rumored that Spanish troops were being sacrificed to protect the mining concessions of foreign capitalists. The situation in Barcelona was, furthermore, already unstable: the textile industry was in recession; haphazard bomb explosions (some apparently financed by police agents) increased public nervousness; the *Solidaridad Obrera* and the Radical Republicans were struggling for control over

Catalan workers' movements. An initial antiwar protest turned almost immediately into a general strike and, under the urgings of Radical Republicans (whose leader, Alejandro Lerroux, was at the time in Argentina), into a week of burning of convents, churches, and Catholic charitable and educational institutions. There were few deaths during the disturbances; the army often stood by while the mob burned Church property; the middle class of Barcelona was not seconded in the rest of Spain; La Cierva, the minister of the interior, isolated the Catalan city; his claim that the disturbances were caused by Catalan nationalists destroyed any possibility of support outside of Catalonia for the rebellion.[1]

Following the *Semana trágica*, military tribunals condemned five insurgents to death. Among these was Francisco Ferrer, an anarchist sympathizer, the organizer of the "rationalist" *Escuela Moderna* in Barcelona, and previously suspected of complicity in the attempted assassination of Alfonso XIII in 1906. Although evidence of Ferrer's involvement in the *Semana trágica* was inconclusive, Ferrer was executed, to a storm of protest from left-wing circles in other European countries. Ferrer's execution, however, aroused little interest at the time inside Spain.

Opposition to the Moroccan campaign and to Maura's suspension of constitutional guarantees provided a rallying point for those determined to bring down Maura's government. The *Bloque de Izquierdas* (a grouping of certain leading Liberals, among whom were Canalejas and Moret, and Republicans, formed in 1908 to combat Maura's proposed antiterrorism law) campaigned vigorously against the Conservative leader. Although Maura's parliamentary majority was sure, Liberal refusal to collaborate in the Cortes with Maura provoked at the end of October a pro forma offer of resignation, an offer that, to Maura's bitter surprise, was accepted by the king.

The government of Antonio Maura had lasted two years and nine months. No other government of the reign of Alfonso XIII (before the suspension of constitutional rule with Primo de Rivera's coup d'etat in 1923) remained in power for so long a period of time. Despite the almost hysterical accusations of tyranny leveled against Maura, the Cortes were in session for nineteen months of his premiership. Constitutional guarantees were suspended in the whole of Spain for only two months of his rule. Maura's ministry was reactionary in its rhetoric, rather than in its conduct.[2]

The Liberal ministry of Moret, who succeeded Maura as prime minister, was short-lived. Spanish political life in the fall of 1909 was polarized between supporters and opponents of Maura, in a vociferous campaign that was often reduced to the shouting of the slogans *Maura sí* or *Maura no*. Maura, believing himself the object of treachery in the manner of his dismissal from power, refused any collaboration with Moret's government. Adopting an increasingly reactionary posture, he accused the Liberal party of including "los partidarios del motín, del saqueo y del incendio, de la revolución."[3] Moret also lacked support inside the Liberal party: Romanones was personally hostile to the prime minister; many Liberal deputies feared that Moret's attempts to attract right-wing Republicans to his policies—a continuation of the tactics of Sagasta and Cánovas during the Restoration—would cost them electoral support. Moret's unpopularity within his own party, Alfonso's desire to reestablish the smooth functioning of the shattered two-party system by removing the target of Maura's bitterness, explain the king's readiness to provoke the resignation of Moret in February 1910.

Moret's successor was José Canalejas (1854-1912). Like Maura, Canalejas represented a further attempt at reforming the Restoration system from within. Despite his rather authoritarian personality, Canalejas was conciliatory in his policies. He developed a friendship with Alfonso XIII, achieved a certain measure of collaboration with Maura, and endeavored, with some success, to woo right-wing Republicans to the monarchic system.

Canalejas offered hope of solution of the major problems facing Spain: Morocco, Catalonia, social unrest, and the religious question. Spanish victories ended for a while attacks by insurgent Moroccan tribes. In an attempt to satisfy Catalan aspirations, Canalejas steered a *Ley de mancomunidades* through the Cortes in May 1912. A vigorous interventionist policy in social matters brought legislation limiting hours of work and improving working conditions for women. (Canalejas's attempted dialogue with Pablo Iglesias was, however, refused by the Socialist leader.) Although Canalejas's commitment to compulsory arbitration in social conflicts—Spain was beset by strikes in the summers and falls of 1910, 1911, and 1912—earned the hostility of employers and workers alike, his energetic ending of the railroad strike of the fall of 1912 (by calling the strikers back to the army reserves) was widely supported. Canalejas's assassination by an anarchist in November 1912 removed not only one of the bulwarks of the monarchy but also the possibility of a moderate to progressive solution to Spain's social problem.

Canalejas earned his greatest notoriety with his religious policies. Although a devout Catholic, he was hysterically attacked in right-wing circles of his day as an enemy of the Church.[4] Governmental decrees of the spring of 1910 established the minimal demands of the Liberal program in religious questions: all religious orders not included in the Concordat were required to register with the state; non-Catholic religious bodies were permitted external manifestations of their cult. Throughout 1910, the *Ley del Candado* polarized Spanish opinion: the law refused the entry of new religious communities into Spain—unless governmental authorization were previously obtained—until such time as a new *Ley de Asociaciones* was voted.

Despite the ardent polemics that they aroused, Canalejas's anticlerical measures had an impact that was more apparent than real. Canalejas intended to accomplish his object, that Spanish legislation in religious matters not be subject to the veto of the papacy, by secret negotiation with the Vatican;[5] his anticlerical policies were in part designed to counteract the marked hostility of the left to his person.[6] In practice, the *Ley de Asociaciones* was used to suspend Pablo Iglesias's *Unión General de Trabajadores* and many workers' circles. E. Aunós has, indeed, cogently argued that Canalejas's anticlerical legislation was a "truco de prestidigitación," a symbolic measure that represented in reality the maintenance of the status quo: "Hallándose ya instaladas en España todas las órdenes religiosas que de momento podían caber en ella, ese cerrar la puerta para que no entrasen otras, era un gesto puramente decorativo, que en el fondo venía a sancionar todo lo contrario de lo que pretendía hacer ver."[7]

Spanish Republicans under the Restoration were divided by the same personal hostilities and doctrinal difficulties as during their chaotic period in power (1873). Emilio Castelar (1832-1899), strongly conservative and opposed to any revolutionary conquest of power, collaborated with, and even viewed "with benevolence," the monarchy. Manuel Ruiz Zorrilla (1834-1895), true to the *progresista* theories of his early career, held that a Republic would only be installed by military revolution. From his bitter self-imposed exile in Paris, he organized Republican conspiracies in the army while awaiting a messianic general to restore Republican fortunes. Francisco Pi y Margall

(1824-1901) remained true to federalist doctrine; more interested in social questions than in politics, he was one of the few Spanish political figures to oppose the war in Cuba. Nicolás Salmerón (1838-1908), choosing "evolution" rather than revolution as the path to power, broke with Ruiz Zorrilla and sat in the Cortes in the years following 1886. The *Partido Republicano Centralista,* which he founded with Azcárate in 1887, espoused the unity of the Spanish nation, the federation of Spain and Portugal, religious freedom, and compulsory military service.

Throughout the Restoration and well into the twentieth century, the history of Spanish Republicanism is one of doctrinal and personal squabbles, which were barely patched over in temporary electoral alliances. The Republicans not only differed as to the nature of the Republic that they wished to establish, but they also disagreed over the means to achieve this Republic, dividing between those who worked within the Restoration system (the "evolutionists") and partisans of Revolution who denied all legitimacy to the monarchy. Sharing only a belief in the Republic and a doctrinaire anticlericalism, Republicans were for all practical purposes without a program. Certainly, with the exception of Pi and his minuscule following, Republicans were for the most part without interest in the social and economic questions that increasingly concerned middle-class Spaniards. The Republicans drew their support from a handful of intellectuals. For the most part right-wing and possessing few contacts with the masses, they had no hope of attaining power.

In 1903 Salmerón, the only surviving paladin of the 1873 Republic, arranged yet another Republican electoral alliance, the *Unión Republicana.* Salmerón had little principle beyond expediency; the *Unión Republicana,* without a social program, soon collapsed. Greatest Republican strength at this time was in Valencia and Barcelona, where left-wing Republican parties followed the revolutionary tradition of Ruiz Zorrilla. In Valencia the Republican leaders Rodrigo Soriano, who inclined toward *Solidaridad Catalana,* and Vicente Blasco Ibáñez, who favored Lerroux, bitterly quarreled. In Barcelona, the Radical Republican party of Alejandro Lerroux, a party that received secret financial support from Sagasta's Liberals who hoped to undercut Catalanist parties, advocated revolutionary violence. In 1907 Salmerón committed political suicide (as far as the Republicans were concerned) by his adherence to *Solidaridad Catalana,* an alliance of Catalanist parties. His embrace of the duke of Solferino, the Carlist leader, so infuriated Spanish Republicans that Salmerón was forced to seek police protection from the ire of his former coreligionaries.

Galdós, dissatisfied with the failure of the Liberals to pursue an aggressive anticlerical policy, joined the Reformist Republicans in early 1907. His presence in the Cortes as Republican deputy for Madrid and, above all, his immense literary prestige immediately made Galdós a leading figure among the ill-organized and mutually antagonistic Republicans. Galdós played a prominent role in the *Bloque de Izquierdas* (1908), which included, among other Republicans, Morote, Azcárate, Sol y Ortega, Melquiades Alvarez, and Costa. The formation of the *Bloque* (to combat Maura's antiterrorism law) gained for the Republicans a forum for propaganda and the political respectability of alliance with leading Liberals. The Republicans at this time were already losing their by no means numerous working-class adherents to Pablo Iglesias's Socialists. The *Bloque,* however, was short-lived. In early 1909 Sol y Ortega launched a campaign against the alleged corruption of Maura's ministers. Leading members of the *Bloque,* including the Liberals Moret and Canalejas and the Republicans Azcárate and Melquiades Alvarez, dissociated themselves from Sol y Ortega to affirm their faith in the honesty of Maura.

Galdós's activities as Republican leader have, regrettably, never been studied. Certainly, his role as president of the *Conjunción Republicano-Socialista* was far from that of a figurehead. The *Conjunción,* founded in the fall of 1909, loosely allied for electoral purposes Reformist Republicans, *progresistas,* Federalists, Soriano's Radicals of the *Conjunción* (to which party Galdós's secretary, Pablo Nougués, belonged), and the Socialists led by Pablo Iglesias. Originally formed to protest Maura's suspension of constitutional guarantees, the *Conjunción* became a channel to protest the war in Morocco, to oppose the return of Maura to power, and, in 1910, to challenge the underhanded means by which Canalejas assumed the premiership.[8] The common program of the *Conjunción* was a conventional enough combination of specific demands and pious generalities:

Supresión del impuesto de consumos; apartamiento de toda política de aventuras belicosas en Marruecos; instauración del servicio militar obligatorio; creación de Milicias coloniales voluntarias; abolición de la ley de Jurisdicciones; reforma del Código de Justicia militar, borrando los absurdos de la parte penal y de la de enjuiciamiento; revisión de los procesos de Baró, Malet, Clemente García, Ferrer y Hoyos; ley de Asociaciones que someta al derecho común a las Congregaciones religiosas, negándoles todo linaje de privilegios; inhabilitación política de la fracción reaccionaria que trocó el Poder público en instrumento de atávicos procederes; desarrollo de la Enseñanza conforme a la Ciencia moderna; fomento intensivo de la Agricultura, la Industria y el Comercio; leyes sociales que, atendiendo las justas demandas del proletariado, eleven su condición moral y material; transformación de la Hacienda nacional, procurando la equitativa aplicación de los impuestos y vertiendo el caudal de los gastos sobre las necesidades más apremiantes del país.[9]

Galdós's role as president of the *Conjunción* was primarily that of conciliator of opposing factions and personalities. It was Galdós who, with Azcárate, first visited Pablo Iglesias in 1909 to persuade the Socialist leader to ally with the Reformist Republicans. In 1910, at Galdós's instigation, Lerroux and the Radical Republicans joined the *Conjunción.* In 1911 Galdós claimed credit for securing the adhesion of the Catalan Republican Nationalists (Galdós chose to emphasize the "nationalist," rather than the "Catalan," element of their creed) and for preventing the departure from the *Conjunción* of the *Unión Nacional Republicana.* Later, in May 1912, Galdós's house provided the "neutral territory" for exploratory talks between Lerroux and other Republican leaders to examine the possibility of Lerroux's return to the *Conjunción.* The conciliatory, moderating role played by Galdós in Republican politics is evident in the interview that he granted to the journalists Olmet and García Carraffa in 1912. Galdós treats with respect all leading Republicans (with the exception of Sol y Ortega, who had violently abandoned the *Conjunción*) and offers high praise of the sincerity and vision of the Socialists.[10]

Despite Galdós's efforts, the *Conjunción,* united only in its opposition to the government, rapidly fragmented. In 1910 Morote (who had originally played an important part in attracting Galdós to Republicanism), wooed by Canalejas, defected to the monarchists. Lerroux and the Radical Republicans withdrew from the *Conjunción* almost immediately after joining, following the revelation of the involvement of the Radical Republicans in corrupt contracts negotiated with the Barcelona municipality. Soriano and the Socialists (who accused Lerroux of betraying Ferrer) bitterly attacked the Radical Republican leader. The disintegration of the *Conjunción* was widely rumored in 1911; the *Conjunción* suffered serious losses in the elections of November of that year. When, in late 1911, death sentences were passed on peasants who had lynched a judge during social disturbances in Cullera, Galdós petitioned Canalejas for the pardon of the condemned men. Alfonso's granting of pardon—Canalejas temporarily resigned—in January 1912 led many Republicans to praise the king in the strongest terms. In 1912 Melquiades Alvarez (who, with Azcárate, most closely shared Galdós's moderate Republicanism) founded the *Partido Republicano Reformista* to work within the monarchical system. In June 1913, against the wishes of Galdós, Alvarez, and Azcárate, the *Conjunción Republicano-Socialista* dissolved. By 1914 Alvarez, Azcárate, and Galdós accepted the monarchy of Alfonso XIII.

Galdós, despite the conciliatory role he had allotted himself as president of the *Conjunción,* expressed bitterness at Republican divisions. Thus, in June 1910, he complained with disgust that the Republican parties were riddled with *caciquismo:* "Este partido está pudriéndose por la immensa gusanera de caciques y caciquillos. Tiene más que los monárquicos . . . Para hacer la revolución, lo primero, lo indispensable, sería degollar a todos. Si estos trajeran la República, estaríamos peor que ahora. Sería cosa de emigrar. Suerte que no hay miedo a que la traigan. ¡Hay cada revolucionario que tiene un miedo feroz a la revolución! . . . Voy a irme con Pablo Iglesias. El y su partido son lo único serio, disciplinado, admirable, que hay en la España política."[11]

Galdós took five years (from October 1907 to August 1912) to compose the six novels that he completed of the fifth series of *episodios. Sagasta,* which was to be the forty seventh *episodio nacional,* was never written. Age (Galdós was in his sixties at the time of composition of the fifth series), blindness (which afflicted Galdós during the writing of *Amadeo I*), and Galdós's time-consuming activities as Republican leader explain the slow pace of composition of these novels.

The *episodios* of this series treat events that took place in Galdós's early adult years, the period when, as journalist and political reporter, he was close to the political life of Madrid. Galdós is thus able to draw on reminiscences of his youth to describe the activities of Vicente Halconero in *España trágica* and the journalism of the early 1870s in

Amadeo I; autobiographical references are, however, rare, guarded, and brief.

Unlike earlier series of *episodios*, there is little semblance of continuous plot in the fifth series. Coherent intrigue—the representation of an ordered progression of events toward a goal—gives way to an almost haphazard presentation of *faits divers,* the novelistic reflection of a period and a society without transcendence, of a Spain—and Galdós's judgment is that of hindsight—moving not to greatness or to reform but only to the *años bobos* of the Restoration. There is, furthermore, no evolution in the character of Tito Liviano, the protagonist of the last four *episodios.* [12] Tito, like the Spain evoked by Galdós, remains forever fixed in instability and weakness.

"History" (the evocation of important events and figures) concerns Galdós even less in the fifth series of *episodios* than in earlier novels. Historical events are treated in a cursory, almost offhand, manner; abstractions play a greater role than does the narration of Spain's past; as in previous *episodios,* novelistic characters resume, in their reactions and psychology, the life of the nation. The atmosphere of the period is evoked in impressionistic, and highly literary, terms. Thus, the first two novels of the series (*España sin rey, España trágica*) are overwhelmingly tragic in tone, the expression of the self-destructive impulses of Spaniards and of the thwarting of Spain's hopes of greatness. The later novels, in which Tito Liviano is the protagonist, represent the degradation and ultimate stagnation of the nation, the movement from comic opera (*Amadeo I*) through boredom (the repetitious mannerisms of "revolutionary" Spain) to the futility of the Restoration.

Galdós's vision of the Spain of the years that followed the Revolution of 1868 and of the Restoration is totally pessimistic. The failure to achieve change does not lie in the inability of nineteenth-century Spaniards to find an adequate constitutional structure (Galdós, disillusioned, has by now rejected the traditional liberal faith that constitutional reform will promote personal happiness and material prosperity); rather, the failure of the revolutionaries to accomplish their avowed goals is to be explained by fundamental flaws in Spanish behavior.

Change of constitution does not, Galdós recognizes, alter the habits of Spaniards. The Spain of the revolutionary period is ruled by the same *caciques* and vain, short-sighted, lying politicians as before. Restoration policies—and Galdós repeats charges uttered by Costa a decade earlier—are based on inertia and fiction ("una política de inercia, de ficciones y de fórmulas mentirosas extraídas de la cantera de la tradición"[13]). The Restoration system enshrines Spanish tendencies to hypocrisy, conformity, and frivolity. It is but one more example of Spanish despotism, a regime that benefits only generals and functionaries and leaves fundamental problems unsolved.

Equally fictitious are the causes for which nineteenth-century Spanish liberals struggled. The overthrow of the Republic, the Third Carlist War, represent no collision of interests or principles, for Republicans and rebellious army officers, Carlist and *alfonsino* generals, share a common background and are linked in amiable *compadrazgo*. The "official" values of Spain (patriotism, revolutionary change, national greatness) are myths, lies that deceive their creators as much as the gullible Spanish people. When the hollow nature of the pretentious claims of Spain's leaders becomes apparent, Spanish governments rule by despotism.

The rhetoric of sentimental patriotism hides a selfish exploitation and neglect of Spain. This neglect, under the Restoration, will constitute a sickness leading to national consumption: "Tu pobre España gemirá, por largos años, bajo la pesadumbre del despotismo que llaman ilustrado, enfermedad obscura y honda, con la cual los pueblos viven muriendo ... y se mueven, gritan y discursean, atacados de lo que llaman *epilepsía larvada* ... Debajo de esta dolencia se esconde la mortal *tuberculosis.*"[14]

The sickness does not only lie in Spain's rulers. Spaniards are out of touch with reality;[15] easily disoriented, they are a facile prey to the glib promises of lying politicians. Ill prepared by despotism for change, Spaniards react with madness and violence when granted liberty. Thus, in *España trágica*, the assassination of Prim is not so much the work of individuals as of the feverish insanity of all sections of the nation.

The inability of the nation to take on a form capable of surviving the pressures of reality is symbolized in two characters, who represent the opposing extremes of excessive idealism and total malleability. The brittle Fernanda, in her excess of idealism, is, when disappointed, destructive of self and others. Tito, on the other hand, lacking commitment to any cause, pursuing one love after another, does no more than react to stimuli with random violence and meaningless activity. Both characters (like Spain) lack that combination of strength and flexibility which would enable them to withstand the buffeting of an uncertain world.

Tito's behavior (which is that of a leaderless nation unable to define worthy goals for itself) is presented by Galdós in terms of sickness. Tito suffers from a neurosis, from a Romantic exacerbation of the ego; his character is dominated by a sterile intellectualism and infantile emotionalism. He lacks perseverance and the ability to learn from experience. When thwarted in his desires, Tito, like Spain, sinks into a life-denying depression: "A los que como tú se inutilizan para el vivir normal solemos dar el nombre de románticos. Románticos son, pero de estofa ínfirma y barata, los que se matan porque la novia se les va con otro, los que se desesperan y reniegan de la Humanidad porque no han podido obtener en un día lo que es fruto de la paciencia en largos años trabajosos."[16]

Galdós's anticlericalism is even more marked in the fifth series of *episodios* than in the fourth. Catholics, whether laymen or clergy, are lustful and hypocritical; priests sacrilegiously lead guerrilla bands; sinister Jesuits plot to overthrow Prim's regime. In the last two *episodios,* Galdós reaches a height of anticlerical venom unattained in previous stages of his career. In *De Cartago a Sagunto,* addressing believing Catholics with a heavy sarcasm, he accuses the Carlists of committing unparalleled atrocities during their sack of Cuenca. In *Cánovas,* Galdós proclaims the "keys" to understanding the degradation of Restoration society: the invasion of foreign friars (a plague rivaling that of the Saracen and Gothic invasions) and the stranglehold of the Church on the educational system, wealth, and even independence of Spain.

Galdós's anticlericalism was certainly not novel. The concentration of his anticlerical fury in the first and last two *episodios* of the fifth series corresponds, however, to Republican campaigns of the period. *España sin rey* (1908) and *España trágica* (1909), written while Maura was prime minister, reinforce charges of clerical intervention in Spanish politics. *De Cartago a Sagunto* (1911) and *Cánovas* (1912) were composed during the bitter debates that accompanied consideration in the Cortes of Canalejas's *Ley de Asociaciones.* Furthermore, the almost paranoiac vision (in *Cánovas*) of an invasion of foreign friars reflects contemporary fears that Portuguese religious orders would seek refuge in Spain, fleeing the Portuguese Republic proclaimed in the summer of 1911.

In obvious warning to his quarreling fellow Republicans, Galdós examines the mistakes of the Republicans of forty years earlier. Republican failures (as those of Spain) are not of doctrine but of personality. Republicans ("románticos de la política") lack knowledge of reality; their personal squabbles, violence, and rhetorical inanity prepared the way for the Restoration.

Galdós is most bitter in his treatment of the Republic of 1873. His comments alert against the repetition of the errors of the past should Republicans again rule in Spain. Republican deputies ("toda esta gente rencillosa y quimerista, sin conocimiento de la realidad ni estímulos de patriotismo"[17]) have the same petty ambitions as the monarchists they replace. Republicans, for temporary advantage, willingly ally with reactionaries (an obvious slap at Salmerón's adhesion in 1907 to *Solidaridad Catalana*). Republicans are indecisive in action; they are overscrupulous (Galdós cites Salmerón's refusal to execute military rebels); they lack discipline; they are riddled with divisions; they behave with cowardice (and again the unfortunate Salmerón is singled out for Galdós's attack); and, like the *progresistas* of a previous generation, they ingenuously mistake histrionic gesture for true revolution: "Creen estos inocentes que las revoluciones se hacen con discursos frenéticos, con abrazos fraternales, con vivas estrepitosas y cantinelas optimistas" (*La primera república*, p. 259).

Galdós portrays, by way of contrast to bickering Republican politicians, one exemplary Republican leader: Nicolás Estévanez. Estévanez combines the virtues of courage, honesty, self-sacrifice, far-sighted vision, energy, and patriotism. Significantly, Estévanez stresses Spain's need for strong leadership: a new "Pizarro" will impose the total reform of the administrative, financial, and educational structures of the nation; a *caudillo* will restore military discipline.

The deliberately exaggerated condemnation of the Revolution in 1868 and of the Restoration served Galdós's contemporary political purpose. The Spain of Maura and Canalejas stood accused in Galdós's harsh portrayal of the degraded and ineffective Spain of the recent past (the Restoration system was in many aspects untouched at the time of composition of the later *episodios*). The necessity for a lay Republic was implicitly argued in the depiction of a monarchy manipulated by clerical interests.

The Revolution of 1868 was, Galdós believes, a false revolution that produced only superficial reforms. Through Mariclío, Galdós in the final paragraph of *Cánovas* advocates *revolución*. The nature of the revolution is, however, without definition by Galdós (save as a contrast to the Restoration system) and is left to the distant future. Despite his manifest contempt for the Restoration, the only note of urgency sounded by Galdós is in his warnings against the clerical invasion of Spanish life. Time (the healer of Calpena in the third series) still has its role: Prim and Cánovas are content to solve the problems of their own day, leaving ideal solutions (such as the Federal Republic) to the passage of the years; similarly, Halconero needs repose to recover from his agitated love for Fernanda.

Galdós in the fifth series exposes past and present weaknesses rather than suggests remedies for Spain's ills.[18] Indications of the means to achieve a better society can, however, be glimpsed in the pages of the later *episodios*. Galdós's prescriptions for reform repeat those of Costa of a decade before: the development of agriculture, education, commerce, and industry, and attention to the well-being of the laboring classes.[19] Like Costa, Galdós (as in the third series of *episodios*) expresses his admiration for strong leaders, such as Prim and Concha; similarly, the exemplary Nicolás Estévanez demands a *cirugía política* to reform Spain.

Despite the attacks in the fourth series of *episodios* on "idealism," on "illusions," political idealism is an important element in Galdós's "program." In the closing lines of *Cánovas*, Galdós (through Mariclío) calls on Spaniards to rebel, to struggle in manly and "Romantic" fashion against the apathy that is strangling Spanish life: "Sed constantes en la protesta, sed viriles, románticos" (*Cánovas*, p. 278). The "Romanticism" that Galdós now advocates is faith in a better future for Spain, a refusal to accept mediocrity and corruption. Significantly, in a conversation with two journalists during the composition of *Cánovas*, Galdós again uses the term Romantic in approving manner, in his protest at the lack of idealism in the Spanish politics of 1912: "Nuestros partidos políticos no tienen ideal. Se va a ellos buscando medros personales. Romanticismo, amor al país. . . . Esos son conceptos arcaicos en los que nuestra política no cree . . . desgraciadamente."[20]

Galdós not only shares with Costa a disgust for Restoration politics and a sense of the need for material reforms, he also, like Costa, propounds as a source of inspiration to his compatriots virtues as abstract and as emptily rhetorical as that sentimental patriotism which he elsewhere condemns in Spain's leaders. Thus, in *España sin rey*, Santiago and Teresa represent for Fernanda an ideal of common sense, will-power, and work. Invisible trumpets sound out the virtues incarnate in the ideal couple: "Invisibles trompetas de oro daban al aire estas voces: *Energía, Dignidad, Amor, Justicia,* y alguna más que no se oía bien."[21]

Equally vague is the vision of the future propounded by Mariclío in *Amadeo I.* The fundamental reform of Spain will be moral rather than political: the true revolution will take place in the hearts of Spaniards. New men ("nueva gente," "hombres que traigan cerebros machos, corazones grandes y ternillas a la medida de los corazones"[22]) will arise from the ranks of workers and soldiers, not from the political class.

The process by which the new Spaniard will be formed is explored in *La primera república.* The cure for the depression that afflicts Tito (and also, in Galdós's eyes, the Spain of the early twentieth century) is to be sought in work, in interest in others (rather than solely in the sickly self), and in limiting ambition to what can reasonably be achieved. By participating in the everyday affairs of men, and above all by working with his muscles, Tito will be healed of his neurotic Romanticism: "Conservando amorosamente el saber que tienes archivado en tu cabeza, ponte a trabajar en una herrería, forjando a fuerza de martillo el metal duro; abre el surco en la tierra, siembra el grano y cosecha la mies; arranca de la cantera el mármol o el granito; agrégate a los ejércitos que entran en batalla; lánzate a la navegación, al comercio, y si logras juntar a tu saber teórico la ciencia práctica que aprenderás en estos trajines, serás un hombre" (*La primera república*, p. 269).

Galdós now reveals an optimism far greater than that of previous series of *episodios.* Fernando Calpena and Santiaguito Ibero were, when cured of Romantic folly, rewarded by individual domestic felicity; a nation that follows the prescriptions of *La primera república* will be utopia itself. The union of the will (symbolized in the smith Titan, the forger of Spanish wills) and education (symbolized in Floriana, the teacher of nations) will lead not only to the regeneration of Spain but also to "la perfecta revolución social."

Galdós's concept of the Spain of the future was no doubt less inane than that expounded in *La primera república.* His intent, however, was inspirational: to move Spaniards to alter modes of behavior that had led to the spiritual morass of the Restoration years and of the first decade of the reign of Alfonso XIII.

In *España sin rey* (October 1907-January 1908) Galdós continues the attack leveled in *La de los tristes destinos* on the values and accomplishments of the Revolution of 1868. Few historical events or movements are treated in the novel. The paucity of historical detail was intentional. The Spain of 1869 (and, Galdós suggests, with an eye to the Spain of his own day, of the following fifty years) lacked moral and historical grandeur: "Y ahora seguiremos presentando anécdotas y sucedidos particulares que son fundamento de la Historia fraguada para medio siglo de Idolatría nacional; un remiendo, más bien chapuza, para tirar hasta 1919."[23]

The problems touched on in the novel reflect as much the concern of 1907 as those of 1869: popular disorder, the sordid manipulations of Spanish politicians, the iron grip on rural regions of *caciquismo* (which Maura, at the time of composition of *España sin rey*, was endeavoring to destroy with his proposed Law of Municipal Reform), and religious freedom. (The Spain of Maura was less tolerant than that of the *Cortes Constituyentes* of 1869.) Galdós's Republicanism is evident in his contemptuous portrayal of Spanish "monarchists," who, in their lack of respect for the national past, profane the recently discovered corpse of the Emperor Charles V.

The anticlericalism of the fourth series of *episodios* continues in *España sin rey*. Priests and Catholics are portrayed as hypocritical, self-seeking, and lustful. Jesuit conspirators are mere cogs in the sinister machinery of their Order: "Ambos iban rectilíneos y sin pestañear al fin que se les señalaba, resortes inflexibles de una máquina tenebrosa y fuerte, soldados de una Orden de caballería que unos creen de Dios, otros del Diablo" (p. 23). Clerical leaders of guerrilla bands are, for the indignant Galdós, guilty of sacrilege: "Era, en fin, un levantamiento general y a la menuda, en la mayoría de los casos organizado y dirigido por indignos clérigos. Y estos bribones, que al verse perdidos se acogían al último indulto, volvían luego tranquilamente a sus parroquias, santuarios o catedrales, y sin que nadie les molestara continuaban ejerciendo su ministerio espiritual, y elevaban la Hostia con sus manos sacrílegas" (p. 211).

The ignoble maneuverings of the politicians of 1869 are only a surface element in Spanish life. Fundamental flaws in the Spanish character, as well as a lack of preparation for change, explain for Galdós the failure to carry out a true revolution in Spain. The sicknesses that afflict the collective life of Spain are symbolized in the novel in four characters:[24] Fernanda (the daughter of Santiago Ibero), Don Wifredo de Romarate (an aging Carlist), Nicéfora (the illegitimate daughter of a Jewish mother and Catholic father), and Don Juan de Urriés (the representative of the Revolution of 1868).

Fernanda and Wifredo represent Spanish idealism, an idealism that is rooted in the past of Spain and that is unable to adapt to present-day reality. Both are deceived by the seductive abstractions of politicians; both abandon the values of their upbringing and yet cannot replace these values with new, more realizable goals; in their disorientation, both—like the Spain which followed the Revolution of 1868—plunge into madness and violence.

Fernanda symbolizes the disappointed hope for a possible happier future of Spain. Like the Spain of the nineteenth century, she has been raised in seclusion and is ignorant of the ways of the world, an easy prey to the honeyed words of the politician Urriés. Representing, like the Rosario of *Doña Perfecta*, a Spain that needs guidance and that is inherently unstable, she can find no middle ground for her passions. Beset by fears and hopes, longing in her dreams for an ideal future of domestic bliss and prosperity, she abruptly descends from the enthusiasm of love to melancholia and homicidal insanity. Like Spain, the brittle Fernanda is incapable of combining idealism with practical caution. Too impetuous, she trusts her heart to the glib promises of a lying Don Juan. When disillusioned, she too readily dismisses not only her past immaturity (her "criterio de cuento de hadas") but also the healthy values of her upbringing.

Don Wifredo is equally unable to adapt to changed circumstances. (A rarity among Galdós's characters, Don Wifredo is a sympathetically portrayed Carlist. The sympathetic treatment may reflect Galdós's disgust with the superficial "liberalism" of the Revolutionaries of 1868.) Don Wifredo has the values of an earlier Spain: he is courteous, chivalric, and charitable, and places friendship above ideology. These values are not challenged by Galdós; however, they are accompanied by a rigid adherence to institutions, such as the Order of Saint John of Jerusalem, which are without meaning in the modern world. Confused by the temptations and verbal manipulations of the prostitutes and politicians of Madrid, suddenly liberated from a lifetime of sexual repression, unable to overcome the conflict between Spain's past (his ideology) and the present (the sordid Spain of 1869), Don Wifredo, like Fernanda, escapes into insanity and violence.

The disturbing element in Spanish life, Galdós suggests, is politics, symbolized by Don Juan Urriés, who appeals alike to Liberals, Democrats, and Carlists. A facile and persuasive speaker—and, as can be seen in his imitation of the style of Echegaray, highly impressionable—he adapts so easily to circumstances that he is without a viewpoint of his own. Willing to make any lying promise to his victims, whether they be electors or women, he is a nineteenth-century degeneration of the traditional Don Juan. His purse (or rather, the National Treasury) ensures the success of his amatory seductions.

Fernanda, Wifredo, and Urriés all symbolize unstable elements in the Spanish character. All, nevertheless, are to a degree (however slight) conscious of their situation. A far more dangerous disequilibrium—that proceeding from unconscious and conflicting religious and ethical values—is represented in the hysterical and neurotic Nicéfora. Mystical and sensuous, concealing the basic vacuum of her soul beneath a veil of hypocrisy, Nicéfora is split between traits derived from her Jewish mother (desire for vengeance, violence) and her Spanish father (religiosity, sensuality, hypocrisy). She is, indeed, in her mental and moral unbalance the expression of the imperfect assimilation in Spain of the values of the New Testament.[25] Because she represents obscure elements in the Spanish soul, elements beyond the reach of any reason, she is for Don Wifredo more evil than the superficial, selfish Urriés: "Era el Diablo mismo en su duplicada encarnación histérica y romántica; era la infernal Antarés, que a don Juan ofrecía sus formas seductoras cuando se hallaba dispuesto a variar de conducta. Con ser tan malo, don Juan era mejor que ella" (p. 304).

The nature of the true revolution, the revolution that Spain still awaited in 1908, is only hinted in *España sin rey*. Real revolution demands the reform of self, for the reform of others is an impossibility. Thus, while Wifredo fatuously and ineffectively dreams of imposing his own form of regeneration on the prostitute *Paca la africana*, Teresa Villaescusa, representing the path that for Galdós Spain should follow, regenerates herself. Teresa's love, unlike that of Nicéfora and Fernanda, is based on common sense and will-power. Teresa's goals are clearly defined and immediate: "Su marido, su trabajo, su casa, y no más" (p. 256). To assist her, she needs neither politician nor flowery promises but rather the solid support of the hard-working Santiago ("un robusto pilar en que asentarla," p. 257).

The ideal of spiritual and material contentment is as yet far from

Spanish reality; Teresa and Santiago live in France. Their blissful union, for Fernanda, is a symbol or myth. The couple personify abstract qualities needed by nation and individual: "Santiago y Teresa eran para ella un símbolo más admirado que comprendido, un mito que representaba la humana vida en su primordial concepto. . . . Invisibles trompetas de oro daban al aire estas voces: *Energía, Dignidad, Amor, Justicia,* y alguna más que no se oía bien" (p. 319).

Perhaps because Galdós is recreating an eventful period of his own youth, there is far greater attention to historical detail in *España trágica* (March 1909) than in *España sin rey.* The events of 1870 evoked in the novel are many and include the duel between Prince Enrique de Borbón and the duke of Montpensier, the masonic burial of the dead prince, the Franco-Prussian War, the vote in the Cortes to offer the Spanish throne to Amadeo of Savoy, the duel between Ducazcal and Paúl y Angulo, and—the lengthiest treatment—the assassination of Prim. Furthermore, Galdós vividly recreates elements of the feverish political atmosphere of the Madrid of the period: the sordid gatherings of Federal Republicans (whom Galdós dismisses as candid and irreflexive), the inane masonic rituals, the street battles between governmental thugs and their opponents, and the frenzied atmosphere in the office of Paúl y Angulo's newspaper *El Combate.*

As in *España sin rey,* Galdós in *España trágica* seeks an underlying reality of which historical events are only a symptom. The Spain of 1870 is consumed by an all-pervading, feverish insanity, a madness that prevents perception of Spain's needs and situation: "El pueblo español padecía de una honda enfermedad del juicio: loco estaba el Patriotismo, loca perdida la libertad, y el año venía con una sarta de locuras trágicas engarzadas una en otra, como cuentas de rosario."[26] For Galdós, it is Spanish madness, rather than the action of individuals, which kills Prim. He thus in *España trágica* deliberately confuses speculation as to the identity of the assassins.[27] Instead, the constant references to tragedy and to Julius Caesar's assassination by Brutus, the death— foreshadowing that of Prim—at the beginning of the novel of Fernanda Calpena ("la mujer trágica") and the repeated prophecies of death by the witchlike *Ecuménicas* relentlessly suggest that all Spaniards, in their collective insanity, bear responsibility for the death of the "hero" Prim.

The protagonist of the novel, Vicente Halconero (the son of the Lucila of the fourth series of *episodios*), resembles in many respects the youthful Galdós. Like Galdós, he is both interested in and repelled by the political scene; he is timid and absent-minded in public gatherings; he lacks commitment to any specific ideology. Halconero shares the pessimism of Spaniards of the nineteenth century, a pessimism with which Galdós associates himself: "Tan sólo Vicente . . . tuvo una rápida visión de la edad futura, visión de sangre, llanto y desconsuelo; pero creyéndola hechura del pesimismo que todos los españoles del siglo XIX llevamos dentro, no se determinó a manifestarla" (p. 188).

Halconero, Galdós declares, is a representative figure of those formed spiritually by the Revolution of 1868. The wills, intelligence, and judgment of the supporters of the Revolution were only partially developed, the consequence of their facile assimilation of a potpourri of foreign systems ill adapted to Spanish life:

De cuanto pudiera decirse acerca de Vicente Halconero, lo más fundamental es que provenía espiritualmente de la Revolución del 68. Esta y las ideas precursoras le engendraron a él y a otros muchos, y como los frutos y criaturas de aquella Revolución fueron algo abortivos, también Vicente llevaba en sí los caracteres de un nacido a media vida. Produjo ciertamente *la Gloriosa* medias voluntades, inteligencias en tres cuartos de madurez con incompleto conocimiento de las cosas, por lo que la gran procesión histórica partida de Cádiz y de Alcolea se desordenó a mitad de su camino, y cada pendón se fue por su lado, La razón de esto era que buena parte de la enjundia revolucionaria se componía de retazos de sistemas extranjeros, *procedentes de saldos políticos*. La fácil importación de vida emperezó en tal manera a los directores de aquel movimiento, que no extrajeron del alma nacional más que los viejos módulos de sus ambiciones y envidias, olvidándose de buscar en ella la esencia democrática, y el secreto del nuevo organismo con que debían armar las piezas desconcertadas de la Nación (pp. 8-9).

Halconero contains within himself both the madness of the Spain of 1870 and its subsequent temporary "cure" (the "peace" that the Restoration would bring). Literature affects him as does political rhetoric the nation: it divorces him from reality and provides false models of conduct. Thus, thwarted in his all-consuming love for Fernanda ("efervescencia de amor y poesía en un cerebro congestionado por la excesiva asimilación literaria"), he meditates suicide. Time, however, heals ("El vacío sentimental se le disminuía gradualmente, y su alma descansaba de los tormentos del pensar solitario, devorándose a sí mismo," p. 135). He replaces his tragic Romantic passion by more readily available, if less inspiring, affections (for the prostitute Eloísa and for his future bride, the frivolous and ignorant Pilar). Renouncing the tragic greatness that he, and Spain, were unconsciously seeking, he thinks increasingly of the practical realities of survival. Spain, he declares, needs a period of repose, in order to reconcile the ideas of the past and those recently introduced: "España acababa de hacer una revolución de tres al cuarto, y anhelaba constituirse en un régimen práctico, ecléctico, que le permitiese vivir . . . No aspiraba por de pronto más que a un vivir de reparación y descanso, con media cabeza en el almohadón del régimen pasado, y la otra media en el de las ideas novísimas" (p. 208).

Abandoning poetry and ancient history, Halconero studies economics to prepare for the safe (and nonrevolutionary) future that awaits him under the Restoration. The last third of the nineteenth century will belong, he decides, to those who avoid extremes (of wealth, of education, of ideology), to the middle class that links rich and poor, democracy and *antiguo régimen:* "Cuando me veo junto a ella, pienso que nuestra clase, la suya y la mía, estas familias medianamente ilustres, medianamente ricas, medianamente aderezadas de cultura y de educación, serán las directoras de la Humanidad en los años que siguen. Este último tercio del siglo XIX es el tiempo de esta clase nuestra, balancín entre la democracia y el antiguo régimen, eslabón que encadena pobres con ricos, nobles con villanos, y creyentes con incrédulos" (pp. 286-87).

Survival demands the lucid assessment of reality, the abandonment of a vision based on literature or the prejudices of upbringing. Santiago Ibero, who in the fourth series of *episodios* had disowned his son rather than countenance his living with the fallen Teresa, now prefers that his daughter Fernanda be dishonored rather than persist in her melancholic state. Lucila protests the male vision that women are passive and doll-like: "Ellos matan a sus rivales, ellos odian, y a nosotras nos mandan que seamos muñecas de amor" (p. 30). Similarly, Fernanda explains to Halconero the difference between a woman of flesh and blood (who has a past, ideas, and passions of her own) and the slave-woman portrayed in novels: "Si te inspiro repugnancia o miedo, retírate tranquilamente a tus libros y busca en ellos el modelo de la mujer esclava del hombre" (p. 31). (The same difference between reality and literature existed, of course, on a national plane, between the turbulent, uncertain Spain of 1870 and that dreamed by the framers of ideal constitutions.)

Halconero's search, after a period of emotional turmoil, for repose, for the slow assimilation of new values, repeats Galdós's teaching of the third series of *episodios*. Galdós also returns in *España trágica* to the theme of a leader who will bring calm to the Spanish madhouse. Prim is approvingly presented as a pragmatist. He thus rejects the federal ideal (an abstraction) in favor of historical reality, the pressing need to find solutions to the problems of his own day: "La historia no es filosófica cuando está pasando, sino después que ha pasado, cuando vienen los sabios a ponerle perendengues ... Los pueblos no entienden la filosofía cuando están descalabrados, febriles y muertos de hambre. El único filósofo que puede crear obras duraderas es el Tiempo, y nosotros, plantados en un *hoy* apremiante, tenemos la misión de resolver el problema de un solo día" (p. 149). The admiration expressed for Prim in *España trágica* is strong: Prim is the "héroe y mártir" (p. 328), "el grande hombre" (p. 329); his energy and intelligence are highly praised. Prim's rashness (a further symptom of Spanish insanity?), on the other hand, leads to his death. His excessive Machiavellianism prevents his winning the trust of his compatriots. Galdós's final judgment on Prim, in *Amadeo I,* is guarded. Prim had established a transitional regime, which had served to brake the course of revolution: "Así fue llevado al sepulcro el hombre que ejercitó en España durante veintisiete meses una blanda dictadura, poniendo frenos a la revolución, y creando una monarquía democrática como artificio de transición, o *modus vivendi* hasta que llegara la plenitud de los tiempos."[28]

One project of Prim's especially interests Galdós: his ambitious plan to grant autonomy to Cuba. The proposal, which, if carried out, would obviously have spared Spain the traumatic wars with Cuban separatists and the United States, was born of a grandiose vision of a new Spain, formed from the moral, linguistic, and ethnic bonds linking the Hispanic nations: "El ensueño de fundar una nueva España más grande y potente, formada de pueblos ibéricos que se aglomeren y unifiquen, no con atadijos administrativos, sino con ligamiento moral, filológico y étnico" (p. 175).

Galdós's anticlericalism is strong in the novel. The witchlike *Ecuménicas,* the harbingers of death, are associated with religious circles. Prim is presented as the key to the future of Spain. His death will return

Spain to the rule of religious *camarillas,* that is, to the clerical interests who, for Galdós, control the Spain of the Restoration and of Maura: "Prim era la clave de la libertad y del povenir de España, y que si aquel hombre faltase, volveríamos tarde o temprano al reino de las camarillas, bajando de tumbo en tumbo hasta ponernos otra vez debajo de las tocas de Sor Patrocinio y del solideo del Padre Claret. Lo que parece vencido y muerto no lo está, y a cada momento sentimos el resuello del fantasmón que quiere volver a darnos guerra y a metérsenos en casa" (p. 141). The final lines of *España trágica* link the death of Prim with approaching religious reaction: "Las devociones reaccionarias y frailunas rezaron por el muerto con esta dulce letanía: 'Vivir para volver' " (p. 330).

Galdós, who, by the time of composition of *España trágica* had long been one of the leading members of the *Bloque de Izquierdas,* reflects in the novel on the role of the proletariate in the revolutionary life of the nation. The lower classes, Galdós holds, are ignorant and easily excited by mob orators. They, however, conserve in their purity the ideals of *Patria* and *Libertad* (p. 229). Politicians, on the other hand, have neither contact with nor knowledge of the elemental life of the nation. Revolutionary philosophical ideas bear no fruit unless they take root in the burning passions of the hungry and the poor: "Como en las grandes crisis políticas de nada sirven las ideas si no vienen vaciadas en pasiones ardientes, la plebe del Sur cumplía muy bien su misión de poner al fuego las ideas para que hirvieran, y con su hervor fuesen cauterio del cuerpo social. La semilla lanzada por filósofos y pensadores, no germina sino cuando cae en los cerebros y en las almas de los que más directamente soportan el mal humano, de los mal comidos y semidesnudos, de los que soportan todas las cargas y no gozan de ningún beneficio" (p. 227). For a revolution to be successful, Halconero comments, thought (philosophy) and impulse (popular passion) must act in harmony: "Para que de las revoluciones salga vida eficaz, es preciso que se casen y procreen la fuerza pensante y la mecánica o impulsiva. De otro modo, todo es barullo estéril" (p. 227).

Reflecting, perhaps, Republican bitterness at Salmerón's defection— Salmerón had adhered to *Solidaridad Catalana* in 1907— and his own difficulties as organizer of the *Bloque de Izquierdas* (Lerroux's rabidly anticlerical Radical Republicans, for example, as well as many Liberals, refused to join the bloc), Galdós laments that left-wing parties cannot see their true interests. They prefer on occasions to ally with the forces of reaction rather than with those who profess a similar creed: "Porque los federales de aquel tiempo, como todo partido español avanzado, padecían ya el mal de miopía, o sea el ver de cerca mejor que de lejos" (p. 138).

In *Amadeo I* (August-October 1910), Galdós touches on numerous events and details of the brief reign of Amadeo (January 1871 to February 1873): the cool reception to the arrival of the Savoyan, the burial of Prim, the virtues of the queen, Amadeo's well-intentioned attempt to rule as a constitutional monarch, his amorous intrigues, the conspiracies of Carlists and Federal Republicans, the virulent quarrels between supporters of Sagasta and those of Ruiz Zorrilla, the abdication of the monarch. The "history" of the period is, however, for Galdós trivial ("ópera cómica, tirando a bufa"[29]). Political creeds are meaningless formulas. Cabinet ministers are "pintorescos personajes de ópera cómica" (p. 146). The formation of a new government is without importance, barely meriting the notice of the historian or novelist: "Ir viviendo, ir trazando una Historia tediosa y sin relieve, sobre cuyas páginas, escritas con menos tinta que saliva, pasaban pronto las aguas del olvido" (p. 39).

Galdós, drawing on personal memories, offers glimpses of his early journalistic career. He treats Albareda, the anglophile who employed Galdós to edit *El Debate* and the *Revista de España*, with sympathy and at length. He gives brief mention of his early colleagues in journalism, Ramón Correa and Pepe Ferreras; the only revelation of note, however, is that *El Debate* was financed in part by Cuban slaveowners. Galdós himself appears in the novel, as a young journalist from the Canary Islands. Although, as was his wont, he evades any insight into his own character, he alludes to the patriotic aims of the *episodios nacionales:* "Años adelante lanzó más de uno [libro] de materia y finalidad patrióticas, contando guerras, disturbios y casos públicos y particulares que vienen a ser como toques o bosquejos fugaces del carácter nacional" (p. 8).

Earlier teachings of the *episodios* are reiterated in *Amadeo I.* Conventional literary Romanticism is satirized in the empty phrases of Obdulia. The pretentious biblical rhetoric of the Federal Republican Roque Barcia meets with Galdós's repeated scorn. Galdós's anticlericalism is unchanged: the "exemplary" priest Don Hilario de la Peña will neither be offered nor wish for a bishopric; the charitable priest

Choribiqueta dismisses friars as "en su mayoría un hatajo de gandules que vienen aquí con hambre atrasada" (p. 199); the Vatican itself, as well as ignorant Basques, takes seriously Tito's tongue-in-cheek proposal that the pope be invited to govern Spain.

Tito (*Proteo Liviano*), the first person narrator of the novel, contains within himself the vices (glibness, seedy amorousness) of the national temperament. In his sickness, confusion, and mediocrity, he resumes the Spain not only of Amadeo but also of subsequent regimes. His ancestry (which includes Carlist and Liberal, Catholic bishop and Protestant cleric, abbess and prostitute) is that of Spain itself. Tito, like the Spain condemned by Galdós, is fickle, mentally unbalanced, and of violent temper. His facility with words—he defends with equal skill and an equal lack of commitment every cause, whether it be the Federal Republic, a *República Hispano-Pontificia,* or Ruiz Zorrilla's radicalism—covers a fundamental emptiness of the soul: "Llevado y traido por fatal corriente misteriosa, yo era el campeón de todas las causas. . . . Era yo, pues, un caso peregrino de proteísmo" (p. 77). His association with unsavory characters (police agents, moneylenders, minor criminals) and ignoble amorous conquests (a washerwoman, servants, a priest's concubine) reflect his, and Spain's, lack of discrimination. Tito's dwarfish stature aptly symbolizes the make-shift illusory nature of the ramshackle monarchy of Amadeo: Tito shrinks in size to that of a baby; he becomes for a time invisible; his actions are without national or personal significance. Buffoonish, he doubts at times his own reality; his loves themselves, Tito conjectures, are perhaps the creation of fantasy; he reacts, like Spain, to stimuli with random violence and meaningless activity.

In June 1910 Galdós expressed his contempt for the divided, *cacique*-ridden Republican coalition that he nominally headed. He repeats in *Amadeo I* his bitter hostility to a political system controlled by those whose concern is not the welfare of a sick nation but only petty personal ambition: "¡Que un país, donde hay sin fin de hombres que discurren con juicio, y sienten en sí mismos y en conjunto el malestar hondo de la Patria; que una Nación europea y cristiana esté en manos de esta cuadrilla de politicajos por oficio y rutinas abogaciles, hombres de menguada ambición, mil veces más dañinos que los ambiciosos de alto vuelo! " (p. 97) "La ambición de estos hombres raquíticos y de cortas luces, se limita, como ves, a la vanidad de ser ministros, sin otros fines que darse tono, repartir empleos, y que la señora y los niños paseen en coche galonado" (p. 98). In obvious criticism of the Republican attitudes of 1910, Galdós accuses the Republicans of Amadeo's reign of lack of knowledge of reality, of dreaming; they were "románticos de la política, constructores clandestinos de una España feliz" (p. 17). The ill-planned violence and inane propaganda of the Federal Republicans served only the cause of the Restoration. The Republican alliance with *alfonsinos* and Carlists is a symptom of Republican shortsightedness. Galdós notes—again with an eye to his own day—Republican divisions and propensity to rhetoric and to personal vendettas: "No había en España voluntades más que para discurrir, para levantar barreras de palabras entre los entendimientos, y recelos y celeras entre los corazones" (p. 118).

In contrast to the unsavory and mediocre Spain of 1872 and 1873, a Spain in which words lack meaning and in which opposition parties offer no more hope of fundamental reform than do the nation's corrupt rulers. Galdós offers a lengthy portrayal of an exemplary Republican, Nicolás Estévanez. Estévanez, the Republican deputy for Madrid, is courageous, honest, self-sacrificing, and far-sighted. His program, which captivates Tito, marks Galdós's renewed acceptance of the forthright measures advocated by the Regenerationists. Estévanez contemptuously rejects the political system, calls for the total reform of all branches of government, and will entrust this task of *cirugía política* to a dictator, to a "Pizarro." Here is Galdós's summary of Estévanez's theories and of the enthusiasm that they inspire in Tito:

Todo cuanto veíamos despedía olor a muerto. Los Gobiernos de don Amadeo no salían de la norma y pauta somníferas de los Gobiernos anteriores a la Revolución. Los vicios se petrificaban, y las virtudes cívicas no pasaban de las bocas a los corazones. Administración, Hacienda, Instrucción Pública, permanecían en el mismo estado de quietismo y pereza oriental. No salía un hombre que alzara dos dedos sobre la talla corriente. Hacía falta un bárbaro, como Pizarro, que sin saber leer ni escribir, creó un mundo hispano en la falda de los Andes.
Estas ideas me cautivaron. Sí, hacía falta un bárbaro que creara otro mundo hispano. . . . Hacía falta un mudo, que hablara con los hechos y con la piqueta, demoliendo los viejos muros, sin pedir permiso a las letras de molde; un mudo, sí, que entendiera de cirugía política, y supiera leer lo escrito con caracteres de fuego en el alma de la Nación. . . . Debajo del pesimismo de mi gran amigo, latía, como es de ley en todo ser superior, un fuerte optimismo. No desconfiaba de la idea, sino de los hombres que en el telar político, llamándose ministe-

riales o de oposición, tejían la misma tela frágil y descolorida, tan fea y tan mala por el derecho como por el revés. . . . En suma, que la oposición republicana, aliándose con los *Nocedales* y *Barzanallanas*, se contagiaba de esa legalidad indigesta que siempre resulta infecunda, y cándidamente hacía el juego a sus naturales enemigos. Los arañaba; pero no supo darles, como debía, muerte y sepultura (pp. 137-38).

Disgusted with the mediocrity that he observes in the Spain of Amadeo, Galdós, through his mouthpiece *Mariclío* (the decayed personification of History), calls for a new race of Spaniards. The "nueva gente"—and Galdós is now as emptily rhetorical as those he elsewhere chastises—will be "hombres que traigan cerebros machos, corazones grandes y ternillas a la medida de los corazones" (p. 152), a generation whose "acciones altas y nobles" can be related with pride. The new Spaniard will arise, not from the class of politicians, but from the ranks of simple soldiers and workers: "Vámonos a la Fuente de la Teja, y allí veremos a los soldados bailando con las criadas. Aquello, en su humildad, es más noble que esto. De allí puede salir algo grande, de aquí no. Iremos también a ver a los chicos jugando al toro o a la tropa, en la Virgen del Puerto. De allí saldrán hombres de poder, ciudadanos, trabajadores, mártires, héroes. Aquello es la sal y el fuego de vida. . . . Aquí no hay más que hombres de humo que burla burlando asfixian a su patria" (p. 149).

In *La primera república* (February-April 1911), Galdós reviews the first seven months of existence of the Spanish Republic proclaimed in February 1873.[30] He treats the abortive Radical revolt of April ("entremés de zarzuela"), the constant schisms in the Cortes, Figueras's "Romanticism" and sudden desertion of the political scene, the programs of Pi and Salmerón, the risings in Málaga and Sevilla, and, at length, the cantonalist revolt in Cartagena and the ill-conceived marauding expeditions of the insurgent fleet.

Republican conduct in power in 1873 serves Galdós as a lesson in what must be avoided if Republicans are again to rule in Spain. The proclamation of the Republic does not of itself cure Spain's rulers of their narrowness of vision and self-centeredness. The ministries are besieged by the same hordes of job-seekers as before. Politicians and their clients have neither patriotism nor practical sense ("toda esta gente rencillosa y quimerista, sin conocimiento de la realidad ni estímulos de patriotismo"[31]). The individualism, rhetorical disputes, and lack of discipline in the Cortes provoke Galdós's contempt: "El individualismo sin freno, el flujo y reflujo de opiniones, desde las más sesudas a las más extravagantes, y la funesta espontaneidad de tantos oradores, enloquecían al espectador e imposibilitaban las funciones históricas" (p. 92).

Galdós blames Republican pusillanimity for the chaos of 1873. Without true commitment to their cause, Republican deputies fraternized with the monarchic-radical rebels of 1873 (a *compadrazgo* that merits Galdós's scorn). Overscrupulous and too timid to rid the Republic of its enemies, Republicans lacks the will and energy to carry out the total revolution which the nation needed: "No se pasa de aquello a esto sin cerrar con cien llaves el arca de los escrúpulos, aplicando calmantes heroicos a las conciencias irritables" (p. 52). "Así no se pasa de un régimen de mentiras, de arbitrariedades, de desprecio de la ley, de caciquismo y nepotismo, a un régimen que pretende encarnar la verdad, la pureza, y abrir ancho cauce a las corrientes de vida gloriosa y feliz" (p. 71). Republican leaders—and the stern Pi y Margall is included in Galdós's indictment—are indecisive in action: "Lucían como faros luminosos en la esfera del ideal; mas en la acción se apagaban sus indecisas voluntades" (pp. 40-41). Republican indiscipline—harebrained provincial revolts, refusal to enforce military discipline, personal rivalries, capricious behavior—plunges Spain into disorder. The same vices are repeated in the miniature republic of Cartagena: unplanned action, histrionic gestures, empty rhetoric, thoughtless bravado, self-interest. The cantonalists, indeed, like the liberal revolutionaries of the fourth series of *episodios,* mistake the appearance of change for its reality: "Creen estos inocentes que las revoluciones se hacen con discursos frenéticos, con abrazos fraternales, con vivas estrepitosas y cantinelas optimistas" (p. 259).

Despite the manifest failure of Spain's "First Republic," Galdós has not renounced his Republican creed. The novelistic title itself is a gesture of faith in the Republican future of Spain. The Federal Republican form of government, Mariclío explains, is a beautiful ideal. (It cannot, however, take root overnight in a nation which is ill accustomed to liberty and where long-established institutions weigh heavily.) Pi y Margall is praised for the severity of his principles, if not for his forcefulness in action. As in *Amadeo I,* Galdós presents Nicolás Estévanez as a model of Republican virtues. As civil governor of Madrid,

Estévanez is honest and energetic; courageous and forceful, Estévanez recognizes the need for a *caudillo* to restore military discipline. As leader of a guerrilla band against the monarchy, Estévanez personifies the age-old Spanish spirit of rebellion against the abuses of authority: "En él veía yo la personificación vigorosa del espíritu de rebeldía que alienta en las razas españolas desde tiempos remotos, y que no tiene trazas de suavizarse con las dulzuras de la civilización, protesta inveterada contra la arbitrariedad crónica del poder público, contra las crueldades y martirios que la burocracia y el caciquismo prodigan a los ciudadanos" (p. 11).

The grave disorders of the Spanish Republic, which are only an extreme expression of a disorder endemic in Spain, are again symbolized in the diminutive and ineffective Tito. Tito's sickness, already marked in *Amadeo I,* is aggravated in *La primera república,* as he proceeds from one low amorous conquest to the next, a prey to panic terrors and to visions born of his fantasy, unable to distinguish between reality and illusion. His malady is that of Spain: an "exacerbación del egoísmo" or "fatalidad del yo," a neurosis (the term is used by his friend Cárceles) provoked by the abuse of emotion and of intellectualism. Because Tito (Spain) is emotionally and mentally ill, immediate possession of an external ideal (Floriana, the Federal Republic) will change nothing, for first Tito (Spain) must undergo a radical restructuring of his nature: "Entiendo yo que es flaqueza del cerebro, resultante del vértigo de los goces fáciles, del ansia de asimilar sabidurías de artes y ciencias, que viene a ser la gula del entendimiento. ¿Cree mi buen Tito que estas generaciones, debilitadas por la continua labor pensante y emotiva en el curso precipitado de la vida mental, pueden arrasar las instituciones caducas, y erigir sobre sus ruinas el monumento del Federalismo, que tiene por base las virtudes y el vigor físico de los pueblos? " (p. 269)

Tito, like the abulic Spaniard described by Ganivet, is depressed by his failure to possess immediately and without effort the object of his desires (the "goddess" Floriana, a utopian republic). He consequently abandons all activity and longs only for death. Nicolás Estévanez and Tito's friend Cárceles independently prescribe the cure for his (and, by extension, national) depression and inactivity: that he work, that he mix with and take an interest in the affairs of others.

Mariclío seconds this sensible advice, with a diagnosis and regimen almost identical to the prescriptions of Ganivet and Costa. The sickness, or lack of adaptation to life, of Tito (Spain) is Romantic in its nature. The remedy, which will make of Tito a man rather than a puppet at the mercy of personal caprice and outside events, is to combine practical physical labor (the material regeneration of Spain) with the theoretical knowledge (his judgment and intelligence) which he already possesses. His ambitions, furthermore, must be directed to what may reasonably be achieved, not to the pursuit of an impossible and sickly ideal:

A los que como tú se inutilizan para el vivir normal solemos dar el nombre de románticos. Románticos son, pero de estofa ínfima y barata, los se matan porque la novia se les va con otro, los que se desesperan y reniegan de la Humanidad porque no han podido obtener en un día lo que es fruto de la paciencia en largos años trabajosos.

Conque ya lo sabes: no quiero verte romántico llorón, ni neurótico, ni flatulento, ni poseído de los demonios, que todos estos nombres han sido aplicados sucesivamente a los enfermos de necedad aguda. Conservando amorosamente el saber que tienes archivado en tu cabeza, ponte a trabajar en una herrería, forjando a fuerza de martillo el metal duro; abre el surco de la tierra, siembra el grano y cosecha la mies; arranca de la cantera el mármol o el granito; agrégate a los ejércitos que entran en batalla; lánzate a la navegación, al comercio, y si logras juntar a tu saber teórico la ciencia práctica que aprenderás en estos trajines, serás un hombre.

No serás hombre sino un muñeco, si en vez de contener tu alma en la norma de ambición que la Naturaleza concede a los humanos, te lanzas al espacio insondable de las ambiciones locas, quiméricas, fuera de los confines de la realidad. Acabarás de perder tu salud, y con la salud tu vida, si te empeñas en remontarte al cielo para coger la estrella más linda que en él has visto desde la tierra, o si te arrojas en medio del Océano para sacar la perla escondida en el seno más hondo de las aguas (pp. 269-70).

In the closing pages of the novel, Galdós, with a symbolism as blatant as that of a political poster, calls on Spain to regenerate itself. Two elements (one from within the individual, one from without) are needed for this task: will-power (symbolized in the mythical smith, the forger of Spanish wills) and education (symbolized in Floriana, the educator of the people). In time, Floriana, by teaching a thousand teachers who will in their turn each instruct a further thousand educators, will regenerate, spiritually and socially, not only Spain but neighboring nations: "Ya puedes comprender que con un millón de maestras como ésta que has visto, tu patria y las patrias adyacentes serán regeneradas, ennoblecidas y espiritualizadas hasta consumar la perfecta revolución social" (p. 288).

Tito (the Spain of the present), suitably chastened by the vision of the ideal combination of worker and educator (the Spain of the future), confesses his moral and physical degeneration, his reliance on the emptiness of words: "Yo, Tito Liviano, el hombre raquítico, enclenque, de ruin naturaleza, residuo miserable de una raza extenuada, politicastro que pretendía reformar el mundo con discursos huecos, con disputas doctrinales, fililíes retóricos y dogmáticos requilorios, me sentí tan humillado, que anhelé con toda mi alma huir de la comparación con aquel ser titánico de infinita grandeza" (p. 289). Tito (Spain) is as yet too weak and ill prepared for the task of reconstruction, which is left by the smith for a future generation (that to which Galdós directs his message of inspiration): "Sería preciso que te dejaras construir de nuevo. Yo y mis compañeros de trabajo somos forjadores de los caracteres hispanos del porvenir" (p. 281).

In *De Cartago a Sagunto* (August-November 1911), Galdós relates the final months of the Canton of Cartagena, the abrupt ending (by military coup) of the Republic, the Battle of Abarzuza (and death of the "hero" Concha), and the brutal sack of Cuenca by Carlist troops. So much historical material is included in the novel that discussion of the military *pronunciamiento* at Sagunto, promised in the title, is left to the following *episodio*.

Novelistic elements are less important in *De Cartago a Sagunto* than in the immediately preceding *episodios*. Tito's confusion—the novelistic reflection of the impossibility of giving a coherent explanation to Spanish history—persists: he still suffers from *desvaríos mentales;* he associates with rogues and prostitutes; he pursues sordid amorous intrigues. Tito's role, however, is now essentially that of observer.

In the first half of the novel (that dealing with the demise of the Canton and of the Republic), Galdós examines the causes of Republican failure during their brief period of rule. The lesson, as Mariclío indicates, is intended for the Republicans of Galdós's day, should Republicans ever regain power in Spain: "Di a tus amigos los republicanos que lloren sus yerros y procuren enmendarlos para cuando la rueda histórica les traiga por segunda vez al punto de . . . ."[32]

The Republicans fail—and Galdós's charge was equally applicable to the Republicans of 1911—because they are divided, split between conservatives and leftists, between partisans of a federation and advocates of a unitary republic. Their internal antagonisms are such that they prefer the monarchy to compromise with Republicans of a different stamp. The Republicans of 1874 also lack courage. In the face of the military coup,[33] Republican politicians react first with bombast and then with cowardice.[34] Looking to the future, Tito demands that Republicans, when they again rule, show thought as well as rashness, that they behave with dignity and courage when faced with danger (p. 103).

As in *La primera república*, Galdós attacks the *compadrazgo* prevailing in Spanish political (and military) life, a *compadrazgo* that makes struggle for principle meaningless. Cantonalist and centralist army officers are quick to reach an accord. Republican leaders and military rebels, the defeated and the victors, easily heal their wounded pride with fresh compacts: "El grave mal de nuestra Patria es que aquí la paz y la guerra son igualmente deslavazadas y sosainas. Nos peleamos por un ideal, y vencedores y vencidos nos curamos las heridas del amor propio con emplasto de arreglitos, y anodinas recetas para concertar nuevas amistades y seguir viviendo en octaviana mansedumbre. En aquel día tonto, el Parlamento y el pueblo fueron dos malos cómicos que no sabían su papel, y el Ejército, suplantó, con sólo cuatro tiros al aire, la voluntad de la Patria dormida" (pp. 102-3). Similarly, the generals fighting on opposing sides in the Third Carlist War are united by ties of career and friendship: "En el llano de Alava, se agolpaban armados hasta los dientes los que compartieron con don Antonio las fatigas de la guerra de Africa y de las contiendas familiares del liberalismo. Habían sido amigos: lo serían siempre" (p. 214). Liberal and Carlist generals were, indeed, fighting for the same cause, that of a despotism that would leave Spain in the hands of traditional rulers and *caciques:* "¿Qué querían, por qué peleaban? Debajo del emblema de la soberanía nacional en los unos y del absolutismo en el otro latía sin duda este común pensamiento: establecer aquí un despotismo hipócrita y mansurrón que sometiera la familia hispana al gobierno del patriciado absorbente y caciquil" (p. 214).

The corruption of Spanish political life is symbolized in the novel in the person of Silvestra, an unstable hypocrite whom Tito in turn woos and flees. Silvestra's violence and capacity to fabricate myths parallel, according to Mariclío, the procedure of Spain's rulers, who govern with alternating patriotic rhetoric and unadorned despotism.

Conforme al voluble proceso mental de tu amiga, gobiernan a España las manadas de hombres que alternan en las poltronas o butacas del Estado, ahora con este nombre, ahora con el otro. También ellos invocan el sentimentalismo patriótico cuando les conviene, o se entregan a los espasmos del despotismo cuando no hallan salida por la vía patriótica, o sea la vía liberal. También ellos inventan historias para domar las fieras oleadas de la opinión y acaban por creer lo que engendró su propia fantasía. Tus gobernantes son creadores de mitos, y mostrándolos al pueblo andan a ciegas sin saber lo que quieren ni a dónde van (p. 244).

Looking to the future, Mariclío declares that the many years of despotism (the Restoration, the reign of Alfonso XIII) which await Spain will only conceal the growth of an obscure sickness, a tuberculosis that will consume the nation: "Tu pobre España gemirá, por largos años, bajo la pesadumbre del despotismo que llaman ilustrado, enfermedad obscura y honda, con la cual los pueblos viven muriendo . . . y se mueven, gritan y discursean, atacados de lo que llaman *epilepsía larvada . . .* Debajo de esta dolencia se esconde la mortal *tuberculosis* (p. 235).

In his treatment of Catholics, Galdós in *De Cartago a Sagunto* goes far beyond the anticlericalism of earlier novels. Believers are hypocrites, whose trust in Divine Providence blinds them to the realities of their situation. (Thus, Don José Ido del Sagrario will praise God for conveying his daughter from a brothel to the safe position of priest's concubine.) The relief of Bilbao leads Galdós to lament the iron grip that the Jesuits would later place on the city: "Al recordar hoy los sublimes momentos de aquel día, ayes de gozo, alaridos de esperanza, me parece que oigo burlona carcajada del Destino. Sí, sí; porque la Restauración primero, la Regencia después, se dieron prisa a importar el jesuitismo y a fomentarlo hasta que se hiciera dueño de la heroica Villa. Con él vino la irrupción frailuna y monjil, gobernó el Papa, y las leyes teñidas de barniz democrático fueron y son una farsa irrisoria" (p. 205).

Perhaps the most vitriolic pages penned by Galdós in his career are those devoted to the Carlist occupation of Cuenca. Sarcastically directing his account to the "Catholic" reader ("lectores muy católicos y muy amantes de nuestra patria," p. 283), Galdós gloatingly describes the atrocities committed by the Carlist hordes. Amid "salvajes gritos y carcajadas infernales," Carlists rape and loot as savages; the Church is the accomplice of their crimes, for the Bishop of Cuenca celebrates the

Carlist victory with a Te Deum. The harshest lines of all are reserved for the Carlist princess, Doña María de las Nieves; Doña María, an "Amazon" who believes she commands by divine right, combines the traits of Attila and Tamerlane (p. 284). In a scene reminiscent of the Blasco Ibáñez of *La araña negra*, Galdós evokes the princess's trampling of the body of a dying officer, murdered by Carlist troops:

El cuerpo chocó contra las piedras, y yacía exánime en medio del arroyo, cuando apareció en la calle abigarrada muchedumbre, a cuya cabeza venía una mujer a caballo, como amazona de circo, radiante de fatuidad, decidida y altanera. Era la tristemente famosa Princesa doña María de las Nieves, esposa de don Alfonso de Borbón. Los que la vieron venir pensaron que desviaría su caballo para no pisar el cuerpo expirante. Pero la terrible capitana de bandidos no se inmutó, y sin dar señales de ninguna emoción ante aquel espectáculo dejó que el animal pisotease a un honrado caballero moribundo (p. 271).

In *Cánovas* (March-August 1912), the last *episodio nacional* to be completed by Galdós,[35] Galdós resumes Spanish life between the end of 1874 and 1880. Events mentioned are numerous: the *pronunciamiento* of Sagunto ("una comedia"), the entry of King Alfonso into Madrid, the repartition of jobs by Cánovas (who pardons the Cantonalists and employs the revolutionaries of 1868), the elections that Romero Robledo organized in 1876 ("la espléndida mentira de la Soberanía Nacional"), the Constitution of 1876, Baldomera Larra's Banco Popular (a swindle), the royal marriage to Mercedes and death of the well-liked princess, cardinals' bickering for the privilege of baptizing the Infanta, the floods of Murcia, and railroad speculation with its accompanying corruption. Because for Galdós the events of the Restoration are significant only as symptoms of the degradation of Spanish life, his treatment is slender and scornful. His lengthiest descriptions are of the more strikingly frivolous activities of the period (the bullfights which celebrate the royal wedding, the career of Alfonso's favorite, the opera singer Elena Sanz).

The portrayal of Cánovas in the novel is favorable. However, the prime minister lacks vision. He fatalistically sees his task as merely one of administration, leaving to the course of time any fundamental change in the soul of a nation that is "petrificada en la tradición y desprovista de toda flexibilidad."[36] Cánovas also lacks will-power. He thus does not carry out the terms of the Peace of El Zanjón negotiated by Martínez Campos, a failure that will ultimately lead to the loss of Spain's Caribbean provinces. Galdós, who had consistently opposed "bookishness" in the *episodios* written after 1898, notes that Cánovas's vast library was of no help to him in the practical art of governing. Neither Alfonso XII nor Sagasta receive treatment in *Cánovas*. Galdós in all probability was reserving their presentation for the novel *Sagasta* which he was never to complete.

The triviality of the historical events described is reflected in the meagerness of the novelistic intrigue. Tito, who has degenerated from the already degraded state in which he found himself in previous *episodios,* is now melancholic, blind, reduced to idiocy, and insanely jealous; he is a fitting representative of a society that has abandoned all hope of reform. To survive, Tito must depend on the assistance that he receives from Casiana ("una criada para todo y una mujer fiel que le proporcione paz, alegría y cariño," p. 28). Casiana, in contrast with the pretentions of the Restoration aristocracy (which also, ironically, depended on the labor of the poor), modestly limits her desires to the care of house and partner: "Muy corto es mi genio, pero más cortos son mis deseos. Con un poquitín de lo que Dios reparte a sus criaturas tengo asegurada la felicidad: un hombre bueno que me quiera, una casa modesta y limpia, un pasar mediano y sin ahogos, un vivir tranquilo, cuidar a mi hombre y tenerle todo a punto y muy arregladito, y para colmo de contento mi plancha, mi aguja y mi estropajo" (p. 96).

The society of the Restoration years ("la era de la hipocresía," "los tiempos bobos") is treated throughout the novel with vitriolic scorn. *Alfonsino* society is symbolized in Leona the prostitute; the new "aristocracy" is composed of former slavers and monopolists. Dress (rather than conduct) becomes of paramount importance in a society based on appearances and of which the dominating characteristics are frivolity, ignorance, and credulity. The Spaniards of the Restoration wish not to create wealth but only to consume. The nation is plagued by "los míseros de levita y chistera," who demand positions in the civil service: "Esta es la plaga, ésta es la carcoma del país, necesitada y pedigüena" (p. 51). The corruption and fictitious nature of the institutions of the period is fittingly resumed in the offer of a post of school inspector to the illiterate Casiana: "Todo era ficciones, favoritismos y un saqueo desvergonzado del presupuesto" (p. 75). In a mediocre society without ethical values or desire for change, Mariclío, the Muse of History, rarely has the need to communicate with Tito. The messages he now receives come from the nymph Efémera, the reporter of transient events.

The Regenerationist charge that the revolutions of nineteenth-century Spain had wrought no change in the fundamental structure of the nation is repeated by Galdós. The dynastic struggle between *alfonsino* and Carlist was only appearance. The reality of Spanish government is, whoever occupies power, the oppressive and arbitrary rule of Throne and Altar. Swarms of job-hungry generals and bureaucrats abet politices of inertia and lies:

El Borbonismo no tiene dos fases, como creen los historiadores superficiales, sino una sola. Aquí y allá, en la guerra y en la paz es siempre el mismo, un poder arbitrario que acopla el Trono y el Altar para oprimir a este pueblo infeliz y mantenerlo en la pobreza y en la ignorancia. Lo único positivo en ese cortejo brillante que ahora atraviesa las calles de Madrid es un sin fin de Generales, Jefes y Oficiales nuevos, agregados a los que ya teníamos, una caterva de funcionarios viejos o novísimos que fundarán sobre el doble catafalco, Altar y Trono, una política de inercia, de ficciones y de fórmulas extraídas de la cantera de la tradición (pp. 127-28).

The *turno* (the two-party system of the Restoration) merits Galdós's total contempt. Members of both parties aspire only to advance the interests of themselves and friends. Liberals and Conservatives are equally lacking in ideals and will fail—and Galdós speaks with hindsight—to make any impression on the religious, economic, and educational problems of Spain. Furthermore, nothing is to be expected of the antimonarchical parties (a reflection, we must assume, of Galdós's disgust with the bickerings of twentieth-century Republicans):

Los dos partidos, que se han concordado para turnar pacíficamente en el Poder, son dos manadas de hombres que no aspiran más que a pastar en el Presupuesto. Carecen de ideales, ningún fin elevado les mueve, no mejorarán en lo más mínimo las condiciones de vida de esta infeliz raza, pobrísima y analfabeta. Pasarán unos tras otros dejando todo como hoy se halla, y llevarán a España a un estado de consunción que de fijo ha de acabar en muerte. No acometerán ni el problema religioso, ni el económico, ni el educativo; no harán más que burocracia pura, caciquismo, estéril trabajo de recomendaciones, favores a los amigotes, legislar sin ninguna eficacia práctica, y adelante con los farolitos. . . . Si nada se puede esperar de las turbas monárquicas, tampoco debemos tener fe en la grey revolucionaria (p. 237).

The society of the Restoration is not only vulgar and ostentatious but it also, in its obsession with politics, fails to perceive the increasing domination of the Church over Spanish life. Galdós, in a return to the violently anticlerical accusations of *Electra,* claims that the role of the Church in the degradation of modern Spain is crucial. The ruling classes blindly allow their children to be educated in Church schools. (Ironically, the Marqués de Beramendi, who had opposed clerical intervention in family life in the fourth series of *episodios,* entrusts his daughters to the Jesuits; other new aristocrats send their daughters to the Order of the Sacred Heart.) Teaching little more than the catechism and a few rudimentary and frivolous social accomplishments, the priestly educators plan for the long term, to gain control of the property of the future husbands of their docile pupils: "—Donde aprenden Catecismo a todo pasto, nociones incompletas de Aritmética y Geografía, mascullar el francés, un machaqueo de piano para romper los oídos de toda la familia, y etiquetas y saluditos a estilo de *París de Francia*. . . Al cuidado de los buenos Padres, éstos aguardan a que las educandas sean señoras para meter las narices en sus hogares, adueñándose del marido y de los hijos, y por fin, esperan cachazudos y tenaces a que se hagan viejas idiotas para quitarles todo lo que tienen" (p. 249).

In a vision bordering on paranoia, Galdós, through Tito and his attendant nymphs, discovers the key to modern Spanish history: hordes of foreign friars ("plaga de insectos voraces") swarm into all regions of Spain to enslave the nation. The clerical invasion is as calamitous in its consequences as those of the Visigoths and Moors: " ¡Pobres majaderos! Desconocían en absoluto la gravísima situación de nuestro país, el momento histórico, semejante a la entrada de los cartagineses ávidos de riqueza, de los bárbaros visigodos o de los insaciables y feroces agarenos. Nada sabían, nada sospechaban: se enterarían de la nueva esclavitud cuando ésta ya no tuviese remedio."[37] The Jesuit Order most alarms Galdós. Avidly appropriating the wealth of Spain, the Jesuits, and not Alfonso XII, are the true rulers of the nation: "Aquí no reina Alfonso XII, sino el bendito San Ignacio, que a mi parecer está en el cielo, sentadito a la izquierda de Dios Padre" (p. 272).

In the bitter closing lines of *Cánovas,* Mariclío expounds what was to be the final teaching of Galdós in the *episodios*. The "peace" of the Restoration is a slow, creeping paralysis that consumes and destroys the nation. Sterile, self-seeking politicians neglect the agriculture, instruction, commerce, and industry of Spain. They surrender the national educational system, wealth, and even independence to the Church. In the face of the approaching death of the nation, but one remedy remains: *Revolution*. Here is Mariclío's exhortation, the closing paragraphs of the *episodios nacionales:*

Pero la paz es un mal si representa la pereza de una raza, y su incapacidad para dar práctica solución a los fundamentales empeños del comer y del pensar. Los *tiempos bobos* que te anuncié has de verlos desarrollarse en años y lustros de atonía, de lenta parálisis, que os llevará a la consunción y a la muerte.

Los políticos se constituirán en casta, dividiéndose hipócritas en dos bandos igualmente dinásticos e igualmente estériles, sin otro móvil que tejer y destejer la jerga de sus provechos particulares en el telar burocrático. No harán nada fecundo; no crearán una Nación; no remediarán la esterilidad de las estepas castellanas y extremeñas; no suavizarán el malestar de las clases proletarias. Fomentarán la artillería antes que las escuelas, las pompas regias antes que las vías comerciales y los menesteres de la grande y pequeña industria. Y por último, hijo mío, verás si vives que acabarán por poner la enseñanza, la riqueza, el poder civil, y hasta la independencia nacional, en manos de lo que llamáis vuestra Santa Madre Iglesia.

Alarmante es la palabra Revolución. Pero si no inventáis otra menos aterradora, no tendréis más remedio que usarla los que no queráis morir de la honda caquexia que invade el cansado cuerpo de tu Nación. Declaraos revolucionarios, díscolos si os parece mejor esta palabra, contumaces en la rebeldía. En la situación a que llegaréis andando los años, el ideal revolucionario, la actitud indómita si queréis, constituirán el único síntoma de vida. Siga el lenguaje de los bobos llamando paz a lo que en realidad es consunción y acabamiento . . . Sed constantes en la protesta, sed viriles, románticos, y mientras no venzáis a la muerte, no os ocupéis de Mariclío. . . . Yo, que ya me siento demasiado clásica, me aburro . . . me duermo (pp. 277-78).

Epilogue

Galdós's message in the third, fourth, and fifth series of *episodios nacionales* has already been summarized. The following remarks address certain biases in Galdós's approach to the past, not the content of his teaching.

In part, Galdós uses the *episodios* to comment directly on the concerns of his own day. The mark of 1898 is apparent in his warnings against fraternal strife, his disgust with rhetoric,[1] and his hostility to Spanish involvement in foreign adventures. He for a while flirts with Costa's authoritarian solutions to Spain's problems. By early 1900, however, he openly satirizes the fatuous arrogance of self-appointed regenerators. Contemporary Liberal campaigns to submit the Church to a *Ley de Asociaciones* have their counterpart in the virulent anticlericalism of certain *episodios*. Such issues of the early twentieth century as the education of princes, the influence of *camarillas*, and Catalan claims to special treatment all provoke Galdós's remark. Portrayal of the past is affected by the politics of the present. Thus, the Revolution of 1868, grudgingly accepted in *Prim* (1906), is, after Galdós's conversion to Republicanism, harshly attacked in *La de los tristes destinos* (1907). Similarly, in novel after novel of the fifth series, Galdós lectures the Republicans of his own day on the shortcomings of their political ancestors.

Galdós's treatment of the past is selective and is strongly colored by hindsight. Within the individual *episodio*, Galdós traces the reactions of those observing and participating in history. His overriding vision, however, reflects less the perceptions of the Spaniards of a previous age than Galdós's preconceived determination that the events he evokes are links in a chain leading to the "disaster" of the end of the century. The wealth of historical detail, the brilliant pastiches, the consistent, if pessimistic, vision of nineteenth-century Spain, will, I believe, deceive the reader anxious for enlightenment on Spain's past. The Spain so vividly created in the *episodios* reflects the fertile imagination of a novelist, not the reasoned assembly of facts and arguments of a historian. Galdós's research for the *episodios* was hasty; he sought from sources and correspondents colorful details rather than an understanding of the past on its own terms. Historical recreation was often accessory[2] to the exigencies of a fictional narrative rooted in a moral vision of Spain.

Galdós's rejection of conventional histories is most apparent in the *episodios* of the fourth and fifth series: "history" is now merely the symptom of an underlying reality, which is best expressed in terms of literary metaphor (the styling of periods or events as "tragic" or "comic opera," the recourse to symbolic characters and to fantasy). Indicative of his increasing aversion to a history based on facts are the "historians" he portrays in the later *episodios:* the unstable Fajardo who seeks, in his history, an abstraction, the essential soul of Spain; the demented *Confusio,* who composes his "logical history" of Spain in a lunatic asylum; and Tito Liviano, who as narrator doubts his own existence.

Galdós's most marked bias in the later *episodios* is that of an all-pervading pessimism. The hostility, and even contempt, with which he regards his compatriots is at times staggering. Galdós's Spain is but one step away from extinction: neglect of agriculture, racial degeneration, civil war, murder, suicide, and mindless despotism characterize a nation driven to self-destruction. The pages of the *episodios nacionales* teem with whores, opportunistic politicians, degenerate aristocrats, Carlist savages, hypocrites, and the fatuous. Rare in these novels are those who, such as the Arratias, contribute in positive fashion to national life. But above all else, Galdós populates the *episodios* with madmen: the schizophrenic Fago; the ranting, suicidal young Calpena; the hysterical Aura Negretti who sets out to kill her guardian; Nelet, murderer and suicide; Santiago Ibero, violent, superstitious, and afflicted by religious melancholia; Alonso de Castro-Amézaga, Montes de Oca, and General Ortega, quixotic dreamers whose idealism masks a suicidal urge; the Fajardo who, guided by his unconscious, murders Bartolomé Gracián; this same Gracián, forever seeking the impossible; a Lucila who, before her marriage, is homicidal and deranged; Santiuste, who acts compulsively and who ends his career in an asylum for the insane; the mentally unbalanced Santiago Ibero the

younger; the homicidally insane Fernanda; Nicéfora, neurotically beyond the reach of any reason; and Tito Liviano, neurotic, fickle, a prey
to panic terrors, reduced at times to idiocy.

Despite Galdós's constant strictures against abstract thought, the
Spain of the later *episodios nacionales* is at heart an abstraction. In his
two historical novels—*El Audaz* and *La Fontana de Oro*—Galdós had
portrayed individuals caught up in a concrete historical situation. In the
episodios, however, novelistic characters embody aspects of the national soul; they symbolize (with corresponding loss of individuality),
rather than respond to, the historical context. Thus, Galdós rarely seeks
to explain the past by the interplay of historical forces or individual
decisions. Instead, historical events are merely symptoms of an insanity
that has afflicted Spanish life throughout the nineteenth century. The
analysis of Spain's madness is consequently of greater concern to
Galdós than the deeds of historic figures.

Because Spain's problems are rooted not in history but in the mind,
Galdós's remedies are those of the alienist, not of the politician or of
the social planner.[3] There are no national solutions; an individual may
with difficulty reform himself, but the reform of others is an impossibility. Ideology is irrelevant; behavior has primacy over thought.
(Thus, our day-to-day activities, rather than our goals or beliefs, determine our mode of being.) Spaniards must avoid excessive excitement
or—the reverse side of Quixotry—skepticism or depression. To this end,
their activities must be ordered by intelligent direction, by the equivalent, indeed, of a parent or director of a lunatic asylum.[4] The new
Spaniard, "cured" by experience and by reflection of compulsive behavior, will view the world dispassionately. He will have self-knowledge
(and the examination in the *episodios* of Spain's past will reveal the
self-defeating pattern of Spanish existence), will devote himself to work
(and Fajardo's writing is presented as a form of therapy), and will be
aware of and interested in others.

If we accept Galdós's initial premises—that nation may be assimilated to individual, that Spaniards, both collectively and individually,
are insane—Galdós's prescriptions for moral reform are unassailable. In
the Spain portrayed in the *episodios,* however, Galdós's remedies are
utopian and without practical consequences. Galdós, in any case, has
little faith that a new Spaniard—aware, decisive, emotionally detached—will replace the old. The appeals for total revolution, which
extend in the *episodios* from *Mendizábal* to the final novel *Cánovas,*

reflect disgust with the past and present behavior of Spaniards, not a vision of the future. The revolution, moreover, is not intended for the Spaniards whom Galdós so harshly castigates in the *episodios:* Tito Liviano must be totally reconstructed before entry into the promised land is possible. Significantly, Galdós is unable to envision in a Spanish context those few Spaniards (the Calpenas and the Iberos, Teresa Villaescusa and Santiaguito Ibero) who do achieve spiritual health. Their moral growth takes place independently of history; they remove themselves from Spanish reality, fleeing to the never-never land of France. Paradoxically, those who have truly learned the lesson of experience can no longer contribute to Spain; thus, Santiaguito Ibero in 1868 immediately abandons the Revolution for which he had so long struggled.

I have been unable to discern in the *episodios nacionales* the "benevolence" that other critics have perceived in these novels; indeed, Galdós's hostility to his fellow countrymen is often savage. Rather than benevolent, Galdós is evasive in his treatment of persons and matters that touch him closely: he is guarded in his judgments of such political figures of his own lifetime as Prim, Cánovas, and Sagasta; he manifestly shirks coming to terms, in *La vuelta al mundo en la Numancia,* with the agrarian problem; he is most reticent in the brief references in the fifth series to his own youth in Madrid. A similar pattern of retreat is evident in the behavior of the protagonists of the *episodios:* involvement in political activity is followed by withdrawal, even flight.[5] Furthermore, the "keys" with which Galdós explains Spanish history—national insanity, atavism, the preponderant role of the Church—represent an oversimplification, a refusal to treat in all its complexity a given historical situation.

I wish to conclude my study on a note that, given the inadequacy of our knowledge of the man Galdós, must necessarily be speculative. In the later *episodios,* Galdós has, I suspect, transferred to the national scene a conflict that has its origins within his own psyche. At the most superficial level, Galdós offers soothing remedies for an overexcited nation: a calm detachment, self-awareness, therapeutic labor, the avoidance of fantasy, even at times the indulgent protection of a loving woman. When outside world and elements from within himself cannot be brought into harmony, Galdós takes refuge in evasion.[6] But at a deeper level—and one that receives free rein in the later *episodios*— Galdós is bitterly hostile and obsessed with themes of madness, of nightmare, and of catastrophe. The "Spain" that Galdós so unsympathetically analyzes in the *episodios* is in part himself; the excesses against which he warns us—of the imagination, of a too great facility with words, of confusing word for deed—are his own; his "remedies" smack of personal defenses against internal demons. It is a common place that Galdós in part portrayed himself in Vicente Halconero (his youth in Madrid, his readings, his "half-will") and in Tito Liviano (his journalism, his seedy amorousness, his temporary physical blindness). It is possible also, I would suggest, that darker elements of Galdós's soul entered the portrayals of Halconero and Liviano: Halconero's suicidal thoughts (after amorous disappointment); Tito Liviano's melancholia, terrors, and depression.[7] Similarly, Bartolomé Gracián's neurotic pursuit of the impossible, so vividly etched in *La revolución de julio*, is also Galdós's own;[8] Gracián's murder, by Galdós's alter ego Fajardo, represents Galdós's brutal disposal of socially destructive elements existing within his own character. The therapeutic message of the *episodios* was not only intended for the nation, it was also, in part, Galdós's dialogue with himself.

Notes

INTRODUCTION

1. Two recent works exemplify the contribution that careful scholarship can make to our knowledge of Galdós's journalism; they are Leo J. Hoar, Jr., *Benito Pèrez Galdós y la "Revista del Movimiento Intelectual de Europa"* (Madrid, 1968), and William H. Shoemaker, *Los artículos de Galdós en "La Nación"* (Madrid, 1972).

2. Geoffrey Ribbans, "Ricardo Gullón and the Novels of Galdós," *Anales Galdosianos* 3 (1968): 163.

3. The mature Galdós is now less concerned with retailing historical "facts" than in the earlier series; the imagination—rather than sources—increasingly directs his recreation of the past; the narratorial awkwardness, so evident in the early novels, has long disappeared.

Chapter One

1. Quoted by Iris M. Zavala, "La prensa ante la revolución de 1868," in *La revolución de 1868*, ed. Clara E. Lida and Iris M. Zavala (New York, 1970), pp. 298-99. For further information on the policies of Albareda and the *Revista de España*, see Brian J. Dendle, "Albareda, Galdós and the *Revista de España* (1868-1873)," in Lida and Zavala, *La revolución de 1868*, pp. 362-77.

2. Cf. Galdós's reference, when discussing this period, to the "pesimismo que todos los españoles del siglo XIX llevamos dentro" (Benito Pérez Galdós, *España trágica* [Madrid, 1909], p. 188).

3. For a discussion of Cánovas's system, see Raymond Carr, *Spain 1808-1939* (Oxford, 1966), pp. 346-88.

4. See, for example, Antonio María Fabié, *Cánovas del Castillo* (Barcelona, 1928), p. 111, for an account of the electoral agreement between Cánovas and Sagasta in 1876. Sagasta agreed to the "election" of thirty of his closest followers; four days before the "election," Romero Robledo (the minister of the interior) exchanged the districts of nearly two hundred prospective deputies, the aim being, apparently, to prevent their building a base of power by representing districts in which they had local roots.

5. "El Parlamento elegido por sufragio restringido ha sido en España mucho más digno, independiente y viril que aquel que la voluntad popular dio de sí. Apenas los pueblos y aldeas se acostumbraron a considerar cada elección como un suplemento de cosecha, o una manera de comer y beber sin tasa durante el período electoral a costa ajena, la emisión del voto convirtióse en una operación de toma y daca y chalaneo" (Fabié, p. 234).

6. For a satirical vision of the operation of the *turno* at the local level, see the opening paragraph of Chapter 8 of Leopoldo Alas, *La regenta* (Barcelona,

1884-1885). Alas describes the mutual assistance and patronage rendered by Conservative and Liberal leaders in a provincial town, despite the bitter disputes of their more ideologically inclined followers.

7. See Melchor Fernández Almagro, *Historia política de la España contemporánea* (Madrid, 1968), I: 336. Subsequent references to Fernández Almagro in this chapter will be to the three volumes of this work.

8. Quoted by Fernández Almagro, 2:149.

9. Quoted by José Cepeda Adán, *El 98 en Madrid* (Madrid, 1954), p. 7.

10. José Francos Rodríguez, *Contar vejeces* (Madrid, n.d.), p. 256.

11. See Francos Rodríguez, pp. 343-49.

12. Quoted by Fernández Almagro, 3:46.

13. Leonard Williams, *The Land of the Dons* (London, 1902), p. 327.

14. Quoted by Cepeda Adán, p. 26.

15. Cepeda Adán, pp. 18-19. See also Fernández Almagro, 3:176-83.

16. Quoted by Luis S. Granjel, *Panorama de la generación del 98* (Madrid, 1959), p. 186.

17. Quoted by Fernández Almagro, 3:157.

18. Polavieja promised to Catalonia a new agreement for compounding taxation, municipal reorganization, the uniting of the four provincial *diputaciones,* increased technical education, and respect for Catalan civil law. This appeal to Catalan regionalist aspirations led to the formation in Barcelona of a *Junta de adhesiones al programa del general Polavieja.* See Fernández Almagro, 3:166-67, and E. Allison Peers, *Catalonia Infelix* (London, 1937), p. 140.

19. See Fernández Almagro, 3:164-65.

20. Although Polavieja's program was neutral on religious matters, his reputation as an ardent Catholic believer (he was commonly referred to as "el general cristiano") led to his obtaining support almost exclusively from the Catholic right, disillusioned equally by the internal quarrels of the Carlists and by the policies of expediency adopted by Cánovas's Conservatives. See Gabriel Maura Gamazo, *Historia crítica del reinado de don Alfonso XIII durante su menoridad* (Barcelona, 1925), 2:64-65.

21. See Carr, pp. 391-94.

22. By 1894, 60 percent of Catalonia's export trade was with Cuba. (See Carr, p. 397.) At the time of the Spanish-American War, 95 percent of Catalan exports of textiles were sold to the overseas possessions; see Joan Connelly Ullman, *The Tragic Week* (Cambridge, Mass., 1968), p. 67.

23. Maura's proposal, fifteen years later, to grant corporative representation was one of the leading causes of Liberal opposition to his municipal reform bill, intended to eliminate *caciquismo* in Spain.

24. "En cada comarca, según su carácter agrícola, industrial, comercial, etc., se establecerán escuelas prácticas de agricultura, de artes y oficios, de comercio, etcétera. Deberá informar los planes de enseñanza el principio de dividir y especializar las carreras, evitando las carreras enciclopédicas." Quoted by Fernández Almagro, 2:174-75.

25. See Peers, p. 139.

26. Weyler, relieved of his post by Sagasta, received a tumultuous welcome in Barcelona; Weyler had been born in Mallorca.

27. Pi y Margall, however, objected that the ministry was "reactionary and regionalist" and denied its popularity: "La significación reaccionaria y regionalista de este Ministerio determinó la frialdad y la desconfianza con que fue por la

opinión recibida." Francisco Pi y Margall and Francisco Pi y Arsuaga, *Historia de España en el siglo XIX*, vol. 7, pt. 2 (Barcelona, 1902), p. 1783.

28. Nevertheless, Silvela's elections were conducted in the same arbitrary manner as those of previous Restoration and Regency ministries; *caciquismo* was as firmly entrenched at the end of his rule as at the beginning.

29. Quoted by Fernández Almagro, 3:221.

30. Julio Busquets has calculated that, after the disaster of 1898, the Spanish army had 499 generals, 578 colonels, and over 23,000 officers to command some 80,000 troops. See Carlos Seco Serrano, *Alfonso XIII y la crisis de la Restauración* (Barcelona, 1969), p. 40.

31. Quoted by Pi y Margall, vol. 7, pt. 2, p. 1834.

32. Pi y Margall (whose own bizarre proposal was that the clerical budget should be suppressed, the money thus saved being sufficient to finance not only regeneration but also most state pensions) commented aptly on the selfishly partisan interest revealed by the *clases productoras*, who at one and the same time demanded a reduction in taxes and massive state investment in public works: "Es gracioso eso de las clases productoras. Por lo que se dice, no pertenecen a esas clases sino los que no producen: los comerciantes, los banqueros, los dueños de fábricas, talleres o minas, los terratenientes" (Quoted in Pi y Margall, vol. 7, pt. 2, p. 1791).

33. Angel Ganivet, *Idearium español* (Buenos Aires, 1949), p. 82.

34. Costa knew the injustices of Spanish society from bitter personal experience. Born in a poor family of Upper Aragon, he won an education at the cost of tremendous sacrifice. An indefatigable worker—he wrote forty-two books, as well as countless articles—he labored as teacher, part-time journalist, functionary, and country lawyer, but at no moment in his life was he able to free himself from poverty. Favoritism denied him the university chairs that he sought; the hostility of local *caciques* interfered with his humble provincial career; his intransigence and irascible temperament—the consequence, perhaps, of his early struggles and a lifetime of ill health—prevented his using to advantage the few opportunities for advancement offered to him. For a while, Costa sought to effect reforms from within the Spanish political system; in the early 1890s, he organized in Upper Aragon groups of agriculturists and taxpayers. His attempts to obtain election to the Cortes as an independent candidate were, however, unsuccessful. His publications include numerous studies of Spanish law, studies of agriculture, research into the early inhabitants of Spain, proposals for African exploration and colonization, and, above all, calls for the total reform of the political and social structure of Spain.

35. See Enrique Tierno Galván, *Costa y el regeneracionismo* (Barcelona, 1961), pp. 157, 240-242. See also, for the utopian, impractical nature of the program hatched by the businessmen of Spain, Fernández Almagro, 3:244.

36. See G. J. G. Cheyne, "From Galdós to Costa in 1901," *Anales Galdosianos* 3 (1968): 95-98.

37. Quoted by Pi y Margall and Pi y Arsuaga, vol. 7, pt. 2, p. 1501. The complete text of the *Consulta* is reproduced in Pi, pp. 1500-1523; my citations are from this text.

38. Joaquín Costa, *Oligarquía y caciquismo* (Madrid, 1967), pp. 20-21.

39. Ramiro de Maeztu, "Un suicidio," *Hacia otra España* (Madrid, 1967), pp. 101-2.

40. Ricardo Macías Picavea, *El problema nacional* (Madrid, 1899). The work

was composed between November 1898 and February 1899, that is, when calls for "regeneration" were most strident and widespread.

Chapter Two

1. Benito Pérez Galdós, *Un faccioso más y unos frailes menos* (Madrid, 1898), pp. 320-21.

2. See José F. Montesinos, *Galdós* (Madrid, 1973), 3:16.

3. See Benito Pérez Galdós, *Memorias* (Madrid, 1930), p. 222.

4. For a discussion of this point, see Montesinos, 3:16.

5. Cf. Calpena's admiration of the domestic and agricultural virtues of Demetria.

6. See *Los Ayachuchos* (Madrid, 1900), p. 19. Cf. also Calpena's coming to terms with *La desconocida,* that is, with the past of Spain. For a lucid discussion of Galdós's exposition of similar "Regenerationist" attitudes in the decades prior to 1898, see Peter B. Goldman, "Galdós and the Nineteenth Century Novel: The Need for an Interdisciplinary Approach," *Anales Galdosianos* 10 (1975): 5-18.

7. Benito Pérez Galdós, *De Oñate a la Granja* (Madrid, 1989), p. 185.

8. Benito Pérez Galdós, *La estafeta romántica* (Madrid, 1899), pp. 38-39. The reference to "statistics" is typical of a Regenerationist viewpoint; see Enrique Tierno Galván, *Costa y el regeneracionismo,* pp. 38, 48-49.

9. Cf. the calls by Costa, Silvela, Polavieja, and others for policies based on "reality."

10. Benito Pérez Galdós, *Bodas reales* (Madrid, 1900), p. 29.

11. Benito Pérez Galdós, *Mendizábal* (Madrid, 1898), p. 44.

12. Benito Pérez Galdós, *La Campaña del Maestrazgo* (Madrid, 1899), p. 242.

13. Benito Pérez Galdós, *De Oñate a la Granja,* p. 112.

14. *Bodas reales,* written in the fall of 1900, represents the abandonment of Galdós's earlier optimism.

15. The only minor exceptions are the references to the pressure of foreign bankers on Don Carlos to take Bilbao and to English intervention to negotiate the Elliot Convention.

16. See E. Gómez de Baquero, "Crónica literaria," *La España Moderna* (July 1898), p. 180.

17. Galdós's hasty "research" for the noval consisted of little more than the adaptation of certain passages of Zaratiegui's *Vida y hechos de Zumalacárregui,* supplemented by a rapidly curtailed visit to the Basque Provinces; see G. Boussagol, "Sources et Composition du *Zumalacárregui,*" *Bulletin Hispanique* 26 (1924): 241-64; and Montesinos, 3: 19-20.

18. Juan Bautista Avalle-Arce, *"Zumalacárregui,"* *Cuadernos Hispano-americanos,* Nos. 250-52 (1970-1971): 356-73. A further sensitive treatment of Fago is that of Alfred Rodríguez, *An Introduction to the Episodios Nacionales of Galdós* (New York, 1967), pp. 116-17.

19. Benito Pérez Galdós, *Zumalacárregui* (Madrid, 1898), p. 115.

20. Cf. Fago's remarks to Zumalacárregui: "Pienso yo, mi General, que nos afanamos más de la cuenta por las que llaman *causas,* y que entre éstas, aun las que parecen más contradictorias, no hay diferencias tan grandes como grandes son y profundos los ríos de sangre que las separan" (p. 303).

21. Note, as metaphor of the role of chance in human affairs, that both characters have a more humble namesake in the novel: Mendizábal, in the person of the porter Méndez, and Muñoz in the police-spy *Edipo.*

22. Benito Pérez Galdós, *Mendizábal*, p. 199.

23. The teaching was not novel; Galdós had indicated a similar lesson in *La desheredada* (1881). Costa's later call for a padlock on the Cid's tomb is identical in purpose.

24. Curiously, in the month following completion of *Mendizábal*, Costa sought to organize these same businessmen (the *clases productoras*) as a pressure group to regenerate the nation.

25. Benito Pérez Galdós, *De Oñate a la Granja*, p. 185.

26. Galdós's malicious remark on religious statues presages the anticlericalism of the later *episodios:* "Le querían a don Carlos de veras, sin conocerle más que como se conoce a las imágenes de iglesia, que no hablan ni se mueven, pues si hablasen, quizás muchas de ellas no tendrían tantos devotos" (p. 204). By way of contrast to Carlist hypocrisy, Demetria and Gracia, the daughters of the liberal paladin Don Alonso de Castro-Amézaga, exemplify a simple religious faith that finds expression in charitable works rather than in ostentatious rites.

27. Note also, in this respect, *La desconocida*'s forceful analysis of the reasons for Mendizábal's failure (his rashness, his lack of experience of Spanish life): "No se gobierna con éxito a un país con los resortes del instinto, de las corazonadas, de los golpes de audacia, de los ensayos atrevidos. Se necesitan otras dotes que da la práctica, y que, unidas al entendimiento, producen el perfecto gobernante. Aquí no hay nadie que valga dos cuartos. Todos son unos intrigantes en la oposición, y unos caciquillos en el poder" (p. 31).

28. Benito Pérez Galdós, *Luchana* (Madrid, 1899), p. 12.

29. Thus, Zoilo Arratia willingly abandons Aura on the night of their betrothal to serve in the position of greatest danger.

30. Galdós is not only defending the values of entrepreneurial capitalism, he is implicitly attacking those whose ambition is to live at public expense. (See *De Oñate a la Granja*, p. 219, for Ildefonso Negretti's contempt for *empleados*.) A reduction in the number of governmental employes was a major feature of Costa's program.

31. Cf. Galdós's admiring portrayal, in *La primera república* (1911), of Vulcan, the "forger of Spanish wills."

32. Curiously, the phrase which Zoilo so often repeats—"yo me basto y me sobro"—is identical to that with which the Mosén Antón of *Juan Martín el Empecinado* celebrated a satanic vanity.

33. Benito Pérez Galdós, *La Campaña del Maestrazgo*, p. 160.

34. Benito Pérez Galdós, *La estafeta romántica*, p. 132. Pilar de Loaysa was overoptimistic: a novelistic generation later, Tito Liviano, in *La primera república* (1911), is advised that he must wait a further generation for the Spanish offspring of the combination of the will and intelligence.

35. Cf. Ildefonso Negretti's matter-of-fact reception of Calpena in *De Oñate a la Granja*, when Calpena's "drama" is converted into a *comedia casera*.

36. Thus, Galdós establishes parallels between the two camps: both Espartero and Maroto are men of courage and ability who serve ungrateful monarchs; both generals impose their authority by executing mutinous troops; both Carlist and liberal camps are split by dissension and personal ambition; in both Carlist and liberal Spain, personal favor, not legality, decides judicial questions.

37. Benito Pérez Galdós, *Vergara* (Madrid, 1899), p. 111.

38. Curiously, the text makes clear that the Navarrese are rebelling against a contumacious general and in loyalty to their monarch, Don Carlos. Disorder, however, is blamed not on military leadership but on the inept governments of

liberal and Carlist Spain. Cf. also Galdós's contempt in *La primera república* for Salmerón's refusal to order the execution of mutinous troops.

39. Benito Pérez Galdós, *Montes de Oca* (Madrid, 1900), pp. 82-83. Galdós can only speculate as novelist, not as historian, at the motives of María Cristina and Montes de Oca.

40. Costa had, of course, leveled similar charges against the admirers of the constitutional revisions and "democratic" revolutions of nineteenth-century Spain. See pp. 29-30.

41. Benito Pérez Galdós, *Los Ayacuchos*, p. 194.

42. In letters written to the novelist Oller between 1884 and 1886, Galdós had berated Oller for writing in Catalan, had proclaimed the advantages to Catalonia of Spain's protectionist policies (separatism and protection were, Galdós declared, antithetical concepts), and had cavalierly dismissed all talk of separatism as empty coffee-house gossip. See W. H. Shoemaker, "Una amistad literaria: La correspondencia epistolar entre Galdós y Narciso Oller," *Real Academia de Buenas Letras* (Barcelona, 1964), pp. 1-60.

43. The end in this case is the satisfaction of Demetria's demand that, before her marriage to Calpena, Santiago Ibero and Gracia be reunited, a reunion that will restore mental and spiritual health to them both. Note also that Santiago Ibero represents a sick Spain; his situation is akin to that of Calpena before his forcible cure by his mother.

44. Romanticism itself is attacked as harshly as in previous novels, in the person of Santiago Ibero who, wallowing in self-humiliation after being disappointed in his love for Rafaela del Milagro, retreats into madness and religious melancholia.

45. Calpena describes his decision (ironically) in quixotic terms: "En fin, miradme, Cielos, nuevamente lanzado a la andante caballería; miradme vestido de todas armas, pronto a combatir por altos ideales de justicia, ansioso de perseguir el mal y aniquilarlo, y de acometer toda obra de reparación en obsequio de la virtud; mirad en mí al infatigable soldado del bien" (p. 178).

46. Benito Pérez Galdós, *Bodas reales*, p. 31. Cf. his protest in *De Cartago a Sagunto* (1911) at the military coup that ended the Republic.

Chapter Three

1. J. M. Carretero, "Don Benito Pérez Galdós," *Por esos mundos,* April 1905, p. 348. Quoted by José F. Montesinos, *Galdós* (Madrid, 1968), 1: 81-82.

2. "Public opinion," at least in Madrid, was in any case created by a press secretly subsidized by the government. The virulent hostility of the press to Maura's rule is in part to be explained by his suppression (when minister of the interior in 1902) of payments to journalists (the "fondo de reptiles").

3. Melchor Fernández Almagro, *Historia del reinado de Don Alfonso XII* (Barcelona, 1934), pp. 2-3. (Subsequent references to Fernández Almagro in this chapter will be to this work and will be given in the text.) Cf. Galdós's attack on a corrosive skepticism destructive of all hope of change in *Narváez* (1902) and his rejection of cynicism in *La de los tristes destinos* (1907).

4. Gabriel Maura Gamazo, *Historia crítica del reinado de don Alfonso XIII durante su menoridad* (Barcelona, 1925), 2: 105.

5. *El Ejército Español* (27 November 1905). Quoted by Fernando Díaz-Plaja, *Antecedentes de la Guerra Española en sus documentos (1900-1923)* (Madrid, 1969), p. 101.

6. See Aurelio Martín Alonso, *Diez y seis años de regencia* (Barcelona, 1914), pp. 494-95.

7. Silvela later explained his resignation as motivated by his loss of hope and faith.

8. For a defense of Alfonso's political role in this period, see Carlos Seco Serrano, *Alfonso XIII y la crisis de la Restauración* (Barcelona, 1969), pp. 55-75.

9. For a similar use, at a slightly later date, of anticlericalism to prop up existing institutions, see Ullman, p. 323.

10. *El Siglo Futuro* (28 December 1900). Quoted by Fernando Díaz-Plaja, *Los antecedentes de la Guerra Civil*, p. 23.

11. See E. Inman Fox, "Galdós's *Electra*," *Anales Galdosianos* 1 (1966): 132.

12. A Jesuit priest was accused of having enticed a girl to enter a religious order without maternal consent, a "secuestro moral," in the words of the mother's lawyer, the Republican Salmerón; the court decided in favor of the mother. Later, upon attaining her majority, Adelaida Ubao returned to the convent.

13. By the Concordat, three religious orders were authorized in Spain: those of Saint Vincent de Paul, Saint Philip Neri, and a third unnamed. The Spanish government had maintained that only one more order was permitted in Spain; the Vatican claimed that a third order was permitted in each diocese.

14. Quoted in Diego Sevilla Andrés, *Antonio Maura. La revolución desde arriba* (Barcelona, 1954), p. 235. For an example of the violent hostility of an anticlerical to the very toleration of religious orders in Spain, see Luis Morote, *Los frailes on España* (Madrid, 1904). Morote was two and a half years after publication of this work to play a key role in the conversion of Galdós to Republicanism. See H. Chonon Berkowitz, *Pérez Galdós Spanish Liberal Crusader* (Madison, Wis., 1948), p. 388.

15. In the same year, Catholics demanded the suppression of lay schools, capitalizing on the arrest of Francisco Ferrer, the director of the *Escuela Moderna* of Barcelona, who was accused of complicity in the anarchist bomb attack on the royal wedding procession in May.

16. Quoted by Luis Antón del Olmet and Arturo García Carraffa, *Galdós* (Madrid, 1912), pp. 115-16.

17. See Fernández Almagro, pp. 29-30. The Liberals were divided on the question of state intervention in economic matters. Thus, Urzaiz, as minister of the treasury, strongly opposed Romanones's proposals for public works to relieve distress in Andalusia in 1905.

18. Benito Pérez Galdós, *O'Donnell* (Madrid, 1904), p. 142.

19. Benito Pérez Galdós, *Las tormentas del 48* (Madrid, 1902), p. 302.

20. Benito Pérez Galdós, *Narváez* (Madrid, 1902), p. 126.

21. Benito Pérez Galdós, *La revolución de julio* (Madrid, 1903), p. 19.

22. Benito Pérez Galdós, *La de los tristes destinos* (Madrid, 1907), p. 311.

23. Benito Pérez Galdós, *Prim* (Madrid, 1906), p. 251.

24. Hans Hinterhauser, *Los "episodios nacionales" de Benito Pérez Galdós* (Madrid, 1963), pp. 202-3.

25. Benito Pérez Galdós, *La vuelta al mundo en la Numancia* (Madrid, 1906), p. 31.

26. Fajardo is an example of that *proteísmo* which I have discussed elsewhere; see Brian J. Dendle, "Galdós and the Death of Prim," *Anales Galdosianos* 3 (1969): 67. Even Fajardo's literary style is not his own; the early part of the "Confessions" is in imitation of the style of the *Guzmán de Alfarache*.

27. Benito Pérez Galdós, *Las tormentas del 48*, p. 255.
28. See Ullman, pp. 35-37, for a discussion of resentment of the reputed financial power of religious orders in the Spain of the early twentieth century. Galdós in *Electra*, the action of which is, according to the stage directions, *rigurosamente contemporánea*, offers a farfetched account of the conveyance by aristocratic speculators of vast sums of money to the Church; in this drama, the sinister clerical Pantoja also speculates for his own account.
29. Cf. Galdós's affirmation of the rights of property in his declaration of war on poverty and injustice in an article of November 1903: "Creemos que la pobreza es un mal y una injusticia, y la combatiremos dentro de la estricta ley del 'tuyo y mío.' " Benito Pérez Galdós, "Soñemos, alma, soñemos," *Memoranda* (Madrid, 1906), p. 238.
30. Benito Pérez Galdós, *Narváez*, p. 190.
31. Cf. the timid claim by the Spanish government in early 1902 to regulate religious orders by the *Ley de Asociaciones*, an assertion vigorously rejected by the Vatican.
32. See Fernández Almagro, pp. 17-18, for details of charges leveled by Canalejas in the late spring and early summer of 1902 of improper palace influences on Alfonso XIII to interfere in the political life of the nation. Fernández Almagro repeats Romanones's accusation that palace pressures at this time delayed the award of the Grand Cross of Alfonso XII to Galdós.
33. For a sensible treatment of the confusion that accompanies Galdós's "symbolic" treatment of the Ansúrez family, see Montesinos, 3:130-33.
34. Benito Pérez Galdós, *Los duendes de la camarilla* (Madrid, 1903), p. 32.
35. The attribution of a superior Christianity to those who doubt the authority and dogmas of the Church was common in anticlerical novelists, from Sue onwards. For Spanish examples, see Brian J. Dendle, *The Spanish Novel of Religious Thesis* (Madrid, 1968), pp. 38-40, 71-74, 95-97.
36. In her tenderness, total sacrifice of self to the object of her love, and subsequent despair at abandonment, Lucila has much in common with *La Salada* of Espronceda's *El diablo mundo; La Salada* is, indeed, the obvious model for Galdós's Lucila. Cf. also the opening scene of the novel, in which the mysterious woman (Lucila) hurries through the sinister night in search of her lover, a scene that recalls the opening passages of *El estudiante de Salamanca*.
37. Costa commented on the period in question: "dos generaciones se pasaron la vida gritando *¡viva la libertad!* y tarareando el himno de Riego, en la calle cuando la dejaban, en el cenáculo cuando la reprimían, y a ese grito sacrificó sangre, caudales y vida en guerras civiles, revoluciones y pronunciamientos." Joaquín Costa, *Oligarquía y caciquismo* (Madrid, 1967), p. 22.
38. Benito Pérez Galdós, *La revolución de julio*, p. 45.
39. P. 97. Note that, during the composition of *La revolución de julio,* Galdós "charged the Army with the responsibility of injecting the scientific spirit of modern education into the soul of Spain" (Berkowitz, p. 385). Galdós's speech was delivered to the Círculo Militar de Cartagena, either in December 1903 (Berkowitz, p. 385) or October 1903 (Berkowitz, p. 479 n.).
40. Benito Pérez Galdós, *O'Donnell*, p. 323.
41. Cf. Fernández Bremón's similar treatment of the poverty of civil servants in 1902: "los subalternos de las oficinas, que tienen 16 duros mensuales, es decir, un jornal que no llega a los once reales, con obligación de vestir decentemente, son más pobres y desgraciados que la mayor parte de los obreros de Bar-

celona. . . . Si se añade a esto la enorme cantidad de aspirantes a plazas de cortísimo sueldo, aun sacadas a oposición, en que figuran médicos, abogados, doctores y licenciados en Ciencias, que para vivir se han prestado a matar como verdugos; si se considera la suerte infeliz de los maestros de última clase, con sueldos irrisorios, teniendo a veces que salir a pedir limosna, como vieron las calles de Málaga, o a trabajar como peones, como se ha visto en algunas carreteras; si añadimos a esto los descubrimientos frecuentes que hace la prensa de miserias casi irremediables en familias que tuvieron buena posición y las que oculta en su rubor la pobreza vergonzante, y todo esto no por vagancia y abandono, sino por contrariedades y mala suerte, tras una vida laboriosa, en que la honradez y la buena fe fueron atropelladas por el crimen, la usura y las exigencias sociales, y esta parte de la burguesía es la más numerosa, vean los agitadores si son justos al generalizar sus ataques." Quoted by Fernández Almagro, *Historia política de la España contemporánea*, 3:276.

42. The characterization of Cándido Nocedal is obviously intended to embarrass his son Ramón Nocedal, the editor of the ultramontane *El Siglo Futuro* in the early years of the twentieth century.

43. The Moroccan question came to the fore with the visit of the kaiser to Vigo (March 1904), the Anglo-French Treaty of April 1904, and the Hispano-French Treaty of October 1904. By the latter treaty, the Spanish zone of influence was reduced to the less productive sections of the north of Morocco. Spanish public opinion was indifferent, even hostile, to intervention in Morocco.

44. Benito Pérez Galdós, *Aita Tettauen* (Madrid, 1905), pp. 48-49.

45. Benito Pérez Galdós, *Carlos VI en la Rápita* (Madrid, 1905), p. 21.

46. Juan Ruiz studies not books but man with all his passions: "mis libros las flaquezas, las pasiones, las envidias, las luchas humanas por el pan o por el palo" (p. 193). The inspiration for the archpriest Juan Ruiz is, nevertheless, entirely literary; the irony of using a novel to inveigh against bookishness would surely not have escaped Galdós.

47. See Chapter 3, note 1, above.

48. "El hambre en Andalucía fue tema preferente durante varios meses, de la prensa de todos matices y hasta en la extranjera repercutieron los clamores." Juan Díez del Moral, *Historia de las agitaciones campesinas andaluzas* (Madrid, 1967), p. 212. For an account of libertarian agitation at this time, see Díez del Moral, pp. 221-24.

49. Benito Pérez Galdós, *La vuelta al mundo en la Numancia*, pp. 30-31.

50. Benito Pérez Galdós, *Prim*, p. 41.

51. Cf. the sensible Lucila's dismissal of Cortés as "un vago, un perdido" (*Aita Tettauen*, p. 28).

52. Benito Pérez Galdós, *La de los tristes destinos*, p. 221.

53. Cf. the flight of the Calpenas and Iberos of the third series from Spain. The concluding novels of both the third and fourth series of *episodios (Bodas reales* and *La de los tristes destinos)* are savagely pessimistic in their treatment of Spain. Galdós's harshness toward his compatriots reflects perhaps his assessment of the periods in question, perhaps also a cathartic release from the pressures of research and composition.

54. Moret, in a direct approach to Alfonso, informed the monarch (in a "papelito") that he could no longer support the Liberal prime minister López Domínguez; Moret's treachery served only to split the Liberals and to bring Maura to power.

55. By way of contrast, Galdós presents an idealized vision of Great Britain and her beloved monarch: "¡Nación como ninguna sólida y potente, porque en ella tiene su imperio la Justicia, es respetada la Ley, y amada la persona que la simboliza! " (p. 249) Galdós's admiration for Great Britain was of long date and is iterated in the scenes of London life in the novel. His praise of Great Britain would reinforce the views of those Liberals who favored the growing friendship between Spain and Great Britain; note that Edward VIII and Alfonso XIII met in Cartagena in April 1907. Note also the fears of international conflict expressed in the final paragraph of Galdós's manifesto of April 6, 1907; the reference is surely to the problem of Morocco, to the territory of which France, Germany, and Spain were making claim.

56. Fajardo claims that the training received by the future Alfonso XII will make of him "un caso más de esta inmensa tristeza española, que ya ¡vive Dios! se nos está haciendo secular" (p. 133). Only Galdós's newfound hostility to the monarchy can explain the attribution of "sadness" to a popular monarch, admired for his charm and courage.

57. In August 1906 Romanones authorized civil marriage in Spain without a declaration from the contracting partners of abjuration of Catholicism; his decree, which had stirred much Catholic protest, was withdrawn by the Maura government on March 1, 1907, that is, while *La de los tristes destinos* was in the process of composition.

58. See, for example, Joan Connelly Ullman's documentation of attempts by Radical Republicans in 1909 to win the sympathies of the military (pp. 293-95). Cf. also Melquiades Alvarez's praise of military discipline at the banquet of the *Conjunción Republicano-Socialista* (which Galdós headed) in July 1911. Alvarez claimed that the army and the school are "the two great organs of national energy": "Nosotros no permitiremos que se quebrante la disciplina militar, que es la ley obligada del honor, porque, sin disciplina, el Ejército no es Ejército, es una mesnada entregada a todos los abusos de la fuerza y a todos los desenfrenos de la impunidad. (*Aplausos*.) Es más, y quiero que lo sepa el Ejército, para que dé un mentis a esos miserables engañadores que nos presentan como enemigos suyos: yo he dicho siempre que mientras existan las nacionalidades, que mientras el país sea lo que es hoy, el cuartel y la escuela son dos grandes órganos de la energía nacional, que se auxilian y completan recíprocamente." Quoted by Fernando Soldevilla, *El año político 1911* (Madrid, 1912), p. 289.

59. See Ullman, p. 295.

60. "En aquella ocasión crítica sentí el horror al vacío, horror a la asfixia nacional, dentro del viejo castillo en que se nos quiere tapiar y encerrar para siempre, sin respiro ni horizonte. No había más remedio que echarse fuera en busca de aire libre, del derecho moderno, de la absoluta libertad de conciencia con sus naturales derivaciones, principo *[sic]* vital de los pueblos civilizados. Es ya una vergüenza no ser europeos más que por la geografía, por la ópera italiana y por el uso desenfrenado de los automóviles." Quoted by Olmet and García Carraffa, p. 116.

Chapter Four

1. For an excellent and detailed treatment of the *Semana trágica* and its background, see Ullman.

2. Cf. the opinion of Francos Rodríguez: "Digámoslo con franqueza—escribe

Francos Rodríguez–: los conservadores de 1908 y 1909 no constituyeron una auténtica tiranía; asegurarlo fuera excesiva hipérbole. Sobre que en estos tiempos las tiranías no son posibles, la que se atribuyó a Maura no merecía tal nombre. Estuvo más en las palabras jactanciosas que en las determinaciones represivas. Fue la del Ministerio de aquellos días una reacción algo retórica, bastante teatral y tan ineficaz como molesta." Quoted by Diego Sevilla Andrés, *Canalejas* (Barcelona, 1956), p. 299.

3. Quoted by Fernández Almagro, *Historia del reinado de Don Alfonso XIII*, pp. 154-55.

4. Carlos Seco Serrano indicates the extent to which Canalejas's policies anticipate those of the Second Vatican Council; see Carlos Seco Serrano, *Alfonso XIII y la crisis de la Restauración*, p. 389.

5. Such negotiations were, of course, anathema to anticlericals. Canalejas's preference for a diplomatic solution to the problem is eatablished in Diego Sevilla Andrés, p. 361.

6. The *Conjunción Republicano-Socialista* never forgave Canalejas for the tortuous means by which he replaced Moret (a member of the *Conjunción*) in power. Maura's "sincerity," on the other hand, was acknowledged by many Republicans. Galdós kept in the vestibule of his house a dedicated portrait of Maura (see Olmet and García Carraffa, p. 13). Galdós praised Maura to the two journalists in 1912: "me parece un hombre de gran talento, y sobre todo, un hombre de indiscutible sinceridad. Acaso es de los hombres más sinceros de la política española.... El hombre es admirable en Maura." (Olmet and García Carraffa, pp. 109-10.)

7. E. Aunós, quoted by Diego Sevilla Andrés, p. 360. Joan Connelly Ullman has also argued that anticlerical policies of the early years of the twentieth century diverted energies from attempting solutions to the structural problems of Spain and, indeed, served as a prop for existing institutions; see pp. 323, 331.

8. Thus, Moret, whom Canalejas had supplanted as prime minister, joined the *Conjunción*.

9. The program is quoted in Fernando Soldevilla, *El año político 1911* (Madrid, 1912), p. 190. Galdós's name headed the list of signatories.

10. On this occasion, Galdós affirms a faith, if somewhat vague, in the Socialist "idea": "Me parece sincera, sincerísima. Es la última palabra en la cuestión social.... ¡El socialismo! Por ahí es por donde llega la aurora" (Olmet and García Carraffa, p. 111).

11. Quoted by Fernández Almagro, *Historia del reinado de Don Alfonso XIII*, p. 166.

12. We do not, of course, know Galdós's intentions for the conclusion of the fifth series; in earlier series, the protagonists reap the fruits of experience and of greater awareness in the final *episodios*.

13. Benito Pérez Galdós, *Cánovas* (Madrid, 1912), p. 128.

14. Benito Pérez Galdós, *De Cartago a Sagunto* (Madrid, 1911), p. 235.

15. Cf. Galdós's repeated attacks on "bookishness": for example, Fernanda's reproach to Halconero that he seek in books the *mujer esclava* of his dreams; the refuge in literature of Halconero (the representative figure of the "half-wills" of the Revolution of 1868); Galdós's assertion that Cánovas's vast library is of no aid in the practical art of governing the nation.

16. Benito Pérez Galdós, *La primera república* (Madrid, 1911), p. 269.

17. Ibid., p. 18.

18. We must, however, assume that, had Galdós completed the fifth series of *episodios*, his teaching would, as in previous series, have been made more explicit in the concluding novels of the series.

19. Cf. also the program of the *Conjunción Republicano-Socialista*, quoted on pages 150-51 above.

20. See Olmet and García Carraffa, p. 109.

21. Benito Pérez Galdós, *España sin rey* (Madrid, 1908), p. 319.

22. Benito Pérez Galdós, *Amadeo I* (Madrid, 1910), p. 152.

23. Benito Pérez Galdós, *España sin rey*, p. 193.

24. Throughout *España sin rey*, Galdós stresses that the deeds of his fictitious characters are representative of national life, thus: "voy a referir hechos particulares o comunes que llevaron en sus entrañas el mismo embrión de los hechos colectivos" (p. 6).

25. The inspiration for Nicéfora's character was obviously suggested by Castelar's speech on the two gods (that of Sinai and that of the New Testament) delivered during the debate on religious freedom in the *Cortes Constituyentes;* the speech is quoted at length in *España sin rey*.

26. Benito Pérez Galdós, *España trágica*, p. 235.

27. Thus, Galdós raises the red herring of the possible complicity of Montpensier, suggests clerical interests were involved, and obscures evidence of Paúl y Angulo's implication in the crime. For an extended discussion of Galdós's treatment of the death of Prim, see Brian J. Dendle, "Galdós and the Death of Prim," pp. 63-71.

28. Benito Pérez Galdós, *Amadeo I*, p. 12.

29. Ibid., p. 251.

30. It was not perhaps Galdós's original intention to leave so much material dealing with the Republic of 1873 to the following *episodio, De Cartago a Sagunto*. Cf. his use of material apparently gathered for *Aita Tettauen* in the sequel novel, *Carlos VI en la Rápita*.

31. Benito Pérez Galdós, *La primera república*, p. 18.

32. Benito Pérez Galdós, *De Cartago a Sagunto*, p. 102.

33. Despite his disgust with the instability and selfish politics of the Republic, Galdós nonetheless reproaches the illegality of the military coup. Thus, the soldiers who are forced to obey the insurgent officers realize that their action is an insult to the nation and its laws: "Obedecían a los autores de aquella infamia sin desconocer que escarnecían a la Patria y pisoteaban las Leyes" (p. 100). Cf. his protest in *Bodas reales* at the overthrow of Espartero's government.

34. Galdós takes especial pains to establish the cowardice of Salmerón; similarly, in *La primera república*, Galdós had attacked Salmerón's refusal to countenance the execution of mutinous soldiers. Salmerón had become the bête noire of many Spanish Republicans, following his acceptance of the presidency of *Solidaridad Catalana* and ostentatious embrace of the duke of Solferino, the Carlist leader.

35. Old age and blindness prevented Galdós from writing the remaining *episodios* of the fifth series. Their announced titles were *Sagasta, Las colonias perdidas, La reina regente,* and *Alfonso XIII*.

36. Benito Pérez Galdós, *Cánovas*, p. 165.

37. *Cánovas*, p. 262. See Chapters 22, 23, and 24 of this novel, passim, for Galdós's extended attack on the wealth and power of the Church and on the monkish invasion of Spain.

Epilogue

1. Laments at national divisions and satirical portrayals of patriotic glibness occur, of course, in the second series of *episodios nacionales* (see, for example, *El equipaje del rey José* and *La segunda casaca*). What is new in the novels of the third and later series is the note of greater intensity and Galdós's attempt at a psychological explanation for Spaniards' readiness to delude themselves with verbal formulas.

2. Cf. Galdós's letter of 1905 to Carretero, in which he confessed that historical events were fitted to the "asunto novelesco" (see p. 79). All too frequently, Galdós's placing of history within the individual *episodio* smacks of composition by formula; the reader soon awaits, within each *episodio,* the brief description of historic personages and the one or two chapters set aside for the recreation of an event from Spanish history.

3. Galdós's "program" (the avoidance of strife, the development of agriculture, industry, and education) is trite and, if we except his anticlericalism, acceptable to Conservative and Liberal alike in the early twentieth century. Despite his pleas in the later novels of the third series for "courtesy" and respect for political opponents, Galdós showed no understanding of the role of the politician in bridging differences, in enabling national life to continue in times of turmoil. Thus, in the fifth series of *episodios,* he denounces as *compadrazgo* the very stuff of politics, the healing of wounds between Republican and monarchist, between *alfonsino* and Carlist.

4. The dependence of Galdós's protagonists on indulgent, maternal figures is remarkable: Fernando Calpena is restored to emotional health by the intelligent protection of his mother, who also arranges his marriage; Fajardo is guarded from overexcitement by his wife, María Ignacia; the wise Teresa Villaescusa guides and cares for Santiago Ibero; Tito Liviano needs the intellectual guidance of Mariclío and the physical tenderness of Casiana.

5. Cf. also Galdós's refusal to develop questions that he has himself raised; thus, in *Montes de Oca,* Rafaela del Milagro magnificently protests woman's role in a male-dominated society. In a later novel (*Las tormentas del 48*), Rafaela is reduced to unhappy conformism. Galdós's similar lack of development in *Tristana* of the limitations that society places on women has recently been remarked by Gilbert Smith ("Galdós, *Tristana,* and Letters from Concha-Ruth Morell," *Anales Galdosianos* 10 [1976]: 108). The limited information we have on Galdós's relations with women (with Emilia Pardo Bazán, Lorenza Cobián, and Concha Morell) suggests that the same pattern of withdrawal from involvement operated in Galdós's private life; in all three cases, it was Galdós who broke off the amorous relationship. Noteworthy also, if we bear in mind the predominant theme of madness in the later *episodios,* is Galdós's attraction to mentally unstable partners: Concha Morell hysterically converted to Judaism; Lorenza Cobián committed suicide, suffering (in Galdós's words) from "delirio persecutorio." It is indeed unfortunate, for our understanding of Galdós, that more information on his intimate life is not available.

6. Galdós's timidity and reticence were notorious. Cf. also the ambiguity that has rendered so baffling the interpretation of certain of Galdós's novels; thus, for examples, see Peter B. Goldman, "Galdós and the Aesthetic of Ambiguity: Notes on the Thematic Structure of *Nazarín,*" *Anales Galdosianos* 9 (1974): 99-112; Brian J. Dendle, "Point of View in *Nazarín:* An Appendix to Goldman,"

Anales Galdosianos 9 (1974): 113-21; and Brian J. Dendle, "Galdós, Ayguals de Izco, and the Hellenic Inspiration of *Marianela*," *Galdós Studies II* (London, 1974), pp. 1-11. A trait related—as symptomatic of inner insecurity—to evasiveness is *proteísmo,* the ability to defend all points of view; García Fajardo and Tito Liviano (both of whom share characteristics of Galdós) are described as "Protean" in the *episodios.*

7. Cf. Berkowitz's descriptions, unfortunately not documented, of Galdós's depressions in 1911 and 1912 (Berkowitz, pp. 411, 418).

8. Cf. the revelatory remarks, in which Galdós contrasts his own restless pursuit of truth with Pereda's serenity: "He is a serene spirit, I a perturbed, restless spirit. He knows where he is going, he starts from a fixed base. Those of us who doubt what he affirms are seeking the truth, and we run constantly toward the place where we think we see it, beautiful and elusive" (quoted by Walter T. Pattison, *Benito Pérez Galdós* [Boston, 1975], p. 18).

Galdós's Characters

Index